Microsoft® A

H. ALBERT NAPIER & PHILIP J. JUDD

COURSE TECHNOLOGY

ONE MAIN STREET, CAMBRIDGE, MA 02142

an International Thomson Publishing company I(T)P®

Cambridge • Albany • Bonn • Boston • Cincinnati • London • Madrid • Melbourne • Mexico City
New York • Paris • San Francisco • Singapore • Tokyo • Toronto • Washington

Mastering and Using Microsoft® Access 97 is published by Course Technology.

Product Managers:	Richard Keaveny, Susan Roche
Associate Product Manager:	Ellina Tsirelson
Production Editor:	Daphne E. Barbas
Development Editor:	India Koopman
Copy Editor:	Joan Wilcox
Composition House:	GEX, Inc.
Text Designer:	Joseph Lee
Illustrator:	Michael Kline
Feature Photographer:	Susan Roche

© 1997 by Course Technology — I(T)P®

For more information contact:

Course Technology
One Main Street
Cambridge, MA 02142

International Thomson Editores
Campos Eliseos 385, Piso 7
Col. Polanco
11560 Mexico D.F. Mexico

International Thomson Publishing Europe
Berkshire House 168-173
High Holborn
London WCIV 7AA
England

International Thomson Publishing GmbH
Königswinterer Strasse 418
53277 Bonn
Germany

Thomas Nelson Australia
102 Dodds Street
South Melbourne, 3205
Victoria, Australia

International Thomson Publishing Asia
211 Henderson Road
#05-10 Henderson Building
Singapore 0315

Nelson Canada
1120 Birchmount Road
Scarborough, Ontario
Canada MIK 5G4

International Thomson Publishing Japan
Hirakawacho Kyowa Building, 3F
2-2-1 Hirakawacho
Chiyoda-ku, Tokyo 102
Japan

0-7600-5061-9

Printed in the United States of America

Napier & Judd

In their over 48 years of combined experience, Al Napier and Phil Judd have developed a tested, realistic approach to mastering and using application software. As both academics and corporate trainers, Al and Phil have the unique ability to help students by teaching them the skills necessary to compete in today's complex business world.

H. Albert Napier, Ph.D. is the Director of the Center on the Management of Information Technology and an Associate Professor in the Jones Graduate School of Administration at Rice University. In addition, Al is a principal of Napier & Judd, Inc., a consulting company and corporate trainer in Houston, Texas, that has trained more than 80,000 people in computer applications.

Philip J. Judd is a former instructor in the Management Department and the Director of the Research and Instructional Computing Service at the University of Houston. Phil now dedicates himself to corporate training and consulting as a principal of Napier & Judd, Inc.

Other Selected Books by Napier & Judd:

Mastering & Using Microsoft Office 97, Professional Edition

Mastering & Using the Internet for Office Professionals Using Netscape Navigator Software

Mastering & Using Microsoft Word 97

Mastering & Using Microsoft PowerPoint 97 for Business Presentations

Mastering & Using Microsoft Excel 97

Mastering & Using Corel WordPerfect 7 for Windows 95

Mastering & Using Microsoft Office for Windows 95, Professional Edition

Mastering & Using Microsoft Word 7 for Windows 95

Mastering & Using Microsoft Excel 7 for Windows 95

Mastering & Using the Microsoft Office, Professional Edition (Windows 3.1)

Mastering & Using Microsoft Word 6.0 for Windows 3.1

Mastering & Using Microsoft Excel 5.0 for Windows 3.1

Mastering Microsoft Word 6 for Windows 3.1

Mastering Microsoft Excel 5 for Windows 3.1

Mastering & Using Microsoft Word for Windows 2.0

Mastering & Using WordPerfect 6.1 for Windows

Mastering & Using WordPerfect 6.0a for Windows

Mastering & Using WordPerfect 5.2 for Windows

Mastering & Using WordPerfect 6.0

Mastering & Using WordPerfect 5.1

Mastering & Using Lotus 1-2-3, Release 5.0 for Windows

Philip J. Judd   H. Albert Napier, Ph.D.

Preface

At Course Technology we believe that technology will transform the way that people teach and learn. We are very excited about bringing you, instructors and students, the most practical and affordable technology-related products available.

The Development Process

Our development process is unparalleled in the educational publishing industry. Every product we create goes through an exacting process of design, development, review, and testing.

Reviewers give us direction and insight that shape our manuscripts and bring them up to the latest standards. Every manuscript is quality tested. Students whose backgrounds match the intended audience work through every keystroke, carefully checking for clarity and pointing out errors in logic and sequence. Together with our own technical reviewers, these testers help us ensure that everything that carries our name is as error-free and easy to use as possible.

The Products

We show both how and why technology is critical to solving problems in the classroom and in whatever field you choose to teach or pursue. Our time-tested, step-by-step instructions provide unparalleled clarity. Examples and applications are chosen and crafted to motivate students.

New in this Edition!

- Thorough coverage of the **new features of Office 97** such as the Office Assistant, the Web Authoring Tools, the ability to draw tables using a drawing tool, new screen tips and automation features, and much more!
- Extensive **Internet coverage** has been integrated into the text and featured in case study exercises (*see page vi*).
- **Additional document integration coverage**, including integration with HTML documents.
- **Microsoft Certification** exam objectives are addressed throughout the text, making this book an excellent preparation tool for Microsoft Certification exams (*see page vii*).

Instructor's Resource Kit

All books in the Mastering & Using series are supplemented with an Instructor's Resource Kit (IRK) that includes an integrated array of teaching and learning tools that offer you and your students a broad range of technology-based instructional options. You can also obtain many of these components by accessing the Faculty Online Companion at **www.course.com**.

Items in the Instructor's Resource Kit Include:

Instructor's Manual

Written by the authors and quality assurance tested, the printed Instructor's Manual includes:

- A suggested syllabus
- Instructors notes and chapter outlines
- Solutions to all end-of-chapter material
- Transparency Masters of key concepts

CD-ROM Including:

Electronic Instructor's Manual

The Electronic Instructor's Manual is an electronic version of the Instructor's Manual that includes a suggested syllabus, instructors notes and chapter outlines, solutions to all end-of-unit material, and Transparency Masters of key concepts, and additional chapters that may be printed, photocopied, and distributed to your students.

Student Files

To use this book students must have student disks. The student disks include student files needed to complete exercises in the text. These files should be copied to floppy disks as indicated to create the student disks. They can also be posted to a network or stand-alone workstations.

Solutions Files

Solutions Files represent the correctly completed files that students are asked to create in the end-of-chapter exercises. These files accompany the solutions that are provided in the Instructor's Manual.

Course Test Manager Version 1.1 Engine

Course Test Manager (CTM) is a cutting-edge Windows-based testing software program, developed exclusively for Course Technology, that helps instructors design and administer examinations and practice tests. This full-featured program allows students to generate practice tests randomly that provide immediate on-screen feedback and detailed study guides for questions incorrectly answered. Instructors can also use Course Test Manager to create printed and Online tests. You can create, preview, and administer a test on any or all chapters of this textbook entirely over a local area network. Course Test Manager can grade the tests students take automatically at the computer and can generate statistical information on individual as well as group performance.

Course Test Manager Version 1.1 Test Bank

The Course Test Manager Test Bank to accompany your text comes along with the engine on the CD-ROM. The test bank includes multiple-choice, true/false, short answer, and essay questions, many of which include graphics from the text.

CourseHelp offers online annotated tutorials that are accessible directly from the Start menu. These on-screen "slide shows" help students understand the most difficult concepts in Access 97. This text includes the following CourseHelp slide shows: Planning a Database; Filtering Records; and Sorting Records.

If you do not have access to a CD-ROM drive, these components are also available on disk through Course Technology's customer service department.

Mastering & Using Microsoft Access 97

Today there are millions of people using personal computers in their everyday lives both as tools at work and for recreational activities. As a result, the personal computer has revolutionized the ways in which people interact with each other. Database management software and the Internet are two of the most influential applications used on personal computers today. Microsoft Access 97 combines these two powerful tools to allow people to do amazing things.

This book introduces students to the power of Microsoft Access 97, Microsoft Office 97, and how Microsoft Access 97 can be used to connect and use resources on the Internet.

This book has been developed to:
- Acquaint the student with database software
- Acquaint the student with the Internet and the World Wide Web (WWW)
- Provide the student with a working knowledge of Microsoft Access 97
- Provide the student with an excellent reference to advance his or her knowledge of Access 97

Distinguishing Features

All of the textbooks in the Mastering & Using series share several key pedagogical features:

Quick Start Approach

In their many years of teaching experience, Napier and Judd have found that students are more enthusiastic about learning a software application if they can see immediate results. With this in mind, the authors have designed a unique system of instruction which allows students to be able to perform the basic application functions quickly.

This book begins with a four chapter unit which introduces students to the Microsoft Office environment. In this unit the students learn the essentials of getting started with Microsoft Office 97, Professional Edition, and the common elements to the applications in the Office 97 Suite.

In the Access unit, the first chapter provides an overview of general database terminology, as well as Access-specific terms and concepts. The second chapter provides a quick start approach to creating a new database, creating and adding records to a table, and creating queries, forms, and reports using Wizards.

Chapter Openers

To help students understand how what they are learning is applicable in a real world setting, chapters in the Mastering & Using series begin with photos and accompanying quotes from office professionals explaining how they apply the chapter material in their daily lives. For more information on the chapter openers, please see pages viii and ix in this preface.

Step-by-Step Instructions and Screen Illustrations

All examples in this text include step-by-step instructions. Screen illustrations are used extensively to help students learn the features of the Access 97 software and the Office 97 suite. The authors have found this approach very useful for both novice and more advanced users.

Quick Tip

Placed in the margins next to the relevant material in the chapter, these boxes of information provide students with shortcuts to perform common business-related functions and increase their productivity.

Caution

Based on their years of experience teaching information technology, the authors have placed notes in the margin next to concepts or steps which often cause students difficulty. Each Caution box anticipates the student's possible confusion, and provides methods for avoiding the problem in the future.

Mouse Tip / Menu Tip

Since many functions can be performed in a number of different ways, the authors provide additional instructions in the margin for students about alternative methods of performing a task than the one that is explained in the body of the chapter.

Internet Coverage

Microsoft Access 97 provides students with a great opportunity to incorporate the power of the Internet with database management. In order to help students use the Internet as they progress through this book, the authors have integrated Internet material throughout. Instructors and students are alerted to Internet coverage by the Internet logo in the section heading.

End-of-Chapter Summary, Commands Review, and Exercises

Each book in the *Mastering & Using* series places a heavy emphasis on providing students with the opportunity to practice and reinforce the skills they are learning through extensive exercises. Each chapter has an extensive summary, commands review, concepts review, skills review, and case problem exercises so that students can learn by doing. For a further explanation of each of the end-of-chapter elements see page xii in this preface.

Appendices

Mastering & Using Access 97 contains four appendices to further help students prepare to be successful in the classroom as well as in the workplace. Appendix A introduces students to Windows Explorer and how to manage files on their desktop computer. Appendices B and C provide students with practice exams similar to ones they may be asked to take when they apply for employment in an office. Appendix D summarizes the proofreader's marks that students learn while working through this book. For more information on the appendices in this book please see page xiii in this preface.

Microsoft Certification

Microsoft Certification is an important accomplishment which is valued by many employers. This book has been written with the objectives of Microsoft Certification in mind in order to make this book suitable to be used as a preparation tool when studying for Microsoft Certification exams. If you are interested in finding out more about the requirements and objectives of Microsoft Certification, please consult Microsoft on the Web at **http://www.microsoft.com/train_cert/cert/certif.htm**.

Acknowledgments

We would like to thank and express our appreciation to the many fine individuals who have contributed to the completion of this book. We have been fortunate to have reviewers whose constructive comments have been so helpful.

No book is possible without the motivation and support of an editorial staff. Therefore, we wish to acknowledge with great appreciation the following people at Course Technology: Joseph Dougherty, President and CEO, Course Technology; Marjorie Hunt, Publisher; Richard Keaveny, Product Manager; Ellina Tsirelson, Associate Product Manager; Susan Roche, Product Manager and Photographer; Daphne Barbas, Production Editor; Deb Kaufmann, Developmental Editor; Greg Bigelow, Quality Assurance Project Leader.

We are very appreciative of the personnel at Napier & Judd, Inc., who helped prepare this book. We acknowledge, with great appreciation, the assistance provided by Ollie Rivers and Nancy Onarheim in preparing and checking the many drafts of this book and the instructor's manual.

We would also like to thank all of the people and their companies that participated in Voices from Business. The participants and their companies appear in this book solely to express how the skills learned in this book are an essential part of their work environment. By appearing in this book, neither the participants nor their companies are in any way endorsing Microsoft or any product or company mentioned in this book.

Tamra LaPierre *Automatic Data Processing*
Mark Lippott *Coldwell Banker Hunneman & Company*
Aviva Yoffe *Massachusetts Financial Services*
Robert Goodman *Pinnacle Enterprises*
Judi Quagliaroli *Simmons College Graduate School of Management (GSM)*
Amy Stoll *Cultural Survival*
Ralph Mancini *Vista Travel*

How to Use this Book

Each chapter in this book begins with a summary of the material covered in the previous chapter, a snapshot of the material that will be covered in the present chapter, and a portrait of someone who works in a business environment.

Office 97

CHAPTER

2

Quick Start for Office 97 Document Integration

Voices from Business— Quotes from people in a wide range of business environments explain how using the skills taught in this book help them in their daily activities.

"

My job as an administrative assistant demands that I am well organized and able to perform multiple tasks efficiently. Microsoft Office helps me to be more efficient. I use Microsoft Word to create memos and letters and I maintain numerous databases to organize and manage the department budget.

"

Yvonne Malcolm
administrative assistant

Department of Psychology
Northeastern University
Boston, MA

Opening Every Chapter

Chapter Overview:

Chapter 1 provided an overview of Office 97 including how to start and close the applications and the common elements of those applications. To complete a project in a business environment, you may need to integrate data from several software applications such as word processing, worksheet, presentation, and database applications. This chapter demonstrates how you would use the Word, Excel, and PowerPoint applications to prepare a weekly sales report.

SNAPSHOT

In this chapter you will learn to:

> Complete a project with Office applications

> Copy information from Excel to Word

> Copy information from Excel to PowerPoint

> Use a Binder to store related documents

> Work with the Office Assistant

Chapter Overview—A concise summary of what students learned in the previous chapter and an outline of the skills they will learn in the present chapter.

Snapshot—A quick reference of the major topics that students will learn in the present chapter.

How to Use this Book

In a few seconds, the Access data is saved in the specified folder as an Excel workbook named "Discontinued" containing a worksheet also named "Discontinued."

To view the "Discontinued" query data as an Excel worksheet:

Numbered Steps—Clear step-by-step directions explain how to complete the specific task. When students follow the numbered steps, they learn quickly how each procedure is performed and what the results will be.

STEP 1 — CLICK — the Open Office Document button [icon] on the Shortcut bar

STEP 2 — SWITCH — to the appropriate disk drive and folder

STEP 3 — DOUBLE-CLICK — DISCONTINUED

The DISCONTINUED workbook opens with one worksheet (also named Discontinued) containing the formatted records from the Access query. Close the Excel application and close the DISCONTINUED workbook. Close the PETSTORE RECORDS database and the Access application.

For more information on integrating Access data and Excel, see Access or Excel online Help.

7.c Creating Hyperlinks and HTML Documents

[INTERNET]

Internet Coverage—Internet material integrated throughout the book provides students with the opportunity to incorporate the power of the Internet with database management.

You can create hyperlinks to link Access data to other Office documents just as you did with Word documents, Excel workbooks, and PowerPoint presentations. You can also use hyperlinks as labels on Access forms and reports to link them to other Office documents, documents on a company intranet, or pages on the Internet. Access tables, queries, forms, and reports can also be published as HTML documents on an intranet or the World Wide Web (WWW).

LINKING ACCESS DATA TO A WORD DOCUMENT WITH A HYPERLINK

Suppose you want to send an interoffice memo to the secretarial staff that contains information about the regional managers. You can type the information in the memo, or you can insert a hyperlink that allows each recipient to open an Access database and review the desired information.

First, open the SOUTHWEST STAFF SECRETARIAL MEMO located on the student disk. This memo advises the secretarial staff to review the new regional managers data maintained in an Access database and specific query. You will create a link to the database in the body of the memo. To create a hyperlink to the BRANCH database:

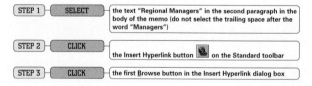

STEP 1 — SELECT — the text "Regional Managers" in the second paragraph in the body of the memo (do not select the trailing space after the word "Managers")

STEP 2 — CLICK — the Insert Hyperlink button [icon] on the Standard toolbar

STEP 3 — CLICK — the first Browse button in the Insert Hyperlink dialog box

Within Every Chapter

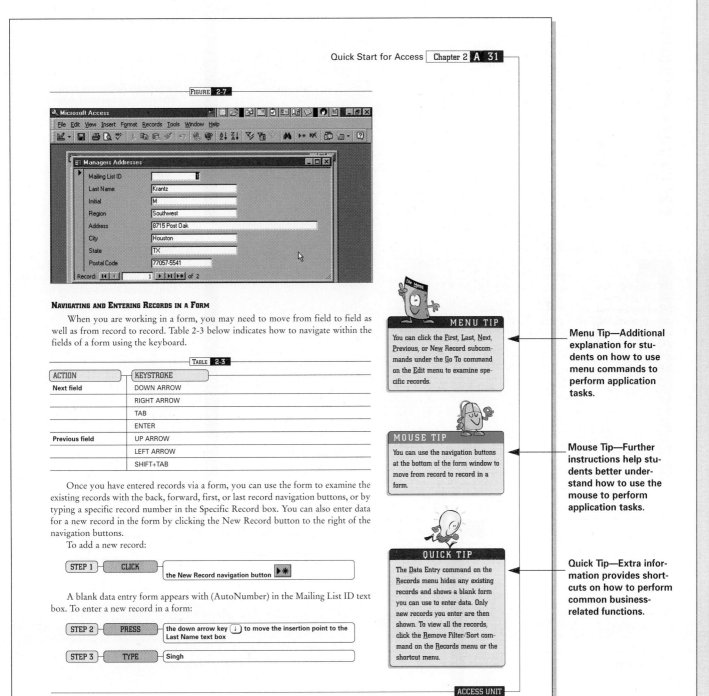

FIGURE **2-7**

NAVIGATING AND ENTERING RECORDS IN A FORM

When you are working in a form, you may need to move from field to field as well as from record to record. Table 2-3 below indicates how to navigate within the fields of a form using the keyboard.

TABLE **2-3**

ACTION	KEYSTROKE
Next field	DOWN ARROW
	RIGHT ARROW
	TAB
	ENTER
Previous field	UP ARROW
	LEFT ARROW
	SHIFT+TAB

Once you have entered records via a form, you can use the form to examine the existing records with the back, forward, first, or last record navigation buttons, or by typing a specific record number in the Specific Record box. You can also enter data for a new record in the form by clicking the New Record button to the right of the navigation buttons.

To add a new record:

STEP 1 — CLICK — the New Record navigation button ▶*

A blank data entry form appears with (AutoNumber) in the Mailing List ID text box. To enter a new record in a form:

STEP 2 — PRESS — the down arrow key ↓ to move the insertion point to the Last Name text box

STEP 3 — TYPE — Singh

MENU TIP

You can click the First, Last, Next, Previous, or New Record subcommands under the Go To command on the Edit menu to examine specific records.

MOUSE TIP

You can use the navigation buttons at the bottom of the form window to move from record to record in a form.

QUICK TIP

The Data Entry command on the Records menu hides any existing records and shows a blank form you can use to enter data. Only new records you enter are then shown. To view all the records, click the Remove Filter/Sort command on the Records menu or the shortcut menu.

ACCESS UNIT

Menu Tip—Additional explanation for students on how to use menu commands to perform application tasks.

Mouse Tip—Further instructions help students better understand how to use the mouse to perform application tasks.

Quick Tip—Extra information provides shortcuts on how to perform common business-related functions.

End-of-Chapter Material

In order to help students reinforce the skills they have learned, each chapter has an extensive summary, commands review, concepts review, skills review, and case problems.

Summary & Commands Review

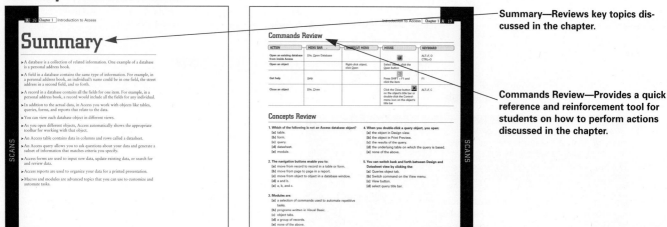

Summary—Reviews key topics discussed in the chapter.

Commands Review—Provides a quick reference and reinforcement tool for students on how to perform actions discussed in the chapter.

Concepts & Skills Review

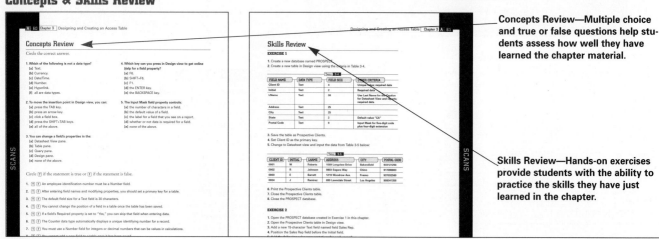

Concepts Review—Multiple choice and true or false questions help students assess how well they have learned the chapter material.

Skills Review—Hands-on exercises provide students with the ability to practice the skills they have just learned in the chapter.

Case Problems

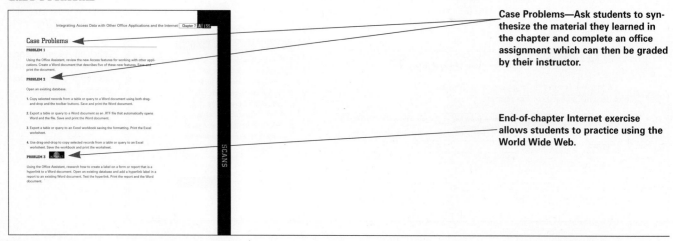

Case Problems—Ask students to synthesize the material they learned in the chapter and complete an office assignment which can then be graded by their instructor.

End-of-chapter Internet exercise allows students to practice using the World Wide Web.

Appendices

Appendix A: Introduction to Microsoft Windows Explorer

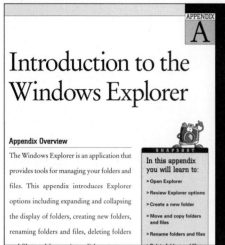

Appendix A—Introduction to Windows Explorer introduces students to using the Windows Explorer through the same step-by-step process found within each Napier and Judd chapter.

Appendices B and C: Sample Assessment Tests

 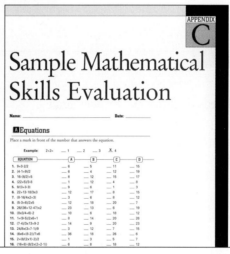

Appendices B and C—A sample language and a sample math skills evaluation provide students with the opportunity to assess their own strengths and weaknesses.

Appendix D: Proofreader's Marks

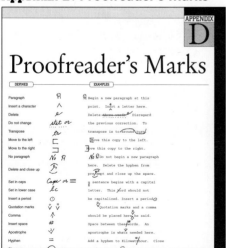

Appendix D—An example of an edited page illustrates the use of proofreader's marks in editing manuscript.

Contents

Access Unit   A 1

Getting Started with Microsoft Office 97 Professional

Chapter Overview:

This book assumes that you have little or no knowledge of Microsoft Office 97. It does assume, however, that you have worked with personal computers and are familiar with Microsoft Windows 95. This unit introduces the capabilities of Microsoft Office 97 and how the applications can assist you in your work. The computer hardware and software requirements for using Microsoft Office 97 applications are defined. Common elements of the Microsoft Office 97 applications are identified. Finally, this chapter illustrates how to start and close Microsoft Office 97 applications.

SNAPSHOT

In this chapter you will learn to:

> **Describe Microsoft Office 97 Standard and Microsoft Office 97 Professional**

> **Determine how Microsoft Office 97 Professional can help you in your work**

> **Determine hardware and software requirements for Microsoft Office 97 Professional**

> **Start Microsoft Office 97 Professional applications**

> **Identify common elements of Microsoft Office 97 Professional applications**

> **Close Microsoft Office 97 Professional applications**

1.a What Are Microsoft Office 97 Standard and Microsoft Office 97 Professional?

Microsoft Office 97 is a package that contains several software applications. If you have Microsoft Office 97 Standard, the software applications included are:

Microsoft Word 97
Microsoft Excel 97
Microsoft PowerPoint 97
Microsoft Outlook 97

If you have Microsoft Office 97 Professional, you have the applications mentioned above as well as the following additional applications:

Microsoft Access 97
Microsoft Bookshelf Basics

> **IN THIS BOOK**
>
> This book assumes that you have Microsoft Office 97 Professional. For the remainder of this book, Microsoft Office 97 Professional is called Office. Rather than include the text *Microsoft* and *97* each time the name of an application is used, the text will refer to the respective software package as *Word, Excel, PowerPoint, Access, Outlook* and *Bookshelf Basics*.

Word provides you with word processing capabilities. **Word processing** is the preparation and production of documents using automated equipment. Today, most word processing activities are completed with personal computers and word processing software. Using personal computers, you can complete word processing tasks as well as a host of other duties, including desktop publishing.

Excel is software that allows you to create worksheets and charts as well as perform other tasks such as sorting data. With Excel, you can create financial budgets, reports, and a variety of other forms. **Worksheets** may also be referred to as **spreadsheets**.

PowerPoint is an application used to create materials for **presentations,** called slides. These **slides** can contain text, graphs, organization charts, and other objects. The slides are placed in a presentation file that you can use to print transparencies for an overhead projector. The slides can also be viewed directly on your computer monitor or on a screen using a projector connected to your computer. You can view and print an outline of a slide presentation and create audience handout materials from a slide presentation.

Access provides **database management** capabilities that allow you to store and retrieve information in a database. You can query, or search, the database to answer specific questions about the data within the database. For example, you can determine which customers in a particular state had sales in excess of a particular value during a specific/particular month.

Outlook is a new desktop information manager that provides tools for managing e-mail as well as maintaining a calendar and "to do" lists. For more information on using Outlook, see the documentation provided with the software.

Bookshelf Basics is a set of reference materials that includes the *American Heritage Dictionary*, third edition, *The Original Roget's Thesaurus*, and *The Columbia Dictionary of Quotations* on CD-ROM. You can use Bookshelf Basics reference materials from Word, Excel, or PowerPoint. For more information on using the Bookshelf Basics reference materials with Office documents, see Bookshelf Basics online Help.

1.b How Office Can Help You in Your Work

The primary advantage of using Office applications is the ability to integrate the applications by sharing information between them. For example, you may want to include a portion of an Excel worksheet or chart in a Word document, use an outline created in a Word document as the starting point for a PowerPoint presentation, import an Excel list into Access, or merge names and addresses from an Outlook Address Book with a Word letter.

Another example of integration is to use the Access database application to store a mailing list for a company's employees that can be used in Word to create form letters. For example, you can use Access to create a list of the employees in a specific department. Then, you can use this specific employee list in a Word merge procedure to create individual letters for the persons appearing on the list.

Information can be shared between applications by copying, linking, or embedding data from a source application into a destination application. You can **copy** data from a **source** application and paste the data into a **destination** application. The data then become part of the destination application.

Whenever you need applications to share data that changes frequently, you can **link** the data between applications. When you link data from a source application to a destination application, the data reside only in the source application. The destination application contains only a representation of the data, which is updated automatically whenever the data in the source application are changed. You can also edit linked data from the destination application. For example, suppose you link data from an Excel worksheet to a Word document. To edit the linked data while you are working in Word, simply double-click the linked data. This opens the Excel application and the workbook that actually contains the data. You then make changes to the data in the Excel workbook, and the Word document is automatically updated.

If you **embed** data from a source application into a destination application, you are actually placing a *copy* of the data (called an embedded object) in the destination application. All editing is done with the menu and toolbars of the source application; however, the editing task is actually accomplished in the destination application. There is no link between the source application and the embedded object; that is, the changes are recorded only in the destination application. When you double-click the embedded object, the source application menu and toolbars used in editing the object appear.

EXAMPLE OF USING OFFICE APPLICATIONS TOGETHER

Suppose you work in the sales department of a lumber company. A weekly progress report is prepared that presents a summary of the week's sales activities. The progress report contains text information on various activities, worksheet information, and charts. The progress report is distributed to several individuals in the organization.

Figure 1-1 contains the first page of the report. This document was created using Word. Note the sales data for each day. This numeric information was created in Excel.

FIGURE 1-1

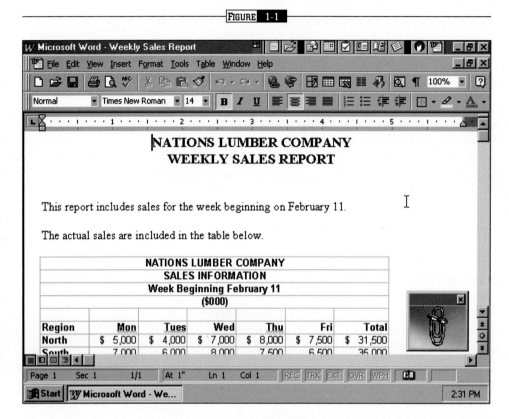

The Excel worksheet appears in Figure 1-2. The values in the worksheet have been copied from the Excel worksheet to the Word document.

At some point, the manager responsible for the progress report will need to make a presentation related to the weekly data. Charts are particularly useful in presentations to illustrate financial results. PowerPoint provides the tools you need to make slides for such a presentation. You can create charts within PowerPoint or link a chart in Excel to a PowerPoint slide. Figure 1-3 contains a PowerPoint slide that includes a chart. The chart was prepared in Excel using the values appearing in Figure 1-2. The chart created in Excel was copied to the PowerPoint slide.

As noted earlier, the weekly sales report is distributed to several individuals. Rather than prepare separate documents to be mailed to several individuals, you can create a single document and then merge the names and addresses of the recipients to create personalized documents. To accomplish this task, you need a mailing list of the names of those people who will receive the report. You can create and save such a list of individuals in Word or Access.

FIGURE 1-2

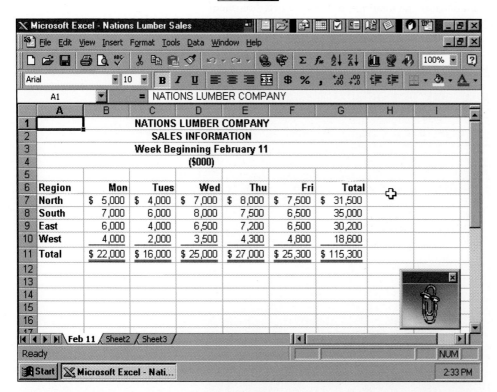

FIGURE 1-3

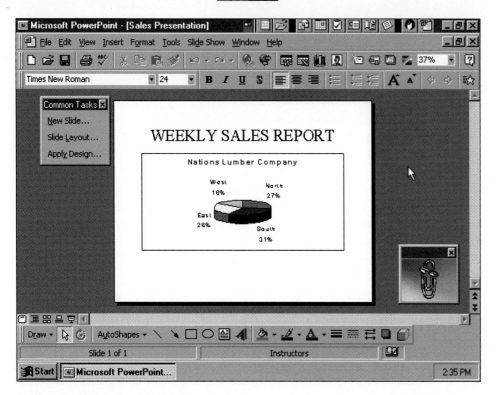

Figure 1-4 illustrates an Access database that includes a mailing list. Through a standard process called **merging**, you can combine the mailing list with a Word document and create the letters for all individuals receiving the report.

FIGURE 1-4

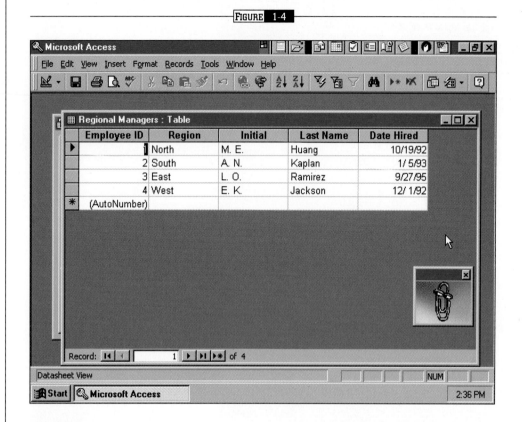

Hardware and Software Requirements

1.c

You must install Office 97 applications in Windows 95, Windows NT Workstation 3.51, or Windows NT 4.0. Office 97 applications will not run in the Windows 3.x, Windows for Workgroups, or Windows NT 3.5 environments.

To use the versions of Word, Excel, PowerPoint, or Access covered in this book, you must have an IBM or compatible personal computer. Microsoft recommends that your computer have a 486 or higher processor, at least 8 MB of RAM for programs other than Access and 12 MB of RAM for the Access application. More memory may be required to run multiple applications simultaneously. For instructions on installing Office on a hard disk or for the hard disk space requirements for a Typical or Custom installation, see the documentation that comes with the software.

SUPPLIES

When using a personal computer, you will need several items. You should have access to the printed documentation that comes with the software. You will also need to have some floppy disks on which to store documents. Make sure you have the proper type of floppy disk for the computer you are using. You can purchase floppy disks at office supply stores and campus bookstores. You may also want a disk storage box to store and protect your disks when you are not using them.

QUICK TIP

If you are left-handed, you can switch the operation of the left and right mouse buttons in the Mouse Properties dialog box. Double-click the My Computer icon on the desktop, double-click the Control Panel folder, and then double-click the Mouse icon to display the dialog box.

1.d Starting Office Applications

Before you attempt to access Office applications and place them in the memory of your computer, first check all computer connections.

To begin:

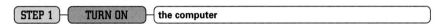

STEP 1 — TURN ON — the computer

You access the Office applications through the Windows 95 desktop. The Windows 95 software is automatically loaded into the memory of your computer when you turn it on. Your screen should look similar to Figure 1-5.

FIGURE 1-5

1. Taskbar
2. Start button

IN THIS BOOK

Your Windows 95 desktop may not look identical to the figures in this book. Your instructor may revise comments, chapter steps, and exercises as necessary if items on your Windows 95 desktop do not agree with desktop items in this book.

IN THIS BOOK

When referring to a mouse operation, **point** means to place the mouse pointer on the command or item. **Click** means to press the left mouse button and then release it. **Right-click** means to press the right-mouse button and then release it. **Double-click** means to press the left-mouse button twice very rapidly. **Drag** means to press and hold the down the left mouse button while you move the mouse. **Right-drag** means to press and hold down the the right mouse button while you move the mouse. **Scroll** means to use the application scroll bar features or the scrolling wheel that is part of the new IntelliMouse™ device that is available for Office 97 applications.

THE MICROSOFT OFFICE SHORTCUT BAR

Efficient and productive employees are an important asset to an employer. When you work in a business environment, you must use the most efficient and productive tools available to accomplish your assignments and tasks. The Microsoft Office Shortcut Bar provides tools to help you perform at peak productivity.

The Microsoft Office Shortcut Bar should appear in the top-right corner of your screen. In the remainder of this book, the Microsoft Office Shortcut Bar is called the **Shortcut Bar**. A series of buttons appears on the Shortcut Bar. Each button represents a shortcut to frequently performed tasks. If the mouse pointer is positioned on one of the buttons, a **ScreenTip** appears with the descriptive name of the shortcut. Initially, the Shortcut Bar should look similar to Figure 1-6. You will learn how to customize the Shortcut Bar in Chapter 3 in this unit.

1. Control menu
2. New Office Document
3. Open Office Document
4. New Message
5. New Appointment
6. New Task
7. New Contact
8. New Journal Entry
9. New Note
10. Microsoft Bookshelf Basics
11. Getting Results Book

FIGURE 1-6

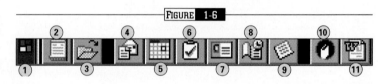

Table 1-1 below illustrates the Shortcut Bar buttons included on the Shortcut Bar displayed in this book:

TABLE 1-1

BUTTON	SHORTCUT
	Shortcut Bar Control menu
	New Office Document
	Open Office Document
	New Message
	New Appointment
	New Task
	New Contact
	New Journal Entry
	New Note
	Microsoft Bookshelf Basics
	Getting Results Book

QUICK TIP

If the Shortcut Bar is not installed, you will have to install it using the add/remove programs feature. See online Help for more information on how to add/remove programs.

If the Shortcut Bar is not displayed, click Start on the taskbar, point to Programs, point to Startup, and then click Microsoft Office Shortcut Bar.

STARTING THE WORD APPLICATION

There are several ways to start an application. Chapter 2 in this unit discusses alternate methods to open an application and a document. To use the taskbar to open the Word application:

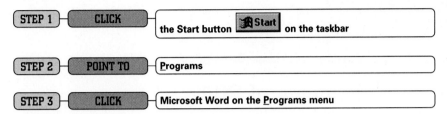

The Word software is placed into the memory of your computer and the initial Word window appears. A **window** is a rectangular area on your screen in which you can view a software application such as Word or an application document. (The first time you start an Office application after installation, the Office Assistant window appears with a "Welcome" message. If you see this message, click the "Start using . . ." command in the Office Assistant balloon.)

Your screen should look similar to Figure 1-7.

FIGURE 1-7

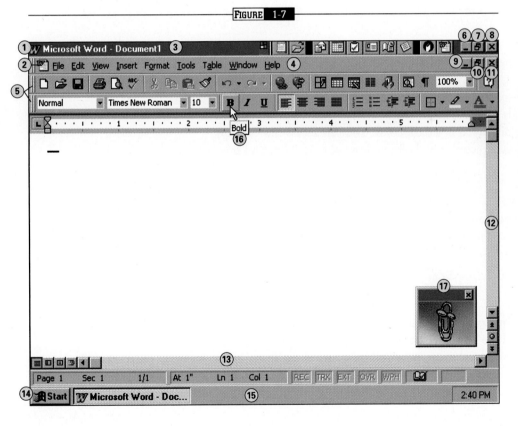

1. Application Control-menu icon
2. Document Control-menu icon
3. Title bar
4. Menu bar
5. Toolbars
6. Application Minimize button
7. Application Restore button
8. Application Close button
9. Document Minimize button
10. Document Restore button
11. Document Close button
12. Vertical scroll bar
13. Horizontal scroll bar
14. Start button
15. Taskbar
16. ScreenTip
17. Office Assistant

IN THIS BOOK

You may sometimes use the keyboard to use Office application features. When the keyboard is used to issue a command, this text illustrates keystrokes as follows:
   Press the Enter key (↵ ENTER)
   If you are asked to press one key and, while holding the key down, to press another key, the instruction will appear as:
   Press the Shift+F7 keys (SHIFT) + (F7)

1.e   Identifying Common Elements of Office Applications

Figure 1-7 notes several common elements of all Office applications. These elements are described below.

TITLE BAR

The **title bar** appears at the top of the Office application window. It includes the application Control-menu icon, the application name, the filename of the active document, and the document Minimize, Maximize (or Restore), and Close buttons.

APPLICATION CONTROL-MENU ICON

The **application Control-menu icon** [W], located in the upper-left corner of the window, is used to display the Control menu. The Control menu typically contains commands such as Restore, Move, Size, Minimize, Maximize, and Close. In some Control menus, all of the commands may not be currently available for use. Commands that are currently available are displayed in a dark color. You can access the Control menu by clicking the Control-menu icon or by holding down the ALT key and then pressing the SPACEBAR key.

APPLICATION MINIMIZE BUTTON

The **application Minimize button** [_] appears near the upper-right corner of the window. Use this button to reduce the application window to a button on the taskbar. When you point to the Minimize button and click, the application window changes to a raised button on the taskbar.

APPLICATION MAXIMIZE BUTTON

The **application Maximize button** [□] sometimes appears in the upper-right corner of the window to the right of the Minimize button. Use it to maximize or enlarge the size of the application window to fill the entire screen display area above the taskbar. If the window is already maximized, the Maximize button will not appear. The Restore button (described below) appears in its place.

APPLICATION RESTORE BUTTON

The **application Restore button** [⊡] appears in the upper-right corner of the window to the right of the Minimize button. Use the Restore button to change the size of the application window to a smaller size on your screen.

APPLICATION CLOSE BUTTON

The **application Close button** appears in the upper-right corner of the window to the right of the Restore or Maximize button. Use the Close button to close the application and remove it from computer memory.

DOCUMENT CONTROL-MENU ICON

The **document Control-menu icon** , located below the application Control-menu icon, contains the Restore, Move, Size, Minimize, Maximize, and Close menu commands for the document. Access the document Control menu by pointing to the document Control-menu icon and clicking, or by holding down the ALT key and pressing the hyphen (-) key.

MENU BAR

The **menu bar** is a special toolbar located at the top of the window below the title bar. The Word menu bar contains the commands File, Edit, View, Insert, Format, Tools, Table, Window, and Help. Menu bar commands will vary between applications.

You can customize the menu bar by adding and removing commands and buttons. Using the menu bar is covered in more detail in Chapter 2 in this unit. Customizing the menu bar is discussed in an application unit later in this book.

DOCUMENT MINIMIZE BUTTON

The **document Minimize button** appears on the menu bar below the application Minimize button. Use this button to reduce the document window to a title bar icon inside the document area.

DOCUMENT MAXIMIZE BUTTON

The **document Maximize button** appears on the title bar icon of a minimized document. Use it to maximize or enlarge the size of the document window to cover the entire application display area and share the application title bar. If the window is already maximized, the Maximize button will not appear. The Restore button (described below) appears in its place.

DOCUMENT RESTORE BUTTON

The **document Restore button** appears in the menu bar to the right of the document Minimize button. Use the Restore button to decrease the size of the document window inside the application window.

DOCUMENT CLOSE BUTTON

The **document Close button** appears in the menu bar to the right of the Restore or Maximize button. Use the Close button to close the document and remove it from computer memory.

DEFAULT TOOLBARS

The **Standard and Formatting toolbars**, located below the menu bar, are displayed by default in most Office applications. They contain a set of icons called buttons. The buttons on the toolbars represent commonly used commands, and they allow you to perform tasks quickly by clicking the button. In addition to the Standard and Formatting toolbars, there are several other toolbars available in each application. You can customize toolbars by adding buttons and commands. Customizing toolbars is discussed in an application unit later in this book.

VERTICAL SCROLL BAR

The **vertical scroll bar** appears on the right side of the document area. This scroll bar includes scroll arrows and a scroll box. The vertical scroll bar is used to view various parts of the document by moving or scrolling the document up or down.

HORIZONTAL SCROLL BAR

The **horizontal scroll bar** appears near the bottom of the document area. This scroll bar includes scroll arrows and a scroll box. The horizontal scroll bar is used to view various parts of the document by moving or scrolling the document left or right.

SCREENTIPS

When the mouse pointer rests on a toolbar button, a **ScreenTip** appears identifying the name of the button. ScreenTips also are provided as part of online Help to describe a toolbar button, a dialog box option, or a menu command.

OFFICE ASSISTANT

The **Office Assistant** is an animated graphic you can click to display online Help for a specific task, search online Help for specific topics, and get user tips. The Office Assistant will also anticipate your needs and provide advice in a balloon-style dialog box when you begin certain tasks.

START BUTTON

The **Start button** is located in the lower-left corner of the Windows 95 Desktop and displays the Start menu or list of tasks you can perform and applications you can use in Windows 95.

TASKBAR

The **taskbar** is located across the bottom of the Windows 95 desktop and displays buttons indicating the applications that are currently open in the memory of your computer. You can switch between applications, close applications, and view other items, such as the system time and printer status, with buttons on the taskbar.

Other common elements of Office applications that are discussed in more detail in Chapter 2 in this unit or in one or more specific application units include:

- Long filenames
- Pop-up menus
- Wizards
- IntelliSense Technology that provides the AutoCorrect, AutoComplete, AutoText, and AutoFormat features
- IntelliMouse™ Navigation, which uses a mouse with a scrolling wheel
- Enhanced document management using features in the Open dialog box
- Binders you can use to keep related documents together
- ActiveWeb Technology that allows you to create hypertext links within or between Office documents, convert Office documents to HTML documents for the World Wide Web, and a Web toolbar
- Shared Drawing toolbar with enhanced drawing features

Leave the Word application open for the next section of this chapter.

ACCESSING THE EXCEL APPLICATION

To start the Excel application:

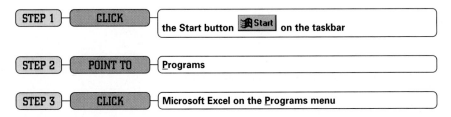

STEP 1 — CLICK — the Start button [Start] on the taskbar

STEP 2 — POINT TO — Programs

STEP 3 — CLICK — Microsoft Excel on the Programs menu

The Excel software is placed into the memory of your computer, and the Excel application window and blank workbook appear. Your screen should look similar to Figure 1-8.

FIGURE 1-8

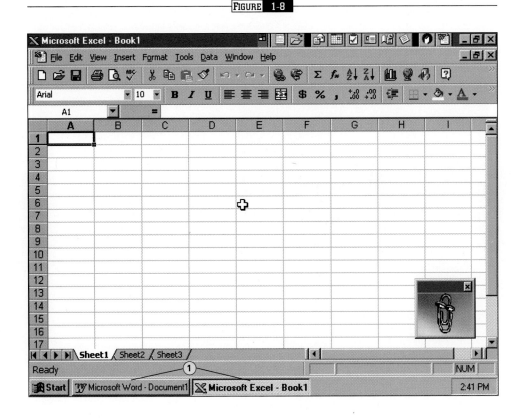

1. Two applications open

Word is still open in the memory of your computer. You can switch to Word by clicking the Word button on the taskbar.

STEP 1 — CLICK — the Word button [Microsoft Word - Document1] on the taskbar

The Word application window appears. Your screen should look similar to Figure 1-7 again. You can start other applications along with Word and Excel. However, your computer's resources may limit the number of applications you can run at the same time.

1.f Closing Office Applications

There are five ways to close open applications and return to the Windows 95 desktop:

1. You can click the E̲xit command on the F̲ile menu to close an application.

2. You can double-click the application Control-menu icon on the title bar.

3. You can click the application Close button on the title bar.

4. You can right-click the application button on the taskbar to display a shortcut menu, and then click the C̲lose command.

5. You can press the ALT+F4 keys.

To close the Word application using the taskbar:

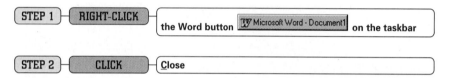

STEP 1 — RIGHT-CLICK — the Word button [W Microsoft Word - Document1] on the taskbar

STEP 2 — CLICK — C̲lose

The Word application closes and the Excel application window appears. To close the Excel application using the title bar:

STEP 3 — CLICK — the application Close button [X] on the title bar

The Excel application closes and the Windows 95 desktop appears.

Summary

> Microsoft Office 97 Standard includes Word, Excel, PowerPoint, and Outlook.

> Microsoft Office 97 Professional includes Access and Bookshelf Basics in addition to the applications included in Microsoft Office 97 Standard.

> The Word application provides word processing capabilities for the preparation and production of documents.

> Financial budgets, reports, charts, and forms are created with the Excel worksheet application.

> Presentation material such as slides, outlines, and audience handouts are created with the PowerPoint application.

> The Access application provides capabilities to store and retrieve information in a database.

> The Outlook application helps you maintain a schedule of appointments, "to do" lists, and the names and addresses of contacts plus other desktop management tasks.

> One major advantage of using Office applications is the ability to integrate the applications by sharing information between them.

> You can copy, link, or embed information between Office applications.

> Linking data enables Office applications to share dynamic data from the source application that automatically update in the destination application when the data change.

> Embedding data places a copy of the data in the destination application.

> Another advantage of using Office applications is that they share a number of common elements such as the title bar, application and document Control menus, Minimize, Maximize, and Restore buttons, application and document Close buttons, scroll bars, ScreenTips, and a menu bar.

Concepts Review

1. Answer Yes or No to indicate whether each application is included in Office 97 Professional and/or Office 97 Standard.

TABLE 2-2

APPLICATION	OFFICE 97 PROFESSIONAL	OFFICE 97 STANDARD
Word 97		
Excel 97		
PowerPoint 97		
Outlook 97		
Access 97		
Bookshelf Basics		

2. Using Figure 1-9 below, identify the common elements of Office application windows.

1. _____   10. _____
2. _____   11. _____
3. _____   12. _____
4. _____   13. _____
5. _____   14. _____
6. _____   15. _____
7. _____   16. _____
8. _____   17. _____
9. _____

FIGURE 1-9

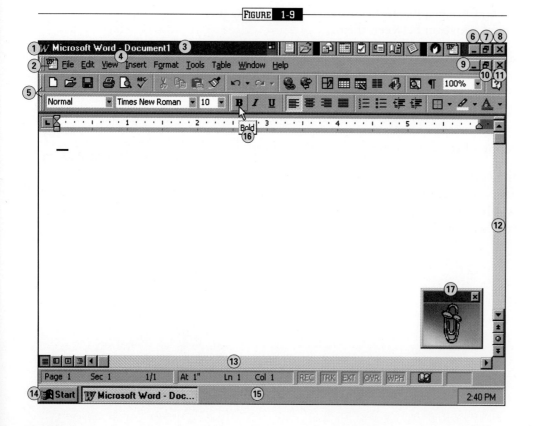

SCANS

Circle the correct answer.

1. **ScreenTips provide:**
   [a] the name of a button on a toolbar.
   [b] a way to view different parts of a document.
   [c] a method for enlarging the application window.
   [d] none of the above.

2. **The document Maximize button allows you to:**
   [a] change the view of your document.
   [b] reduce the size of the application window to a button on the taskbar.
   [c] perform a task using a shortcut.
   [d] enlarge the document window to cover the full area of the screen.

3. **The title bar displays:**
   [a] the application Control-menu icon.
   [b] the application Close button.
   [c] the application and document name.
   [d] all of the above.

4. **You can use the Excel application to:**
   [a] prepare financial reports.
   [b] maintain a list of tasks to accomplish.
   [c] store lists of related data.
   [d] create letters.

5. **The primary advantage of using Office applications is:**
   [a] the ability to store mailing lists.
   [b] the ability to communicate with other employees.
   [c] the ability to integrate applications by sharing information.
   [d] the ability to sort data.

6. **Bookshelf Basics contains the:**
   [a] Excel application.
   [b] *American Heritage Dictionary.*
   [c] *The Columbia Dictionary of Quotations.*
   [d] Outlook.
   [e] a and b.
   [f] b and c.

7. **Word processing is:**
   [a] used to create materials for presentations called slides.
   [b] used to store and retrieve information in a database.
   [c] the preparation and production of documents using automated materials.
   [d] used to maintain a calendar and "to do" lists.
   [e] none of the above.

8. **Right-click means to:**
   [a] press the left mouse button twice very rapidly.
   [b] place the mouse pointer on a command or item.
   [c] press and hold down the right mouse button while you move the mouse.
   [d] press the right mouse button and then release it.
   [e] none of the above.

9. **A window is:**
   [a] a new word processing software application.
   [b] a rectangular area on your screen in which you can view a software application.
   [c] a shortcut to performing tasks.
   [d] the same thing as a computer.
   [e] none of the above.

10. **The taskbar is located:**
   [a] in the upper-right corner of the Word application window.
   [b] in the lower-left corner of the Word application window.
   [c] in the upper-left corner of the desktop.
   [d] across the bottom of the desktop.
   [e] in the lower-right corner of the Word application.

SCANS

Circle Ⓣ if the statement is true or Ⓕ if the statement is false.

1. Ⓣ Ⓕ Office 97 consists of a set of software applications that work compatibly together.

2. Ⓣ Ⓕ Office 97 Professional includes only Word, Excel, and PowerPoint.

3. Ⓣ Ⓕ Excel is an application used to create materials, called slides, for presentations.

4. Ⓣ Ⓕ Word processing is the preparation and production of documents using automated equipment.

5. Ⓣ Ⓕ The primary reason for using Office 97 applications is to increase productivity.

6. Ⓣ Ⓕ The title bar appears at the bottom of an Office 97 application window.

7. Ⓣ Ⓕ When the mouse pointer rests on a toolbar button, a ToolTip appears identifying the name of the button.

8. Ⓣ Ⓕ The application Minimize button is used to enlarge the size of the window on your screen.

9. Ⓣ Ⓕ The menu bar is a special toolbar located at the top of the window below the title bar.

10. Ⓣ Ⓕ When you run multiple applications simultaneously, your computer may require more than 12 MB of memory.

SCANS

Skills Review

EXERCISE 1

Start the Word application using the taskbar. Close the Word application using the taskbar.

EXERCISE 2

Start the Excel application using the taskbar. Close the Excel application using a button on the title bar.

EXERCISE 3

Give three examples of how you can integrate Microsoft Office applications.

EXERCISE 4

List and briefly describe the software applications included in Microsoft Office 97 Standard.

EXERCISE 5

List and briefly describe the software applications included in Microsoft Office 97 Professional that are *not* included in Microsoft Office 97 Standard.

EXERCISE 6

Start the PowerPoint application using the taskbar. Close the PowerPoint application using the taskbar.

EXERCISE 7

Start the Access application using the taskbar. Close the Access application using the Control-menu icon.

Quick Start for Office 97 Document Integration

" My job as an administrative assistant demands that I am well organized and able to perform multiple tasks efficiently. Microsoft Office helps me to be more efficient. I use Microsoft Word to create memos and letters and I maintain numerous databases to organize and manage the department budget. "

Yvonne Malcolm
administrative assistant

Department of Psychology
Northeastern University
Boston, MA

Chapter Overview:

Chapter 1 provided an overview of Office 97 including how to start and close the applications and the common elements of those applications. To complete a project in a business environment, you may need to integrate data from several software applications such as word processing, worksheet, presentation, and database applications. This chapter demonstrates how you would use the Word, Excel, and PowerPoint applications to prepare a weekly sales report.

SNAPSHOT

In this chapter you will learn to:

> **Complete a project with Office applications**

> **Copy information from Excel to Word**

> **Copy information from Excel to PowerPoint**

> **Use a Binder to store related documents**

> **Work with the Office Assistant**

2.a Completing a Project with Office Applications

Object Linking and Embedding

Suppose you are a sales analyst for Nations Lumber Company. Each Monday, you must prepare a sales report that includes the sales data for the previous week and a slide presentation illustrating that sales data.

The sample project in this chapter has been prepared to provide an overview of how you can use Word, Excel, and PowerPoint together to accomplish such a task. The basic sales report text is in a Word document. The sales data by day and a chart representing the percentage of each day's sales to total sales is in an Excel workbook. To complete the project, you will copy the Excel data and chart and paste it into the Word document. Additionally, you will create a PowerPoint slide presentation consisting of one slide. You will copy the Excel chart and paste it into the slide. When you have completed the steps in this chapter, your sales report document should look like Figure 2-1. (Note: The Excel data and chart are not centered in this document. You will learn to do this in the Word unit.)

| FIGURE | 2-1 |

NATIONS LUMBER COMPANY
WEEKLY SALES REPORT

This report includes sales for the week beginning on February 11.

The actual sales are included in the table below.

NATIONS LUMBER COMPANY
SALES INFORMATION
Week Beginning February 11
($000)

Region	Mon	Tues	Wed	Thu	Fri	Total
North	$ 5,000	$ 4,000	$ 7,000	$ 8,000	$ 7,500	$ 31,500
South	7,000	6,000	8,000	7,500	6,500	35,000
East	6,000	4,000	6,500	7,200	6,500	30,200
West	4,000	2,000	3,500	4,300	4,800	18,600
Total	$ 22,000	$ 16,000	$ 25,000	$ 27,000	$ 25,300	$ 115,300

The sales for each region as a percent of total weekly sales are indicated in the following chart.

Nations Lumber Company
West 16%
North 27%
East 26%
South 31%

The next sales report will be sent next Monday.

This report was prepared by Student Name.

Verify that the Windows 95 desktop is showing. To start the Word application:

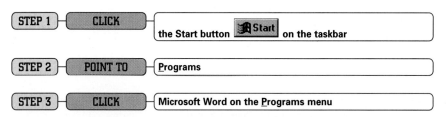

STEP 1 — CLICK — the Start button ▊Start on the taskbar

STEP 2 — POINT TO — Programs

STEP 3 — CLICK — Microsoft Word on the Programs menu

The Word application opens with a blank document. Now open the existing Word document named SALES REPORT located on the student disk. This document contains the basic text for the sales report.

> **IN THIS BOOK**
>
> All document, workbook, presentation, and database filenames will be shown in uppercase letters for easier identification. For example, the previous paragraph advises that you will open a document named SALES REPORT. The actual filename on the student disk is Sales Report, in mixed-case letters.
>   Your instructor will assist you in accessing the student files used in this book.

When working with Office applications, there usually are multiple ways to accomplish a task. The **Taskbar method**, the **Shortcut icon method,** the **Shortcut menu method**, the **Toolbar method**, the **Shortcut Bar method**, the **Menu bar method,** and the **Keyboard Shortcut method** are all common ways to access commands.

Table 2-1 below describes methods to open an existing Word document and the Word application.

TABLE 2-1

METHOD	ACTION
Taskbar	1. Click the Start button ▊Start, point to Documents, then click the name of a Word document on the Documents menu.
	2. Click the Start button ▊Start, point to Programs, click Windows Explorer on the Programs menu, select the appropriate disk drive and folder, then double-click a Word document icon.
	3. Click the Start button ▊Start, click Open Office Document, select the appropriate disk drive and folder, click a Word document icon, then click the Open button in the dialog box.
Shortcut Bar	Click the Open Office Document button 🗁, select the appropriate disk drive and folder, click a Word document icon, then click the Open button in the dialog box.
Shortcut icon	1. Double-click the My Computer icon on the Windows 95 desktop, double-click the appropriate disk drive and folder, and double-click a Word document icon.
	2. Create a shortcut icon on the desktop for a Word document.

Table 2-2 below describes methods you can use to open an existing Word document after the Word application is running:

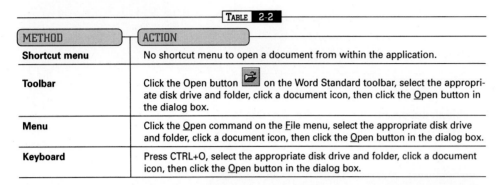

METHOD	ACTION
Shortcut menu	No shortcut menu to open a document from within the application.
Toolbar	Click the Open button 📂 on the Word Standard toolbar, select the appropriate disk drive and folder, click a document icon, then click the Open button in the dialog box.
Menu	Click the Open command on the File menu, select the appropriate disk drive and folder, click a document icon, then click the Open button in the dialog box.
Keyboard	Press CTRL+O, select the appropriate disk drive and folder, click a document icon, then click the Open button in the dialog box.

IN THIS BOOK

In Chapters 1-4 in this unit, the **Taskbar** and **Menu** methods to start an application and open an existing document are shown. In the remaining units of this book, the **Shortcut Bar**, the **Shortcut menu**, and the **Toolbar methods** will be emphasized.

To open the SALES REPORT document using the Menu method:

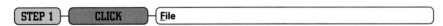

STEP 1 — CLICK — File

A drop-down menu containing buttons, commands, and keyboard shortcuts appears. Your screen should look similar to Figure 2-2.

FIGURE 2-2

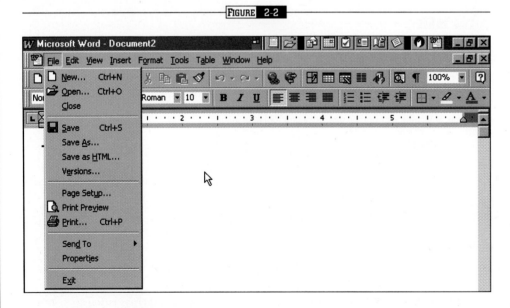

An ellipsis (...) after a command on a menu indicates that a dialog box opens when that command is clicked. A **dialog box** provides additional options within a command.

STEP 2 — CLICK — Open

The Open dialog box opens. Your screen should look similar to Figure 2-3.

FIGURE 2-3

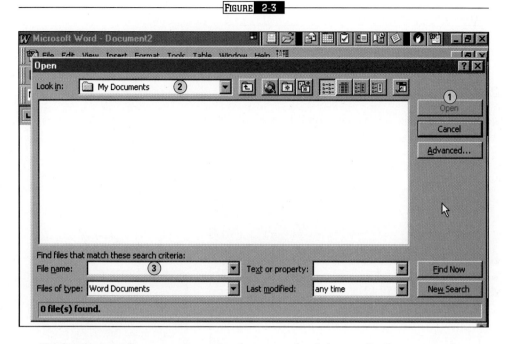

1. Command button
2. List box
3. Text box

Dialog boxes often contain option buttons, check boxes, list boxes, text boxes, and command buttons. These and other elements of a dialog box are described below.

- **Option buttons** are round buttons. Whenever these option buttons appear in a group box within a dialog box, only one can be active. You can activate the appropriate option by clicking it.
- **Check boxes** are small square boxes that you can click to insert a check mark. A check mark in a check box means that feature is active. If the check box is blank, then that feature is inactive. To activate a check box, click on the box to insert a check mark. To deactivate the feature, click the box to remove the check mark.
- **List boxes** provide a list of choices. Sometimes you cannot see the entire list. When the entire list is not visible, a vertical scroll bar appears to the right of the list. You can use this scroll bar to view all the items in the list. To select an item from a list, click the item.
- **Text boxes** provide an area in which you can type text. For example, in Figure 2-3 the File name: text box is the area that will contain the name of the file to be opened. To move the insertion point into a text box, click inside the text box area.
- **Command buttons** are rectangular buttons, such as the Open button shown in Figure 2-3. Other common command buttons include the OK and Cancel buttons. To select a command button, click it. If the command button has a dark outline, you can also press the ENTER key to select it.
- **Spin boxes** are small text boxes with up and down triangle buttons to the right of the text area. To change the value in the box, click the up or down triangle button to increase or decrease the value, or select and retype the number in the spin box.

QUICK TIP

You can use the keyboard to access dialog box items by pressing the ALT key together with the underlined character in the dialog box item name. An alternative for moving between various items in a dialog box is to press the TAB key. Pressing the TAB key selects the next item in a dialog box.

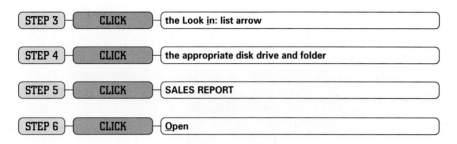

STEP 3	CLICK	the Look in: list arrow
STEP 4	CLICK	the appropriate disk drive and folder
STEP 5	CLICK	SALES REPORT
STEP 6	CLICK	Open

The SALES REPORT document appears and your screen should look similar to Figure 2-4.

FIGURE 2-4

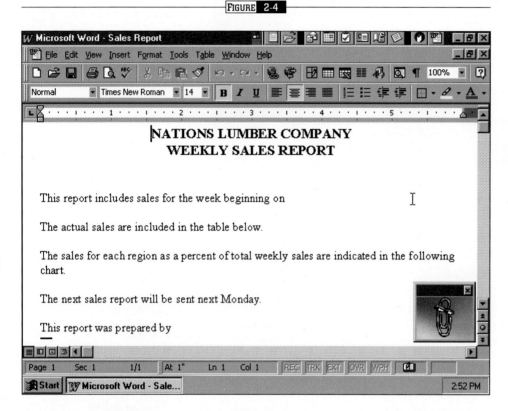

> **QUICK TIP**
>
> An alternate method of opening a file is to double-click the document name in the Open dialog box.

When the mouse pointer is positioned in a text area, its shape changes to an **I-beam**. The I-beam mouse pointer shape is used to position the **insertion point**, or typing position indicator, in a text area. To add a date to the first sentence:

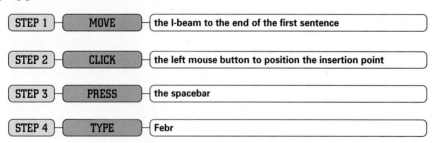

STEP 1	MOVE	the I-beam to the end of the first sentence
STEP 2	CLICK	the left mouse button to position the insertion point
STEP 3	PRESS	the spacebar
STEP 4	TYPE	Febr

Notice that even though you did not completely type the month name, a small yellow box containing the text "February" appears above the insertion point. This is the **AutoComplete** feature, which suggests alternative text for common words or abbreviations. Your screen should look similar to Figure 2-5.

FIGURE 2-5

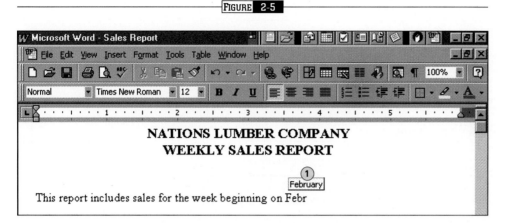

1. AutoComplete suggestion

AutoComplete is one of several Word automatic formatting features. In this example, when you type the first few characters of a month name, the AutoComplete feature displays the entire month name in a ScreenTip box. You can accept the AutoComplete suggestion by pressing the ENTER key or you can ignore the AutoComplete suggestion by continuing to type the text. To accept the AutoComplete suggested text "February" and add the day of the month:

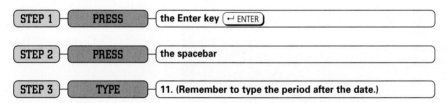

STEP 1 — PRESS — the Enter key (↵ ENTER)

STEP 2 — PRESS — the spacebar

STEP 3 — TYPE — 11. (Remember to type the period after the date.)

Leave the Word application and the SALES REPORT document open to continue working in the next section.

2.b Copying Information from Excel to Word

You are ready to place the weekly sales data in the sales report. The data are stored in an Excel worksheet. To copy data from Excel to Word, you first must open the Excel application:

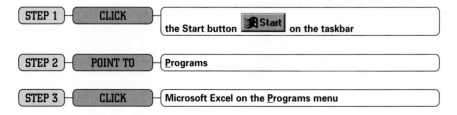

STEP 1 — CLICK — the Start button [Start] on the taskbar

STEP 2 — POINT TO — Programs

STEP 3 — CLICK — Microsoft Excel on the Programs menu

The Excel application and a blank workbook open. The data for the sales report are stored on the student disk in the workbook named NATIONS LUMBER SALES. To open the workbook:

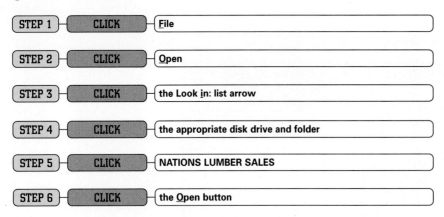

STEP 1	CLICK	File
STEP 2	CLICK	Open
STEP 3	CLICK	the Look in: list arrow
STEP 4	CLICK	the appropriate disk drive and folder
STEP 5	CLICK	NATIONS LUMBER SALES
STEP 6	CLICK	the Open button

The Feb 11 worksheet in the NATIONS LUMBER SALES workbook appears. Your screen should look like Figure 2-6.

FIGURE 2-6

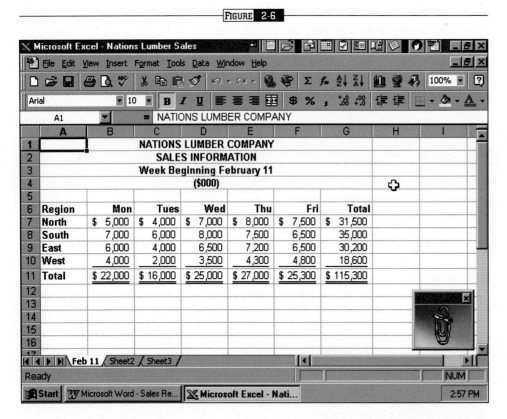

With Office applications, you can use the Clipboard to copy and paste information from one document to another. The **Clipboard** is a reserved storage area in the memory of the computer that temporarily stores a selection of data to be copied. In this example, you will copy the data from the Feb 11 worksheet in the NATIONAL LUMBER SALES workbook to the Clipboard and then paste it into the SALES REPORT Word document. Before you copy the data, you must first select them. To select the data:

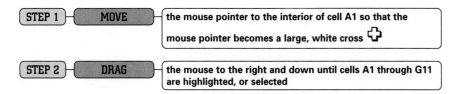

The selected cells are called a **range**. Cell A1 is the anchor, or beginning cell, of the range. The anchor in a range remains white, whereas the other cells in the range are shaded.

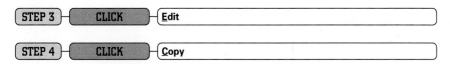

Observe the dashed-line marquee that moves around the selected cells. This marquee indicates the range has been copied to the Clipboard.

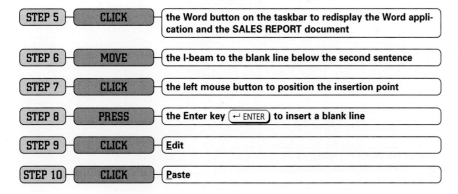

After a few seconds, the selected Feb 11 worksheet data is pasted into the document as a Word table. Your screen should look similar to Figure 2-7.

FIGURE 2-7

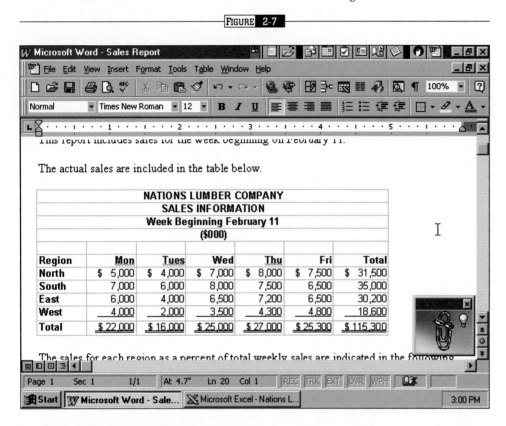

You will now copy the chart in the Excel worksheet and paste it into the Word document. Before you can copy the chart, you must first select it.

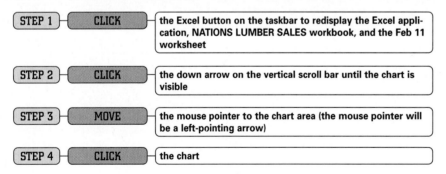

STEP 1	CLICK	the Excel button on the taskbar to redisplay the Excel application, NATIONS LUMBER SALES workbook, and the Feb 11 worksheet
STEP 2	CLICK	the down arrow on the vertical scroll bar until the chart is visible
STEP 3	MOVE	the mouse pointer to the chart area (the mouse pointer will be a left-pointing arrow)
STEP 4	CLICK	the chart

Your screen should look similar to Figure 2-8.

FIGURE 2-8

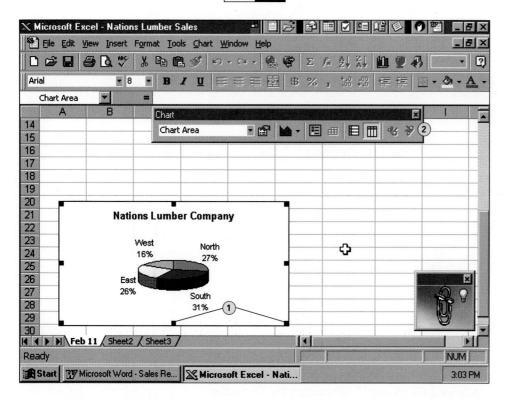

1. Sizing or selection handles
2. Chart toolbar

Small black squares, called **selection**, or **sizing**, **handles**, appear around the chart to indicate that it is selected. These sizing handles will be used later in this chapter to change the size of the chart. The Chart toolbar also appears, by default, when a chart is selected.

To paste the chart into the SALES REPORT document:

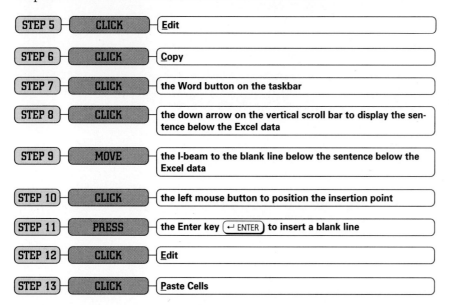

STEP 5	CLICK	Edit
STEP 6	CLICK	Copy
STEP 7	CLICK	the Word button on the taskbar
STEP 8	CLICK	the down arrow on the vertical scroll bar to display the sentence below the Excel data
STEP 9	MOVE	the I-beam to the blank line below the sentence below the Excel data
STEP 10	CLICK	the left mouse button to position the insertion point
STEP 11	PRESS	the Enter key (↵ ENTER) to insert a blank line
STEP 12	CLICK	Edit
STEP 13	CLICK	Paste Cells

After a few seconds, the chart appears in the document as an embedded chart object. Because you pasted an embedded chart object, Word automatically switches from the default Normal editing view to the Page layout editing view. Different editing views are discussed in the Word unit. Your screen should look similar to Figure 2-9.

FIGURE 2-9

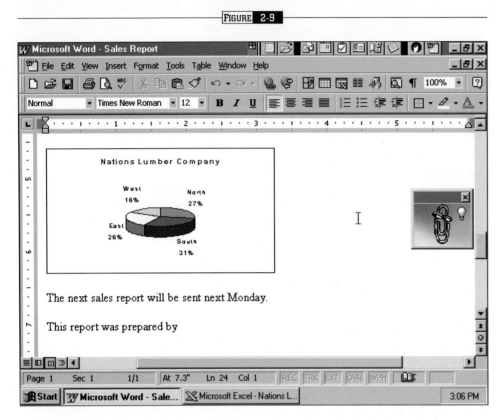

To add your name to the report:

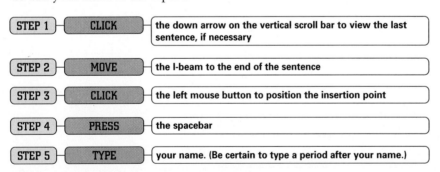

STEP 1 — CLICK — the down arrow on the vertical scroll bar to view the last sentence, if necessary

STEP 2 — MOVE — the I-beam to the end of the sentence

STEP 3 — CLICK — the left mouse button to position the insertion point

STEP 4 — PRESS — the spacebar

STEP 5 — TYPE — your name. (Be certain to type a period after your name.)

IN THIS BOOK

You can set up your Office applications to save files on a disk or directory different from the one established during installation. Save your documents to the disk and folder specified by your instructor. As you use this book, save a document only when you are instructed to do so.

When you are asked to save a document, the filename will be shown in uppercase letters; however, you can type the filename in either upper-, mixed-, or lowercase letters. Unless otherwise advised by your instructor, type the filename in mixed-case letters.

The SALES REPORT document is complete.
To change the editing view back to Normal view:

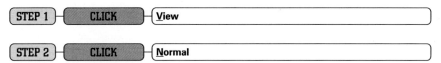

STEP 1 — CLICK — View

STEP 2 — CLICK — Normal

To save the document with a new name:

STEP 1 — CLICK — File

STEP 2 — CLICK — Save As

Notice that the current filename, SALES REPORT, is highlighted, or selected, in the File name: text box. This means the insertion point, or typing position, is already in the File name: text box.
To give the document a new name, simply begin typing the name:

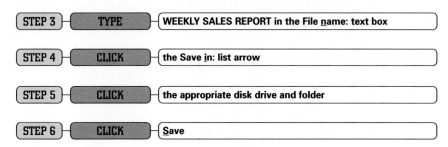

STEP 3 — TYPE — WEEKLY SALES REPORT in the File name: text box

STEP 4 — CLICK — the Save in: list arrow

STEP 5 — CLICK — the appropriate disk drive and folder

STEP 6 — CLICK — Save

The document is now saved in the specified folder.
To print a copy of the WEEKLY SALES REPORT document:

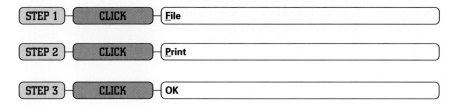

STEP 1 — CLICK — File

STEP 2 — CLICK — Print

STEP 3 — CLICK — OK

One copy of the WEEKLY SALES REPORT prints. You will learn more about changing printing options in an application unit of this book.

2.c Copying Information from Excel to PowerPoint

The sales manager wants you to create a one-slide presentation using the chart in the Feb 11 worksheet in a slide presentation. The PowerPoint application is used to create such presentations. To create a presentation you must copy the chart from the Feb 11 worksheet and paste it into a PowerPoint slide. To do this, first open the Power-Point application and a presentation file named WEEKLY SALES PRESENTATION located on the student disk.

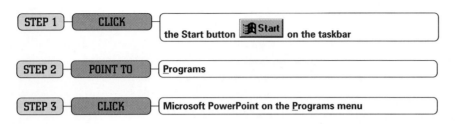

STEP 1 — **CLICK** — the Start button [Start] on the taskbar

STEP 2 — **POINT TO** — Programs

STEP 3 — **CLICK** — Microsoft PowerPoint on the Programs menu

The PowerPoint application window and dialog box appear. Various menu and toolbars also appear. Your screen should look similar to Figure 2-10.

FIGURE 2-10

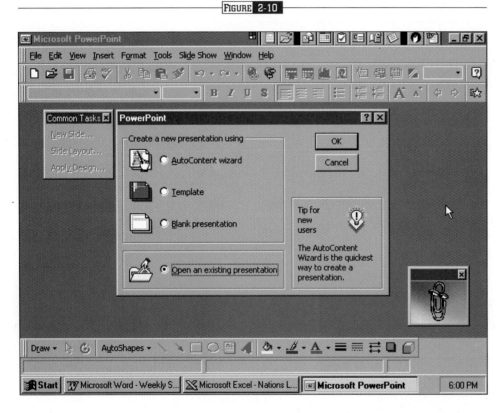

The PowerPoint dialog box displays a tip for new users as well as options for opening an exiting presentation or creating a new, blank presentation. To open an existing presentation:

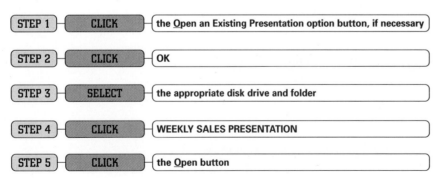

STEP 1 — **CLICK** — the Open an Existing Presentation option button, if necessary

STEP 2 — **CLICK** — OK

STEP 3 — **SELECT** — the appropriate disk drive and folder

STEP 4 — **CLICK** — WEEKLY SALES PRESENTATION

STEP 5 — **CLICK** — the Open button

The WEEKLY SALES PRESENTATION slide presentation appears. Your screen should look like Figure 2-11.

FIGURE 2-11

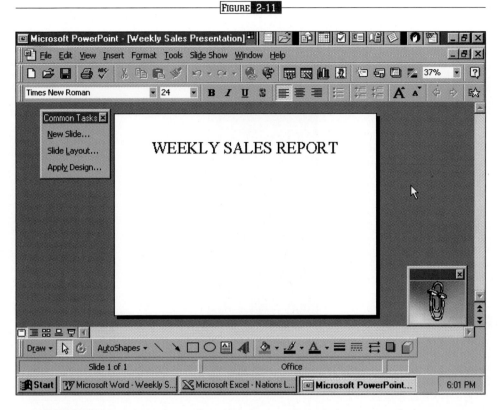

Because the Excel chart is still stored on the Clipboard, you simply have to paste it into the slide.

| STEP 6 | CLICK | Edit |
| STEP 7 | CLICK | Paste |

In a few seconds, the small Excel chart object appears on the slide. Notice the white sizing handles surrounding it. You will use these sizing handles to enlarge the chart.

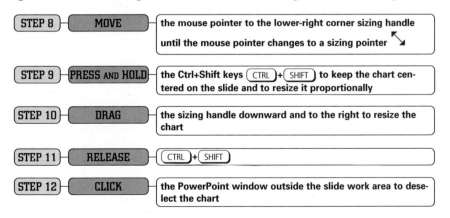

STEP 8	MOVE	the mouse pointer to the lower-right corner sizing handle until the mouse pointer changes to a sizing pointer ⬊
STEP 9	PRESS AND HOLD	the Ctrl+Shift keys (CTRL)+(SHIFT) to keep the chart centered on the slide and to resize it proportionally
STEP 10	DRAG	the sizing handle downward and to the right to resize the chart
STEP 11	RELEASE	(CTRL)+(SHIFT)
STEP 12	CLICK	the PowerPoint window outside the slide work area to deselect the chart

After you have resized and deselected the chart, your screen should look similar to Figure 2-12.

FIGURE 2-12

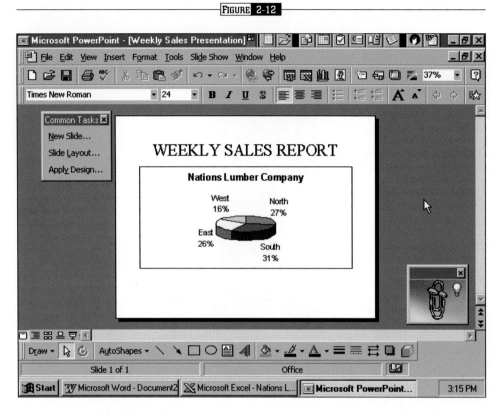

To save the slide presentation with a new name:

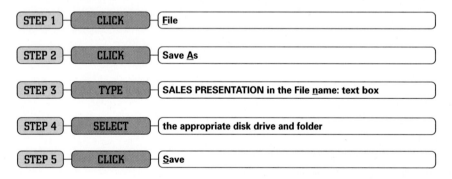

STEP 1 — CLICK — File

STEP 2 — CLICK — Save As

STEP 3 — TYPE — SALES PRESENTATION in the File name: text box

STEP 4 — SELECT — the appropriate disk drive and folder

STEP 5 — CLICK — Save

At this point, you have copied or integrated information between Word, Excel, and PowerPoint. As a next step, you could prepare a cover letter and distribute the WEEKLY SALES REPORT document to the appropriate personnel. You could save the mailing list in a database using the Access application. The individual letters could be prepared using the Mail Merge feature in Word with the Access database or Outlook Address Book as a data source.

Close the three applications used in this chapter. As each application closes, do not save changes to any open documents. When the applications and documents are closed, only the Windows 95 desktop, desktop icons, the taskbar, and the Shortcut Bar should be visible on your screen.

2.d Using a Binder to Store Related Documents

You can use a **Binder** to store related documents together. For example, the WEEKLY SALES REPORT document, the NATIONS LUMBER SALES workbook, and the SALES PRESENTATION slide presentation can be stored together in a Binder. You can then open the Binder for easy access to all three files and the three Office applications used to create the files. Each document stored in a Binder is in a **section**. You can edit the individual sections, print selected sections, or print the entire contents of the Binder.

To open a Binder named WEEKLY SALES DATA located on the student disk:

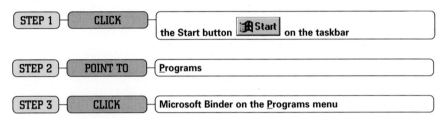

STEP 1	CLICK	the Start button **⊞Start** on the taskbar
STEP 2	POINT TO	Programs
STEP 3	CLICK	Microsoft Binder on the Programs menu

The Microsoft Office Binder - Binder1 window appears. Your screen should look similar to Figure 2-13.

FIGURE 2-13

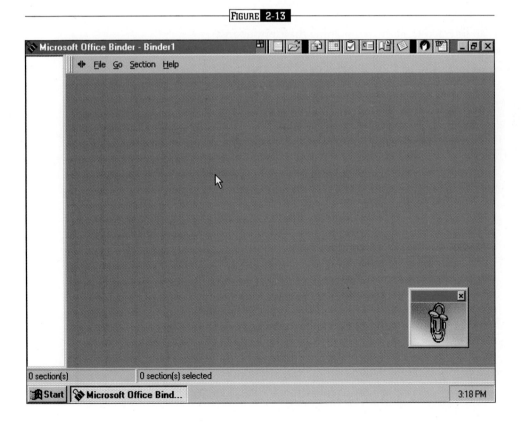

To open the WEEKLY SALES DATA Binder:

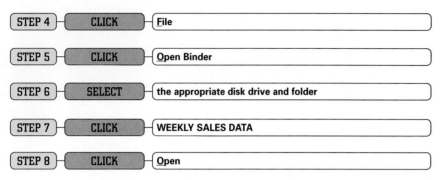

STEP 4 — CLICK — File

STEP 5 — CLICK — Open Binder

STEP 6 — SELECT — the appropriate disk drive and folder

STEP 7 — CLICK — WEEKLY SALES DATA

STEP 8 — CLICK — Open

The WEEKLY SALES DATA Binder containing the sales report documents appears. The document sections are displayed in the narrow left pane of the window. The selected document and application are displayed in the larger right pane of the window. You can select a section by clicking on the section icon. When you select a section, the application and document appear in the right pane of the window. After reviewing the WEEKLY SALES DATA Binder, you can close it.

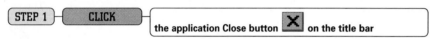

STEP 1 — CLICK — the application Close button ✕ on the title bar

2.e Working with the Office Assistant

The Office Assistant is an interactive, animated graphic that appears in a separate window of the Word, Excel, PowerPoint, and Access application windows. When you activate the Office Assistant, a balloon-style dialog box opens that contains options for searching online Help by topic or displaying user tips. The Office Assistant will also automatically offer suggestions when you begin certain tasks. In addition, if you are performing a task, such as selecting text or data, that requires the screen space occupied by the Office Assistant, the Office Assistant automatically will move out of the way or temporarily disappear from the screen. You can customize the Office Assistant by changing the animated graphic image or turning on or off various options. Any customization is shared for all Office applications.

AUTOMATICALLY ACTIVATING THE OFFICE ASSISTANT

Suppose you want to type a personal letter to Aunt Sue. The Office Assistant will automatically suggest help for writing the letter. First, start the Word application.

To open the application:

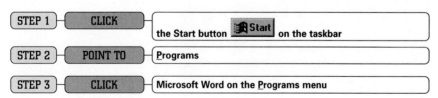

STEP 1 — CLICK — the Start button ⊞Start on the taskbar

STEP 2 — POINT TO — Programs

STEP 3 — CLICK — Microsoft Word on the Programs menu

To begin the letter:

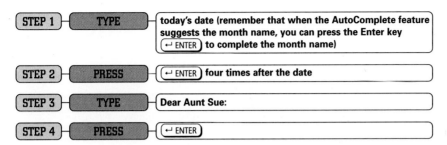

STEP 1 — TYPE — today's date (remember that when the AutoComplete feature suggests the month name, you can press the Enter key (↵ ENTER) to complete the month name)

STEP 2 — PRESS — (↵ ENTER) four times after the date

STEP 3 — TYPE — Dear Aunt Sue:

STEP 4 — PRESS — (↵ ENTER)

The Office Assistant balloon appears, and the Office Assistant asks if you want help writing the letter. Your screen should look similar to Figure 2-14.

FIGURE 2-14

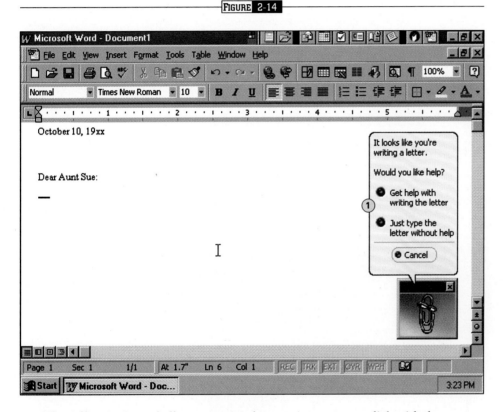

1. Office Assistant balloon

The Office Assistant balloon contains three options you can click with the mouse. If you click the "Get help with writing the letter" option, the Letter Wizard dialog box opens. A **wizard** is a step-by-step process with a series of dialog boxes you can use to complete a task. If you click the "Just type the letter without help" option or the Cancel option, the balloon closes.

To close the Office Assistant balloon:

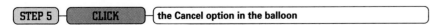

STEP 5 — CLICK — the Cancel option in the balloon

The Office Assistant balloon and window close.

CAUTION

Once you cancel the balloon containing the help options for writing a letter, the letter-writing help options will not appear again until you create a new, blank document.

MANUALLY ACTIVATING THE OFFICE ASSISTANT

You can activate the Office Assistant at any time to search online Help for specific topics, get tips, or customize the Office Assistant. To review the customization options for the Office Assistant:

STEP 1 — CLICK — the Office Assistant button 🔲 on the Standard toolbar

The Office Assistant balloon appears and the Office Assistant asks what you would like to do.

STEP 2 — CLICK — Options in the Office Assistant balloon

The Office Assistant dialog box opens.

STEP 3 — CLICK — the Options tab in the dialog box, if necessary

Your screen should look similar to Figure 2-15.

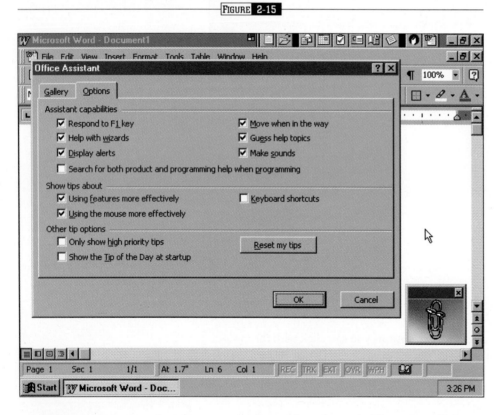

FIGURE 2-15

Take a moment to review the customization options shown in Figure 2-15. To learn more about each option, you can use the ScreenTips help feature. To use ScreenTips in a dialog box, you place the mouse pointer on a dialog box item and click the right mouse button.

To display a ScreenTip for the <u>K</u>eyboard shortcuts item in the Show tips about group:

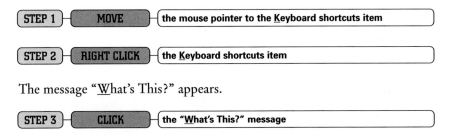

| STEP 1 | MOVE | the mouse pointer to the **K**eyboard shortcuts item |

| STEP 2 | RIGHT CLICK | the **K**eyboard shortcuts item |

The message "<u>W</u>hat's This?" appears.

| STEP 3 | CLICK | the "**W**hat's This?" message |

A ScreenTip appears with a description of the dialog box item. Your screen should look similar to Figure 2-16.

FIGURE 2-16

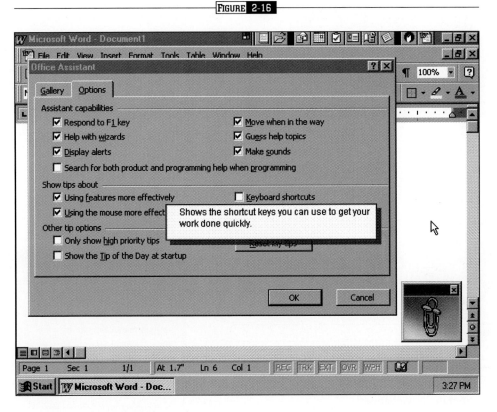

To close the descriptive message:

| STEP 4 | PRESS | the Esc key (ESC) |

The Office Assistant comes with a gallery of images you can use to represent the Office Assistant on the Windows 95 desktop. The default image is Clippit.
<u>G</u>allery:

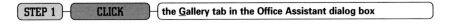

| STEP 1 | CLICK | the **G**allery tab in the Office Assistant dialog box |

Your screen should look similar to Figure 2-17.

FIGURE 2-17

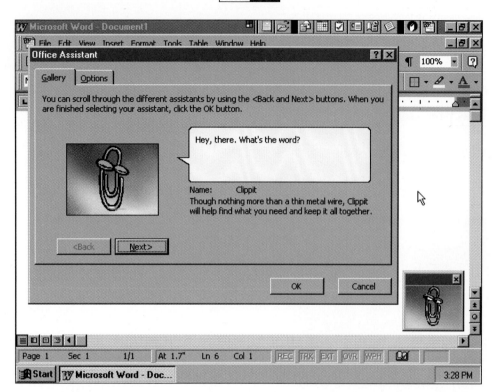

To display a new Office Assistant:

| STEP 2 | CLICK | Next > |

The Dot icon appears. Review the description for The Dot.
To view other assistants:

| STEP 3 | CLICK | Next > |

| STEP 4 | CONTINUE | to review the remaining images |

To close the dialog box without making any changes:

| STEP 5 | CLICK | Cancel |

You can choose to display or hide the Office Assistant.
To hide the Office Assistant:

| STEP 1 | RIGHT CLICK | the Office Assistant |

| STEP 2 | CLICK | Hide Assistant |

The Office Assistant window no longer appears.

MENU TIP

If the Office Assistant is hidden, you can display it by clicking the Microsoft Word Help command on the Help menu. You can hide the Office Assistant by right-clicking the Office Assistant to display a shortcut menu, and then clicking the Hide Assistant command.

MOUSE TIP

When the Office Assistant is hidden, you can click the Office Assistant button on the Standard toolbar to display it. You can hide the Office Assistant by clicking the Close button on the Office Assistant window title bar.

To display the Office Assistant:

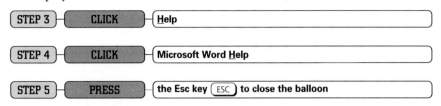

STEP 3	CLICK	Help
STEP 4	CLICK	Microsoft Word Help
STEP 5	PRESS	the Esc key (ESC) to close the balloon

Close the Word application and document without saving any changes.

OTHER METHODS OF GETTING ONLINE HELP FOR OFFICE APPLICATIONS

There are many other ways to get online Help when working in Office applications. Table 2-3 below describes various methods of getting online Help.

TABLE 2-3

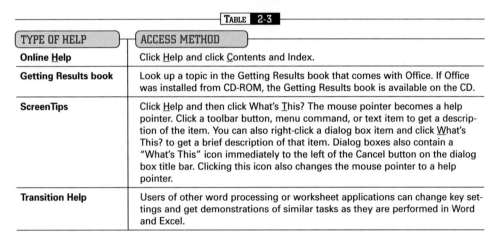

TYPE OF HELP	ACCESS METHOD
Online Help	Click Help and click Contents and Index.
Getting Results book	Look up a topic in the Getting Results book that comes with Office. If Office was installed from CD-ROM, the Getting Results book is available on the CD.
ScreenTips	Click Help and then click What's This? The mouse pointer becomes a help pointer. Click a toolbar button, menu command, or text item to get a description of the item. You can also right-click a dialog box item and click What's This? to get a brief description of that item. Dialog boxes also contain a "What's This" icon immediately to the left of the Cancel button on the dialog box title bar. Clicking this icon also changes the mouse pointer to a help pointer.
Transition Help	Users of other word processing or worksheet applications can change key settings and get demonstrations of similar tasks as they are performed in Word and Excel.

Summary

> Office applications can be used together to improve your productivity in preparing business documents and reports.

> There are multiple ways to accomplish a task when using Office applications.

> Common ways of accessing Office application commands are the Taskbar method, the Shortcut icon method, the Shortcut menu method, the Toolbar method, the Shortcut Bar method, Menu bar method and the Keyboard Shortcut method.

> Dialog boxes contain option buttons, check boxes, list boxes, text boxes, command buttons, and spin boxes.

> The mouse pointer changes shape to the I-beam in a typing area of a dialog box or word processing document.

> The Clipboard can be used to temporarily store information copied or cut from an Office application.

> In a worksheet, highlighted cells are called a range.

> Objects such as embedded charts will have selection, or sizing, handles around them when they are selected. These selection handles are used to change the size of the object.

> You can copy data and charts from Excel to Word and PowerPoint.

> Binders are used to store related Office documents together and allow you easy access to both the documents and their associated Office applications.

> Office applications provide several way to get help: Office Assistant, Contents and Index Help, a Getting Results book, ScreenTips, and Transition Help.

Concepts Review

Circle the correct answer.

1. When you click the Start button to open a document, you are using the:
[a] Toolbar method.
[b] Taskbar method.
[c] Keyboard method.
[d] Menu method.

2. You can increase the number in a spin box by:
[a] clicking the down triangle to the right of the spin box.
[b] selecting the number and typing a new number.
[c] clicking the up triangle to the right of the spin box.
[d] a and b.
[e] b and c.

3. You can position the insertion point in a document by:
[a] clicking the OK button.
[b] moving the Help pointer to the new position and clicking the left mouse button.
[c] moving the I-beam to the new position and clicking the left mouse button.
[d] dragging the mouse pointer to the new location.

4. The first step in copying Excel worksheet data to a Word document after the applications are open is to:
[a] press the ENTER key to insert blank lines.
[b] click Paste on the Edit menu.
[c] click the chart area.
[d] drag to select the worksheet data.

5. When you click the yellow lightbulb in the Office Assistant window, you get:
[a] useful tips about recently performed tasks.
[b] key settings and demonstrations of tasks like those performed in other vendors' products.
[c] a list of possible responses to a question.
[d] all of the above.
[e] none of the above.

6. An ellipsis after a command on a menu indicates:
[a] the command is not available.
[b] the command is a toggle switch that turns on and off.
[c] the command is only available in Word.
[d] the command displays a dialog box.
[e] none of the above.

7. Which of the following items are not found in a dialog box?
[a] command buttons.
[b] check boxes.
[c] option buttons.
[d] list boxes.
[e] spin boxes.
[f] all of the above are found in a dialog box.

8. The Clipboard is:
[a] a place to write notes on your assignments.
[b] the location where you install the Office 97 applications.
[c] a reserved storage area in your computer's memory.
[d] an option in a dialog box.

9. The Office Assistant can:
[a] be hidden or displayed as needed.
[b] contain options to display user tips.
[c] be customized.
[d] display help automatically for some tasks.
[e] a and d.
[f] a, b, c, and d.

10. You can change the size of a pasted object with the:
[a] sizing handles.
[b] the object name.
[c] the Change Size command on the Edit menu.
[d] the Change Size command on the View menu.
[e] none of the above.

SCANS

Circle ⒯ if the statement is true or ⒡ if the statement is false.

1. ⒯ ⒡ The Menu bar method and the Toolbar method are two common ways to access commands.

2. ⒯ ⒡ A dialog box provides options within a command.

3. ⒯ ⒡ Text boxes provide a list of names from which you can make a choice.

4. ⒯ ⒡ In a dialog box, only two option buttons can be active at the same time.

5. ⒯ ⒡ If a check box contains a check mark, then that feature is inactive.

6. ⒯ ⒡ You can click an item to select it in a list box.

7. ⒯ ⒡ Only Excel and Word allow you to integrate data.

8. ⒯ ⒡ You can use the Office Assistant button on the Standard toolbar to display or hide the Office Assistant.

9. ⒯ ⒡ You can store related documents in a Binder for easy access, editing, and printing.

10. ⒯ ⒡ You cannot open a file in Word using the keyboard.

Skills Review

EXERCISE 1

1. Open the Word application.
2. Open the EXPENSE REPORT Word document located on your student disk.
3. Open the Excel application.
4. Open the MAY EXPENSES Excel workbook located on your student disk.
5. Copy the district expense information in cells A1 through E12 to the Clipboard.
6. Paste the district expense information into the EXPENSE REPORT Word document between the second and third sentences.
7. Save the Word document as OF02EX01.
8. Print the document, then close the Word and Excel applications.

EXERCISE 2

1. Open the Word application.
2. Open the OF02EX01 document created in Exercise 1 in this chapter.
3. Open the Excel application.
4. Open the MAY EXPENSES Excel workbook located on your student disk.
5. Copy the embedded pie chart to the Clipboard.
6. Paste it into the OF02EX01 document at the end of the document.
7. Save the document as OF02EX02.
8. Print the document, then close the Word and Excel applications.

EXERCISE 3

1. Open the Excel application.
2. Open the MAY EXPENSES Excel workbook located on your student disk.
3. Copy the embedded pie chart to the Clipboard.
4. Open the PowerPoint application.
5. Open the EXPENSE PRESENTATION slide presentation file located on your student disk.
6. Paste the chart on the slide.
7. Resize the chart so that it is larger and easier to read.
8. Save the presentation as OF02EX03.
9. Print the slide, then close the PowerPoint and Excel applications.

EXERCISE 4

Describe the process for copying Excel worksheet data to a Word document.

EXERCISE 5

Describe the process for copying a chart in Excel to a Word document.

EXERCISE 6

1. Open the Word application.
2. Open the SALES REPORT Word document located on your student disk.
3. Open the Excel application.
4. Open the SOUTHWESTERN DIVISION SALES REPORT Excel workbook located on your student disk.
5. Copy the sales report information in cells A1 through B10 to the Clipboard.
6. Paste the sales report information into the SALES REPORT Word document in the appropriate position.
7. Type "February 11." at the end of the first sentence. (Do not type the quotation marks.)
8. Save the Word document as OF02EX06.
9. Print the document, then close the Word and Excel applications.

EXERCISE 7

1. Open the Word application.
2. Open the OF02EX06 document created in Exercise 6 in this chapter.
3. Open the Excel application.
4. Open the SOUTHWESTERN DIVISION SALES REPORT Excel workbook located on your student disk.
5. Copy the embedded pie chart to the Clipboard.
6. Paste the pie chart into the OF02EX06 Word document in the appropriate place.
7. Save the Word document as OF02EX07.
8. Print the document, then close the Word and Excel applications.

EXERCISE 8

1. Open the Excel application.
2. Open the SOUTHWESTERN DIVISION SALES REPORT Excel workbook located on your student disk.
3. Copy the embedded pie chart to the Clipboard.
4. Open the PowerPoint application.
5. Open the SALES REPORT PRESENTATION slide presentation file located on your student disk.
6. Paste the chart on the slide and resize the chart so that it is larger and easier to read.
7. Save the presentation as OF02EX08.
8. Print the slide, then close the PowerPoint and Excel applications.

Case Problems

PROBLEM 1

Open the Word application. Using the Contents and Index command on the Help menu, find the online Help topic "Insert a Microsoft Embedded Chart." (Hint: Click the Contents tab to display the Table of Contents and then click the "Sharing Data with Other Users and Applications" topic.)

PROBLEM 2

Using the Office Assistant, search for information about exchanging data between applications.

PROBLEM 3

After completing Problems 1 and 2 above, write a brief explanation of how you can share, link, and embed information between Office applications.

The Shortcut Bar

"The nature of my job is very fast-paced and deadlines are always imminent. I must be able to switch among several computer applications quickly. Microsoft Office allows me to move from one task to another easily. I can layout a publication, write a media release, send an e-mail, and use the internet within a short period of time."

Alison Steeves
community and public affairs officer

Sunnybrook Health Science Centre
Toronto, Canada

Sunnybrook Health Science Centre is one of the largest hospitals in Canada, housing the first and largest regional trauma unit in the country.

Chapter Overview:

In the previous chapters, you were introduced to Office 97 applications including document integration. This chapter discusses using the Office 97 **Shortcut Bar**, which provides buttons that help you efficiently start Office applications, open existing documents and their applications, and access Outlook features. Chapter 1 introduced you to the default buttons on the Shortcut Bar. In this chapter, you will learn to access the Shortcut Bar Control menu, add additional buttons to the Shortcut Bar, change the appearance and location of the Shortcut Bar, and add other toolbars to the Shortcut Bar.

SNAPSHOT

In this chapter you will learn to:

> Display the Shortcut Bar Control menu

> Add, reposition, and remove buttons on the Shortcut Bar

> Change the appearance and location of the Shortcut Bar

> Add other toolbars to the Shortcut Bar

3.a Displaying the Shortcut Bar Control Menu

The Shortcut Bar Control menu contains commands you can use to customize the Shortcut Bar, add or remove Office programs, or close the Shortcut Bar so that it no longer appears on the desktop. You will display the Control menu and add additional buttons to the Shortcut Bar. While it is not necessary to close all applications before you customize the Shortcut Bar, doing so will make the steps below easier to follow on your screen.

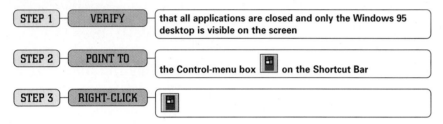

STEP 1	VERIFY	that all applications are closed and only the Windows 95 desktop is visible on the screen
STEP 2	POINT TO	the Control-menu box ▣ on the Shortcut Bar
STEP 3	RIGHT-CLICK	▣

The Shortcut Bar Control menu displays. Your screen should look similar to Figure 3-1.

FIGURE 3-1

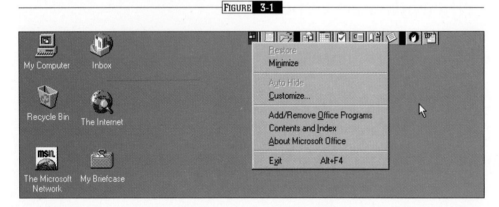

The first two sections of the menu include commands to Restore, Minimize, Auto Hide, and Customize the Shortcut Bar. The **Restore command** returns the Shortcut Bar to its position in the upper-right corner of the desktop window after the Shortcut Bar has been minimized. The **Minimize command** shrinks the Shortcut Bar to a button on the taskbar.

The Auto Hide command hides the Shortcut Bar and displays only a thin border where the Shortcut Bar resides. When you move the mouse pointer to the area of the thin border, the Shortcut Bar appears. When you move the mouse pointer away from the thin border, the Shortcut Bar is hidden again.

You can install or uninstall Office applications with the Add/Remove Office Programs command. You can use the Contents and Index command to access online Help. The About Microsoft Office command provides access to systems information, and the Exit command closes the Shortcut Bar.

QUICK TIP
You can close the Control menu by pressing the ESC key

3.b Adding, Repositioning, and Removing Buttons on the Shortcut Bar

In some situations, you may want to add or delete an application button on the Shortcut Bar. You may also need to change the location of one of the buttons on the Shortcut Bar.

> **IN THIS BOOK**
>
> Your Shortcut Bar may look different from the figures in this book. The following steps to modify the Shortcut Bar assume your Shortcut Bar shows only the default buttons as described in Chapter 1 in this unit and is in the default size to fit into an application title bar. If your Shortcut Bar looks different, your instructor may wish to revise these steps.

ADDING A BUTTON

Suppose you want to add the Word application button to the Shortcut Bar so that you can open the Word application and a blank document with a single click of the mouse button. You can add this button by customizing the Shortcut Bar. To customize the Shortcut Bar, you have to first verify that the Shortcut Bar Control menu is still displayed:

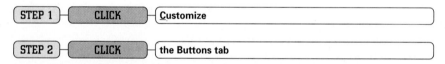

STEP 1 — CLICK — <u>C</u>ustomize

STEP 2 — CLICK — the Buttons tab

The Buttons tab in the Customize dialog box opens. Your screen should look similar to Figure 3-2.

FIGURE 3-2

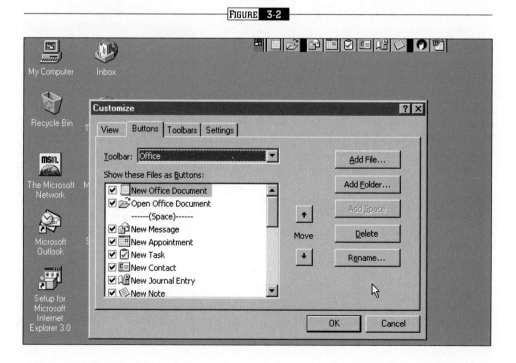

The shortcut button for a particular application or file appears on the Shortcut Bar if a check mark appears in the check box to the left of an application or file icon in the Show these Files as <u>B</u>uttons: list box.

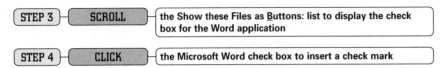

A button for the Word application immediately appears on the Shortcut Bar to the left of the Microsoft Bookshelf Basics button. Your screen should look similar to Figure 3-3.

REPOSITIONING A BUTTON

You can easily reposition a button on the Short-cut Bar. Suppose you want the Word application button to be the first button following the Control-menu box. You can select the application name and use the Move buttons to reposition it. To reposition the Word application button:

FIGURE 3-3

1. Word application button

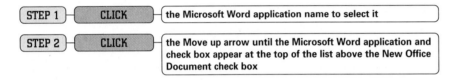

Notice that the Word application button immediately moves to the first position on the Shortcut Bar following the Control-menu box.

DELETING A BUTTON

You can also delete an application button from the Shortcut Bar. To remove the Word application button from the Shortcut Bar:

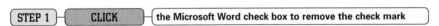

The check mark is removed from the Word check box, and the Word application button no longer appears on the Shortcut Bar.

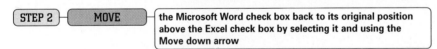

Keep the Customize dialog box open so you can continue working in the next section.

> ### QUICK TIP
>
> You can hide a button quickly on the Shortcut Bar by right-clicking the button and then clicking Hide <u>B</u>utton. To redisplay the button, you must click the appropriate check box in the Customize dialog box.
>
> You can rename a button on the Shortcut Bar by right-clicking the button and then clicking Rename.

3.c Changing the Appearance and Location of the Shortcut Bar

The default location of the Shortcut Bar is in the upper-right corner of your screen, where it is sized to fit within an application title bar. By default, the Shortcut Bar always displays on top of the active application and appears with small buttons. You can enlarge the buttons and place the Shortcut Bar in its own window so that it can be moved elsewhere on the screen. You can also hide and redisplay the Shortcut Bar as needed.

USING LARGE BUTTONS

To use large buttons on the Shortcut Bar:

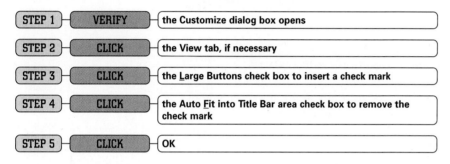

STEP 1	VERIFY	the Customize dialog box opens
STEP 2	CLICK	the View tab, if necessary
STEP 3	CLICK	the Large Buttons check box to insert a check mark
STEP 4	CLICK	the Auto Fit into Title Bar area check box to remove the check mark
STEP 5	CLICK	OK

The appearance of the Shortcut Bar changes: It appears across the top of the screen and contains large buttons. Your screen should look similar to Figure 3-4.

REPOSITIONING THE SHORTCUT BAR

You can drag the Shortcut Bar downward to place it in its own window. When the Shortcut Bar is in its own window, you can move it to a different location on your screen by dragging the window.

FIGURE 3-4

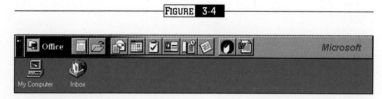

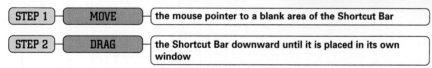

| STEP 1 | MOVE | the mouse pointer to a blank area of the Shortcut Bar |
| STEP 2 | DRAG | the Shortcut Bar downward until it is placed in its own window |

Your screen should look similar to Figure 3-5.

FIGURE 3-5

| STEP 3 | DRAG | the Shortcut Bar window to the far-right side of the screen until the window changes to a long vertical rectangle |

Suppose you want the Shortcut Bar to display vertically along the right side of the screen. You drag it to the right just the way you previously dragged it downward.

The Shortcut Bar is now placed vertically along the right edge of the screen. Your screen should look similar to Figure 3-6.

FIGURE 3-6

To return the Shortcut Bar to its default appearance and location:

| STEP 1 | RIGHT-CLICK | a blank area on the Shortcut Bar |

| STEP 2 | CLICK | Customize |

STEP 3	CLICK	the View tab, if necessary
STEP 4	CLICK	the Large Buttons check box to remove the check mark
STEP 5	CLICK	the Auto Fit into Title Bar area check box to insert a check mark
STEP 6	CLICK	OK
STEP 7	DRAG	the Shortcut Bar upward to the upper-right area of the title bar

The Shortcut Bar is again in the default position, has small buttons, and is sized to fit within the title bar of an open application.

HIDING THE SHORTCUT BAR

The Auto Hide command hides the Shortcut Bar until you move the mouse pointer to the Shortcut Bar area. Then the Shortcut Bar redisplays. Hiding the Shortcut Bar until you need it allows more viewing area for your desktop or application windows. Before you can use the Auto Hide command, however, you first must turn off the Auto Fit into Title Bar area in the Customize dialog box.

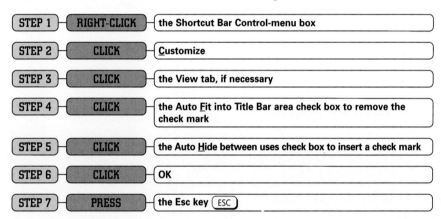

STEP 1	RIGHT-CLICK	the Shortcut Bar Control-menu box
STEP 2	CLICK	Customize
STEP 3	CLICK	the View tab, if necessary
STEP 4	CLICK	the Auto Fit into Title Bar area check box to remove the check mark
STEP 5	CLICK	the Auto Hide between uses check box to insert a check mark
STEP 6	CLICK	OK
STEP 7	PRESS	the Esc key (ESC)

The Shortcut Bar no longer appears. Notice the thin line across the top of the screen. This is the Shortcut Bar area. You can redisplay the Shortcut Bar by moving the mouse pointer to the Shortcut Bar area. After the Shortcut Bar is redisplayed you can return it to the default size and position.

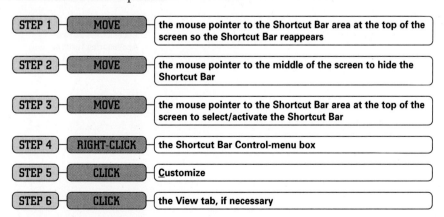

STEP 1	MOVE	the mouse pointer to the Shortcut Bar area at the top of the screen so the Shortcut Bar reappears
STEP 2	MOVE	the mouse pointer to the middle of the screen to hide the Shortcut Bar
STEP 3	MOVE	the mouse pointer to the Shortcut Bar area at the top of the screen to select/activate the Shortcut Bar
STEP 4	RIGHT-CLICK	the Shortcut Bar Control-menu box
STEP 5	CLICK	Customize
STEP 6	CLICK	the View tab, if necessary

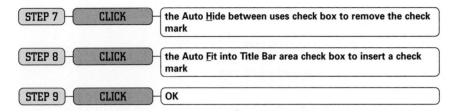

STEP 7	CLICK	the Auto **H**ide between uses check box to remove the check mark
STEP 8	CLICK	the Auto **F**it into Title Bar area check box to insert a check mark
STEP 9	CLICK	OK

The Shortcut Bar is returned to the default size and position at the upper-right area of the screen.

3.d Adding Other Toolbars to the Shortcut Bar

It is possible to add a button to the Shortcut Bar that will allow you to display and access other toolbars. For example, you can add a button to access the various applications on the Accessories menu with a single click of the mouse button.

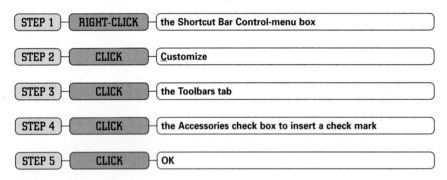

STEP 1	RIGHT-CLICK	the Shortcut Bar Control-menu box
STEP 2	CLICK	**C**ustomize
STEP 3	CLICK	the Toolbars tab
STEP 4	CLICK	the Accessories check box to insert a check mark
STEP 5	CLICK	OK

Buttons for the Accessories applications appear on an Accessories toolbar, which replaces the Shortcut Bar. Your screen should look similar to Figure 3-7.

Notice that a new button, the Office button, appears to the right of the Shortcut Bar Control-menu box. To exhibit the Shortcut Bar with this button:

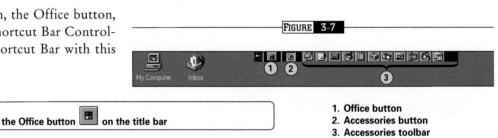

| STEP 6 | CLICK | the Office button ▦ on the title bar |

1. Office button
2. Accessories button
3. Accessories toolbar

The Shortcut Bar appears. Now a new button, the Accessories button, appears to the right of the Shortcut Bar. Your screen should look similar to Figure 3-8. The Accessories button activates the Accessories toolbar.

FIGURE 3-8

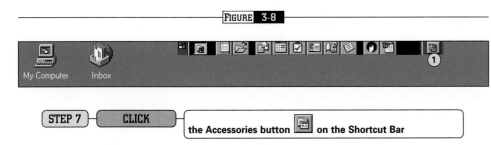

1. Accessories button

| STEP 7 | CLICK | the Accessories button 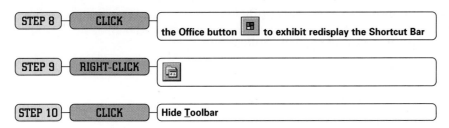 on the Shortcut Bar |

The Accessories toolbar reappears. You easily can hide any additional toolbars that have been added to the Shortcut Bar.

| STEP 8 | CLICK | the Office button to exhibit redisplay the Shortcut Bar |

| STEP 9 | RIGHT-CLICK | |

| STEP 10 | CLICK | Hide Toolbar |

The Shortcut Bar returns to the default display. The Accessories button no longer appears on the Shortcut Bar.

Summary

> You can customize the Shortcut Bar by adding or removing Office applications and moving or hiding the Shortcut Bar.

> You can add buttons to the Shortcut Bar that allow you to display and access other toolbars, such as the Accessories toolbar.

> The Shortcut Bar provides buttons that help you efficiently use Office applications.

> The default location and size of the Shortcut Bar is in the upper-right corner of your screen and is sized to fit within an application title bar.

> The Shortcut Bar appears by default at the top of the active application.

> You can drag the Shortcut Bar downward to place it in its own window.

> You can hide the Shortcut Bar with the Auto Hide command and then display it by moving the mouse pointer to the Shortcut Bar area.

> You can add other toolbars to the Shortcut Bar.

Concepts Review

Circle the correct answer.

1. The Shortcut Bar provides:
[a] buttons to open applications.
[b] additional toolbars.
[c] access to Outlook features.
[d] a choice of button sizes.
[e] all of the above.

2. You can change the location of the Shortcut Bar by:
[a] dragging the Shortcut Bar into its own window.
[b] minimizing the Shortcut Bar.
[c] restoring the Shortcut Bar.
[d] hiding the Shortcut Bar.
[e] all of the above.

3. The default position and size of the Shortcut Bar is:
[a] vertical on the right side of the display with large buttons.
[b] minimized on the taskbar.
[c] in its own window with large buttons.
[d] sized to fit into an application title bar with small buttons.
[e] none of the above.

4. The Auto Hide command:
[a] repositions the Shortcut Bar at the right side of the screen.
[b] permanently removes the Shortcut Bar.
[c] hides the Shortcut Bar.
[d] minimizes the Shortcut Bar.
[e] none of the above.

5. To display systems information, you can click the:
[a] Exit command.
[b] Restore command.
[c] Customize command.
[d] Auto Hide command.
[e] none of the above.

Circle [T] if the statement is true or [F] if the statement is false.

1. [T] [F] You cannot change the location of the Shortcut Bar.

2. [T] [F] Buttons can be added or deleted on the Shortcut Bar.

3. [T] [F] You can move a button on the Shortcut Bar.

4. [T] [F] When you turn on your computer, the Shortcut Bar appears by default.

5. [T] [F] You can hide or display the Shortcut Bar as needed.

6. [T] [F] If a check mark appears in the application check box in the Show these Files as Buttons: list, a button for the application does not appear on the Shortcut Bar.

7. [T] [F] The default location for the Shortcut Bar is in the upper-left corner of the desktop.

8. [T] [F] Shortcut menus are not available to customize buttons on the Shortcut Bar.

9. [T] [F] The buttons on the Shortcut Bar appear in large size by default.

10. [T] [F] You can close the Shortcut Bar Control menu by pressing the DELETE key.

Skills Review

EXERCISE 1

1. Add the Windows Explorer button to the Shortcut Bar.

2. Move the Windows Explorer button to the first position on the Shortcut Bar.

3. Remove the Windows Explorer button from the Shortcut Bar.

4. Reposition the Windows Explorer button back to its original position in the Show these Files as Buttons: list.

EXERCISE 2

1. Add the PowerPoint button to the Shortcut Bar.

2. Move the PowerPoint button and place it after the Add a Contact button on the Shortcut Bar.

3. Remove the PowerPoint button from the Shortcut Bar.

4. Reposition the PowerPoint button back to its original position in the Show these Files as Buttons: list.

EXERCISE 3

1. Change the size of the buttons on the Shortcut Bar to large buttons.

2. Move the Shortcut Bar to the far right of your screen.

3. Change the size of the buttons to small buttons.

4. Move the Shortcut Bar back to the default position.

5. Auto Fit the Shortcut Bar into the Title bar area.

EXERCISE 4

1. Add the Excel button to the Shortcut Bar.

2. Move the Excel button and place it after the Open a Document button on the Shortcut Bar.

3. Remove the Excel button from the Shortcut Bar.

4. Reposition the Excel button back to its original position in the Show these Files as Buttons: list.

EXERCISE 5

1. Add the Control Panel button to the Shortcut Bar.

2. Move the Control Panel button to the first position on the Shortcut Bar.

3. Remove the Control Panel button from the Shortcut Bar.

4. Reposition the Control Panel button back to its original position in the Show these Files as Buttons: list.

EXERCISE 6

1. Add the Desktop toolbar to the Shortcut Bar.

2. Exhibit the Shortcut Bar.

3. Exhibit the Desktop toolbar.

4. Hide the Desktop toolbar.

EXERCISE 7

1. Hide the Shortcut Bar.

2. Redisplay the Shortcut Bar by moving the mouse pointer to the Shortcut Bar area.

3. Change the Shortcut Bar back to the default size and position.

EXERCISE 8

1. Move the Shortcut Bar to the far left of your screen.

2. Change the size of the buttons to large buttons.

3. Move the Shortcut Bar back to the default position.

4. Change the size of the buttons to small buttons.

SCANS

Case Problems

PROBLEM 1

Using the Contents and Index command, research the following topics:

a. moving the Shortcut Bar

b. hiding the Shortcut Bar

c. adding a toolbar to the Shortcut Bar

PROBLEM 2

Explore adding toolbars to the Shortcut Bar and moving the Shortcut Bar to different positions on the screen. Return the Shortcut Bar to the default position, button size, and button configuration when you are finished.

SCANS

Introduction to the Internet

> *Everybody at HDM needs to have computer skills. We use word processing to enhance our technical packages from product documentation to technical presentation material and project reports.*

Kija Kim
president

Harvard Design and Mapping Co., Inc.
Cambridge, MA

Harvard Design and Mapping Company provides geographic information systems (GIS), mapping integration, and technology solutions to end users in corporations and government agencies.

Chapter Overview:

In the first three chapters of this book, you learned about the uses and features of Office 97 applications. In this chapter you will learn about another important capability of Office 97—the capability to interact with the Internet from each application. This chapter introduces you to the Internet by describing the Internet and its origins, and by identifying methods of and common challenges to accessing the Internet. You will also learn how to load a Web page, use a search engine, and return to your default home page.

SNAPSHOT

In this chapter you will learn to:

> Define the Internet

> Access the Internet

> Recognize the challenges of using the Internet

> Load a Web page

> Use a search engine

> Return to the default home page

> Access the Internet from Office applications

4.a What Is the Internet?

Today, millions of people use the Internet to shop for goods and services, listen to music, view artwork, conduct research, get stock quotes, keep up-to-date with current events, and send electronic mail to other Internet users. More and more people are using the Internet at work and at home to view and download multimedia computer files containing graphics, sound, video, and text. The **World Wide Web**, or **WWW**, is a subset of the Internet that uses computers called **Web servers** to store multimedia files called **Web pages** that are stored at locations called **Web sites**. You can use the Office 97 applications to create Web pages, to link to existing Web pages, and to download or upload files to the Internet.

DEFINING THE INTERNET

The name "Internet" gives you a clue to just what this electronic world is—computers that are somehow interconnected, or networked. A **computer network** is a group of two or more computers linked by communication media such as cables or telephone lines. See Figure 4-1.

FIGURE 4-1

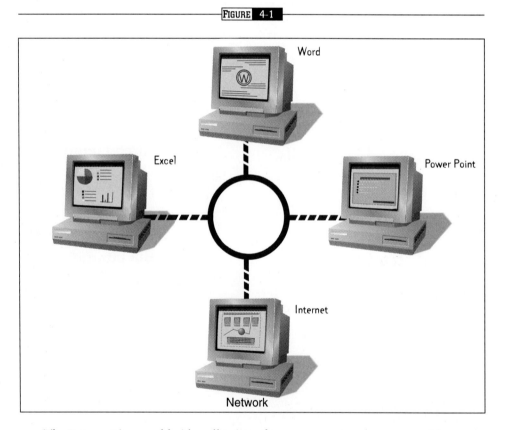

The **Internet** is a worldwide collection of computer networks connected by communication media that allow users to view and transfer information between computer locations. See Figure 4-2.

FIGURE   4-2

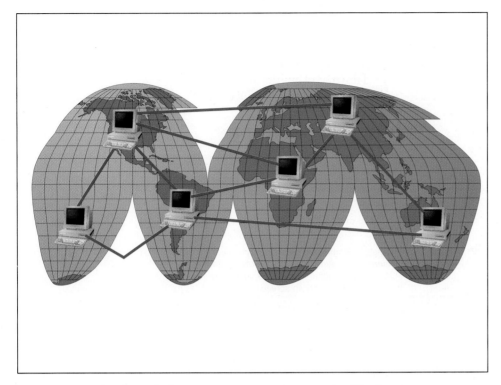

For example, through the Internet, a computer user in Illinois can access a computer in Canada, Australia, or Europe to view the contents of files stored there or to quickly and easily download files to his or her own computer.

THE HISTORY OF THE INTERNET

The Internet is not a single organization or entity but a cooperative effort by multiple organizations managing a variety of computers and different operating systems. In the late 1960s, the U. S. Department of Defense developed an internet of dissimilar military computers called the ARPAnet. Computers on this internet communicated by using a newly developed standard of communication rules called the Transmission Control Protocol/Internet Protocol, or **TCP/IP**. Additionally, the creators of ARPAnet developed a new technology, called "packet switching," allowed data transmitted between computers to be broken up into smaller "packets" before being sent to its destination over a variety of communication routes. The data was then reassembled at its destination. These changes in communication technology enabled data to be communicated more efficiently between different types of computers and operating systems.

Soon, scientists and researchers at colleges and universities began using this internet to share data. In the 1980s, the military portion of this internet became a separate entity called the **MILNET**, and the National Science Foundation began overseeing the remaining non-military portions, which were called the **NSFnet**. Thousands of other government, academic, and business computer networks began connecting to the NSFnet. By the late 1980s, the term *Internet* became widely used to describe this huge worldwide "network of networks."

SERVICES AVAILABLE ON THE INTERNET

Internet users today can choose from a wide variety of services, many of which are described in Table 4-1.

TABLE 4-1

CATEGORY	NAME	DESCRIPTION
Communication	Electronic Mail	Electronic messages sent or received from one computer to another, commonly referred to as e-mail.
	Newsgroups	Computer discussion groups where participants with common interests (like hobbies or professional associations) post messages called "articles" that can be read and responded to by other participants around the world via electronic "bulletin boards."
	Mailing Lists	Similar to Newsgroups except participants exchange information via e-mail.
	Chat	Real-time online conversations where participants type messages to other chat group participants and receive responses they can read on their screens.
File Access	FTP	Sending (uploading) or receiving (downloading) computer files via the File Transfer Protocol communication rules, or FTP.
Searching Tools	Search Engines	Programs that maintain indices of the contents of files at computers on the Internet; users can use search engines to find files by searching indices for specific words or phrases.
World Wide Web (WWW)		A subset of the Internet using computers called Web servers that store multimedia files, or "pages," that contain text, graphics, video, audio and links to other pages that are accessed by software programs called browsers.

4.b Accessing the Internet

> **IN THIS BOOK**
>
> There are many ways to access Internet resources; however, for the activities in this chapter you will use Microsoft Internet Explorer 3.0, a software program called a browser, which makes accessing resources on the Internet easier.

To access the Internet you need some physical communication medium, like network cable or a dial-up modem, that connects your computer to a telephone line. You will also need the Internet communication protocol software TCP/IP Stack. If you are using a dial-up modem, you will need a version of TCP/IP Stack for telephone lines, such as **Serial Line Internet Protocol (SLIP)** or **Point-to-Point Protocol (PPP)**.

You should also have front-end browser software like Internet Explorer to help you use the Internet resources. All the communication software you need to access the Internet generally is included when you purchase browser software.

INTERNET SERVICE PROVIDERS

After you set up your computer hardware and install the communication and browser software, you must make arrangements to connect to a computer already on the Internet called a "**host.**" Usually, you will connect to a host computer via a commercial Internet Service Provider. An **Internet Service Provider (ISP)** maintains the host computer, serves as a gateway to the Internet, and provides an electronic "mail box" with facilities for sending and receiving e-mail. Commercial ISPs usually charge a flat monthly fee for unlimited access to the Internet and e-mail services. Often, a commercial ISP will supply the communication protocols and front-end tools you will need to access the Internet.

QUICK TIP

Internet Service Providers also are called Internet Access Providers.

INTERNET ADDRESSES

All host computers on the Internet are identified by a unique Internet address, or **IP address**, that consists of a series of numbers. Computers on the Internet use these IP address numbers to communicate with each other. Your ISP will provide this IP address so that you can enter it as part of the setup process when you originally set up your communication connection to the ISP.

Host computers also are identified by a descriptive name that specifies the individual computer within a level of organization called an Internet domain. The descriptive host name is easier for you to use and remember than the IP address. For example, a host computer in the math department at a university might be identified as:

computername.math.unv.edu

where "computername" identifies the specific computer, "math" identifies the department, "unv" identifies the university, and "edu" identifies the top-level educational institution domain. The parts of a descriptive address are separated by a period, which is called a "dot."

Table 4-2 below identifies several top-level Internet domain names you will see as you work with Internet resources. The top-level domain names identify the largest overall category to which a host computer can belong.

TABLE 4-2	
TOP-LEVEL DOMAIN	TYPE OF ORGANIZATION
.com	Commercial enterprise
.gov	Government institution
.edu	Educational institution
.mil	Military institution
.net	Computer network
.org	Other organizations
.au, .ca, .uk, .us	Country designation such as Australia, Canada, United Kingdom, and United States

USER NAMES

When you make arrangements to access the Internet via an ISP, you will also set up a **user name** that identifies your particular account with the ISP. A user name usually consists of a name you select and the descriptive name that identifies your host computer. User names can be full names, first initial and last names, nicknames, or a combination of letters and numbers. For example, the user name for a user named Michelle Stone who accesses the Internet via a commercial ISP named ABC Data Systems might be:

Michelle_Stone@abc.net

Here "Michelle_Stone" is the user's name, and "abc.net" is the descriptive name for the ISP's host computer. See Figure 4-3.

FIGURE 4-3

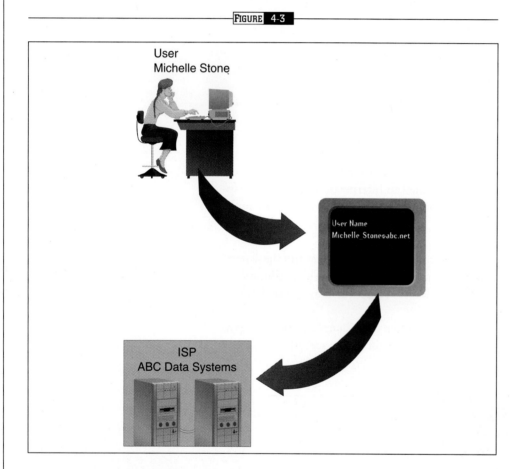

User
Michelle Stone

User Name
Michelle_Stone@abc.net

ISP
ABC Data Systems

OTHER INTERNET ACCESS METHODS

Large commercial enterprises, colleges, universities, and government institutions may already have networks that are part of the Internet, and users can often connect free of charge to the Internet through these existing networks. Public library systems are increasingly providing free Internet access to their patrons. Other kinds of Internet-access providers may charge their users fees. For example, commercial networks such as America Online, CompuServe, and the Microsoft Network provide fee-based Internet access. See Figure 4-4.

FIGURE 4-4

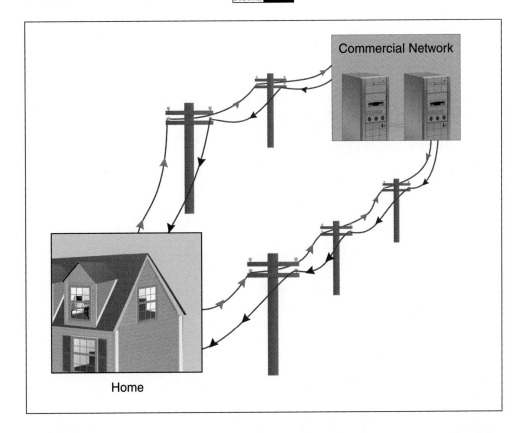

Home

Commercial Network

4.c Challenges of Using the Internet

Using the Internet to send e-mail, read and post articles to newsgroups, chat online, send and receive files, and search for information is fun and exciting. However, there are several challenges using the Internet successfully and productively.

Because the Internet is global, there is a seemingly endless source of data and information available. The sheer size of the Internet can sometimes be intimidating. Using Uniform Resource Locators (URLs) and search engines to find specific information can help minimize the effect of such a huge volume of information. URLs and search engines are discussed in more detail in later chapters.

Many Internet users communicate via modem and telephone lines, which adversely affect the communication speed of the Internet. Communication speeds, that is, how fast data can be shared between computers, can be improved by using high-speed modems and special telephone lines. Because of advances in cable technology, faster Internet communication should be more widely available in the near future.

Because the Internet is a cooperative effort and was created rather piecemeal over the years, no one standard for presenting information was developed. Therefore, how you access information at one site, and what it looks like when you access it, might differ considerably from information stored at another site. This presentation inconsistency can make maneuvering around the Internet frustrating.

Another challenge to users is the Internet's dynamic environment. The information on Internet changes daily, with new host computers being added and other computer sites no longer being maintained. Also, during the peak day and evening traffic hours, millions of users are accessing the Internet. Because of this dynamic environment and heavy usage, users may have difficulty accessing their host computer or other computer sites on the Internet.

In addition, Internet users face a variety of privacy and security issues. Because information travels circuitously from one Internet user to another, a user can never be absolutely sure where his or her information will end up and who can gain access to it along the way. Because there is no automatic security of information traveling over the Internet, there is always the the potential for someone other than the intended recipient to access information and copy or alter it.

In order to enhance Internet security, browser and server software has been developed. This technology encrypts or scrambles information during transmission and then decrypts or unscrambles it at its destination. Commercial Internet activities such as purchasing an item via credit card or online banking can take place in this type of secure environment; however, most Internet activity currently takes place in an insecure environment.

When you access a page on the World Wide Web, it is possible that the site owner is "capturing" certain information about you without your knowledge. This can include your e-mail address; which pages or files at the site you view and for how long; the type of computer, operating system, and browser you are using; and how you linked to that page. Software is available that prevents this type of information from being captured. Also, government regulations and technological methods to assure privacy and security on the Internet continue to be developed.

IN THIS BOOK

Unless your instructor advises you otherwise, before you begin any activities in this chapter, you should connect to an ISP. An ISP connection must be established before you can start the Internet Explorer application or other browser applications.

4.d Loading a Web Page

INTERNET

As explained earlier in this chapter, a Web server location on the Internet is often called a Web site. Web pages are files stored at a Web site that are created with a special markup language called **Hypertext Markup Language**, or **HTML**.

Web pages can contain text, graphics, video, audio, and links to other areas of the same Web page, other Web pages at the same Web site, or to a Web page at a different Web site. These links, called **hypertext links**, are used to connect Web pages, and they allow you to move from one Web page to another in much the same way you use the "jump topics" in any Windows application online Help to connect to and display different Help topics. When you click a link with the mouse pointer, another area of the same Web page, another Web page at the same Web site, or a Web page at a different Web site appears in your browser window. These hypermedia Web pages are transmitted via a special communication protocol called **Hypertext Transfer Protocol**, or **HTTP**.

Each Web page on the World Wide Web is identified by a special code called a **Uniform Resource Locator**, or **URL**. For example, the URL for the Microsoft primary Web page is:

http://www.microsoft.com/

where "http://" is the communication protocol and syntax, and "www.microsoft.com/"

is the descriptive name of the Web server that contains the Web page. This is a simple URL. As you will see when you continue browsing the World Wide Web, some URLs are very lengthy and contain additional information about the path and filename of the Web page.

To access the Internet, be sure to connect to your ISP, then start the Internet Explorer Web browser:

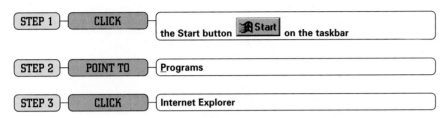

The Internet Explorer application starts and the window opens.

IN THIS BOOK

Many schools have a special school home page as the default home page in their computer labs. In this book, it is assumed the default home page is the Microsoft home page. Your default home page may be different.

Your screen should look similar to Figure 4-5.

FIGURE 4-5

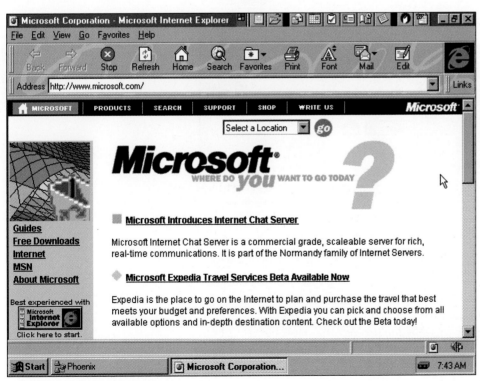

IN THIS BOOK

The World Wide Web is a dynamic environment where pages continually are added or modified. For this reason, the Web page illustrations in this book may not be identical to the Web page you see in the hands-on activities. Your instructor may modify the hands-on activities as necessary to select different Web pages.

The World Wide Web is an exciting place to look for information about a wide variety of topics. You can use the World Wide Web to search for specific information, shop for and purchase goods and services, make travel arrangements, review popular entertainment venues, play games, get vendor product support, and much more.

To access the Web, you use menu commands to display a dialog box and then enter the URL of the Web page you wish to load, or you can type the URL in the Address text box located below the Explorer toolbar. Suppose you want to load the home page for the White House. To load the White House home page:

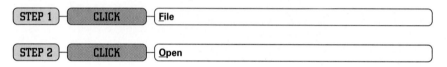

| STEP 1 | CLICK | File |

| STEP 2 | CLICK | Open |

The Open dialog box opens. You will enter the URL for the White House home page in this dialog box. Your screen should look similar to Figure 4-6.

FIGURE 4-6

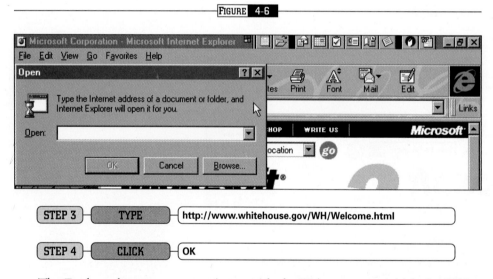

| STEP 3 | TYPE | http://www.whitehouse.gov/WH/Welcome.html |

| STEP 4 | CLICK | OK |

The Explorer browser communicates with the Web server on which the White House home page is stored, and the process of downloading that Web page begins. Notice that the Stop button on the Explorer toolbar is red and that the Explorer icon to the right of the Explorer toolbar is animated, or in motion, indicating the Web page transmission is in progress. During the transmission process, the status bar at the bottom of the Explorer window contains messages about the progress of the transmission. Also during the transmission process, a progress bar to the right of the status bar is animated, illustrating the progress of the transmission.

When the Web page is completely downloaded, the Stop button becomes inactive, and the Explorer icon stops moving. In addition, the message "Done" appears in the status bar.

After the White House home page is completely downloaded, your screen should look similar to Figure 4-7.

FIGURE 4-7

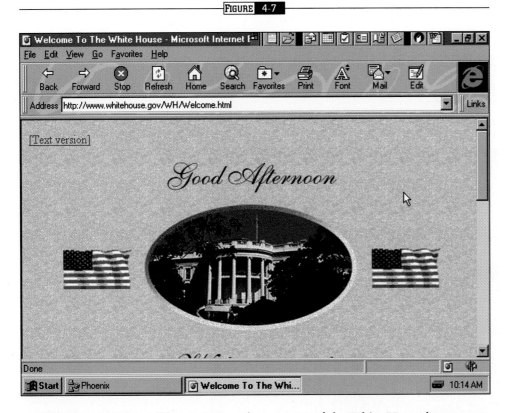

Use the vertical scroll bar to review the contents of the White House home page, then scroll to the top of the page.

4.e Using a Search Engine

INTERNET

Search engines are programs that allow you to search their indices using a keyword or phrase to find Web pages that contain that keyword or phrase. There are many search engines available on the WWW. Explorer provides a button on the Explorer toolbar that displays a Web page with search engine options called a "search page."

Suppose you want to retrieve the student files that accompany this textbook. These files are stored on a computer called an FTP server. You can load a Web page provided by the publisher, Course Technology, to access these files.

To search for a Course Technology Web page that provides access to student files:

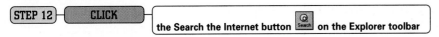

STEP 12 — CLICK — the Search the Internet button on the Explorer toolbar

After a few seconds, the Internet Searches page appears on your screen. It contains a search form for use with the featured search engine and options for using other search engines.

| STEP 2 | SCROLL | until the Search the World Wide Web search form appears |

The AltaVista search engine is a fast keyword search engine that contains thousands of keywords in its index. You will use the AltaVista search engine to find the Course Technology Web page.

| STEP 3 | TYPE | "Course Technology" in the *alta vista* search text box |

Your screen should look similar to Figure 4-8.

FIGURE 4-8

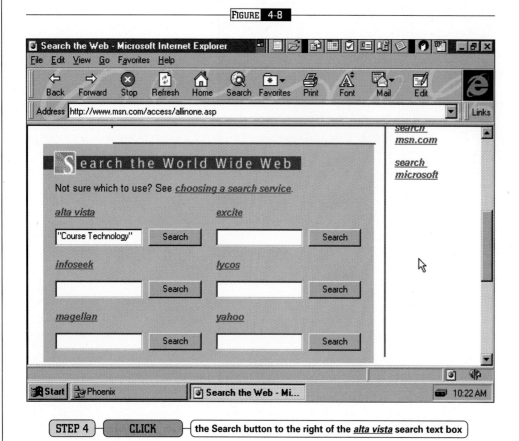

| STEP 4 | CLICK | the Search button to the right of the *alta vista* search text box |

After a few seconds, the AltaVista search engine displays a list of Web pages that contain the keyword phrase "Course Technology." Scroll the list to find the "Course Technology Data Disk Files" Web page. Notice that both the title and the URL listed below the Web page description are a different color and are underlined. This indicates that they are both links to the Web page.

To display the "Course Technology Data Disk Files" Web page:

| STEP 1 | CLICK | either Course Technology Data Disk Files or the URL http://www2.coursetools.com/cti/disks.html |

QUICK TIP

Hypertext links can be text or graphics. If you position your mouse pointer on text or graphics and it changes shape to a hand with a pointing finger, the text or graphic is a hypertext link.

After a few seconds, the Web page is loaded. Your screen should look similar to Figure 4-9.

FIGURE 4-9

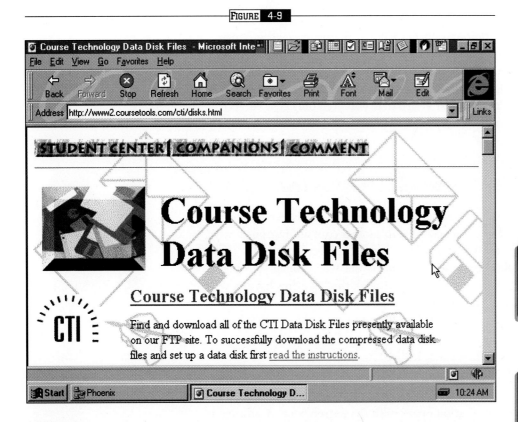

MENU TIP
You can go back to the default home page by clicking the Start Page command on the Go menu.

MOUSE TIP
You can click the Start Page button on the Explorer toolbar to view the default home page. If you click the Explorer icon status indicator to the right of the Explorer toolbar, the default home page will appear.

You can print a Web page by clicking the Print button on the Explorer toolbar.

4.f Returning to the Default Home Page

Sometimes you may want to return to the default home page after you have been "browsing" the World Wide Web.

To view the default home page:

STEP 1 ━ CLICK ━ the Start Page button  on the Explorer toolbar

After a few seconds, the Microsoft Corporation default home page appears. Close the Internet Explorer application.

IN THIS BOOK

Your instructor may provide additional materials on other features of the Internet Explorer browser or the features of a different browser. Your instructor also may provide additional materials on using the Internet to send e-mail, download files, or participate in Mailing Lists or Newsgroups.

4.g Accessing the Internet from Office Applications

INTERNET

You also can access the Internet directly from Office applications such as Word or Excel. Suppose you are working in the Word application and want to search the WWW or link to a specific document. You can display the Web toolbar and use the toolbar buttons to open the Internet Explorer application and load a specific Web page or the Explorer Search page. First, you must verify that you are connected to your ISP; then you can open the Word application.

To display the Web toolbar:

STEP 1 — CLICK — the Web Toolbar button [icon] on the Standard toolbar

The Web toolbar appears below the Formatting toolbar. Use the ScreenTips feature to review the buttons on the Web toolbar. The Web toolbar contains buttons similar to those on the Explorer toolbar. For example, to open Explorer and display the Explorer Search page, click the Search the Web button on the Web toolbar. To open Explorer and display a Web page saved as a "favorite," click the Favorites list arrow and then click the Web page name. To open Explorer and load a specific Web page, type the URL in the Address text box on the Web toolbar and press the ENTER key.

To load the Explorer Search page:

STEP 1 — CLICK — the Search the Web button [icon] on the Web toolbar

After a few seconds, the Explorer application opens with the Search page. If you are asked if you want to save the current blank Word document, click No. After the Search page loads, close the Explorer browser and disconnect your ISP connection.

Summary

> A network is a group of two or more computers linked by communication media such as cable or telephone lines.

> An internet is a group of two or more computer networks, or a "network of networks," linked by communication media such as cables or telephone lines.

> The Internet is a worldwide "network of networks."

> The Internet began in the late 1960s as the military internet ARPAnet. By the 1980s the National Science Foundation assumed oversight of the non-military portions and the term Internet became widely used.

> Internet users can communicate with others via e-mail, computer discussion groups, and online chat groups.

> Programs that maintain indices of the contents of files on the Internet are called search engines.

> The World Wide Web is a subset of the Internet that uses computers called Web servers on which multimedia files called pages are stored at locations called Web sites.

> To access the Internet, your computer must have some physical communication medium (network or modem) and the special communication protocol TCP/IP.

> Access to the Internet is provided by Internet Service Providers who maintain host computers on the Internet.

> Each host computer has an Internet address or IP address consisting of a series of numbers and a descriptive name based on the computer name and domain of the host.

> In addition to the host computer IP address and descriptive name, each user has a name that identifies his or her account with the Internet Service Provider.

SCANS

> Large commercial enterprises, colleges, and universities may have a computer network on the Internet and can provide Internet access to their employees or students.

> There are many challenges to using the Internet, including the global size and volume of available information, slow communication speed, a dynamic environment, lack of presentation standards, and privacy/security issues.

> A Web server location on the Internet is also called a Web site.

> Hypermedia files or Web pages stored at a Web site are created with a special markup language called Hypertext Markup Language, or HTML.

> Links, called hypertext links, connect Web pages and allow you to move from one Web page to another in the same way you move from topic to topic in any Windows application online Help.

> Web pages are transmitted via a special communication protocol called Hypertext Transfer Protocol, or HTTP.

> Each Web page on the World Wide Web is identified by a special code called a Uniform Resource Locator, or URL.

> Search engines are programs that allow you to search an index by keyword or phrase to find Web pages that contain that keyword or phrase.

> Using the Start program command, you can quickly return to the default home page, if desired.

> You can access the Internet from Office applications using the Web toolbar.

Commands Review

ACTION	MENU BAR	SHORTCUT MENU	MOUSE	KEYBOARD
Load a Web page by typing the URL	File, Open			ALT+F, O CTRL+O
Access the Internet from an Office application	View, Toolbars, Web	Right-click a toolbar, click Web		ALT+V, T

Concepts Review

Circle the correct answer.

1. A network is:
[a] a group of two or more computers linked by communication media.
[b] a group of two or more computer networks linked by cables or telephone lines.
[c] an internet.
[d] the Internet.
[e] none of the above.

2. The Internet began as the:
[a] NSFnet.
[b] ARPAnet.
[c] MILNET.
[d] SLIPnet.
[e] none of the above.

3. Which of the following is not a service available on the Internet?
[a] electronic mail.
[b] file access.
[c] searching for files.
[d] computer discussion groups.
[e] all are services available on the Internet.

4. To access the Internet you need:
[a] some physical communication medium.
[b] a TCP/IP Stack.
[c] an Internet Service Provider.
[d] an IP address.
[e] a user name.
[f] all of the above.

5. Which of the following is not a challenge to using the Internet?
[a] global size and volume of information.
[b] communication speeds.
[c] dynamic environment and heavy usage.
[d] security and privacy.
[e] chat groups.

6. Which of the following is *not* a top-level domain name?
[a] .com
[b] .edu
[c] .mlt
[d] .org
[e] .net

7. The World Wide Web:
[a] is a subset of the Internet.
[b] is made up of computers called Web servers.
[c] stores multimedia files called Web pages.
[d] a and b.
[e] a, b, and c.

8. The Hypertext Markup Language is:
[a] often referred to as http.
[b] is a special markup language used to create Web pages.
[c] is a special communication protocol for the World Wide Web.
[d] a special code that identifies each page on the World Wide Web.
[e] none of the above.

9. Hypertext links on a Web page allow you to display:
[a] another area on the same Web page.
[b] another Web page at the same Web site.
[c] a Web page at a different Web site.
[d] a and c.
[e] a, b, and c.

10. Search engines are:
[a] programs that allow you to find Web pages by searching an index.
[b] programs providing special communication protocols for the World Wide Web.
[c] programs that define a default home page.
[d] programs that link pages together.
[e] none of the above.

11. HTTP is the abbreviation for:
[a] Transmission Control Protocol/Internet Protocol.
[b] Hypertext Markup Language.
[c] Uniform Resource Locator.
[d] Hypertext Transfer Protocol.
[e] none of the above.

SCANS

Circle T if the statement is true or F if the statement is false.

1. T F If you are using a dial-up modem to access the Internet, you will need either the SLIP or PPP Internet communication protocol.

2. T F An IP address is a unique identifying number for each host computer on the Internet.

3. T F A host computer's descriptive name identifies it by name and organizational level on the Internet.

4. T F The World Wide Web is a large network that is separate from the Internet.

5. T F Internet users in Boston or New York can access computer files on computers located in the United States only.

6. T F Computer discussion groups are called newsgroups.

7. T F Search engines are programs that maintain indices of the contents of files at computers on the Internet.

8. T F Very few people use the Internet to shop for goods and services, listen to music, view artwork, conduct research, get stock quotes, or send e-mail.

9. T F The primary Web page at a Web site is called the "start page."

10. T F Hypertext links are used to connect Web pages just like the "jump topics" in Windows applications online Help.

11. T F The correct format for a URL is "http://www.computer.com/."

12. T F Because the World Wide Web is dynamic, you can always expect the format and contents of a Web page to be the same each time you load it.

13. T F When a Web page transmission is complete, "Web Page Completed" appears on the Explorer status bar.

14. T F Text hypertext links are usually displayed in a different color from the main text and are usually underlined.

15. T F You must close all Office applications before you can access the Internet.

Case Problems

PROBLEM 1

You are the executive secretary to the manager of the Information Services Department in your company. She has asked you to search for the online bookstore "Amazon.com" that has a catalog of technical books. Connect to your ISP, start the Internet Explorer browser, and use a search engine to search for the "Amazon.com" bookstore. Review the "Amazon.com" home page and print it. Display the default home page and close the Internet Explorer application. Disconnect your ISP connection.

PROBLEM 2

As the administrative assistant to the sales manager of an athletic equipment wholesaler, you have been asked to locate information about the National Football League, the National Basketball Association, and the National Hockey League. The Sales Manager wants to use some information about these professional sports leagues at the next sales meeting.

Connect to your ISP, start Internet Explorer browser, and using the Open dialog box, enter the URL for the National Basketball Association, http://www.nba.com. When the NBA home page appears, print it.

Using the Address text box located below the Explorer toolbar, enter the URL for the National Football League, http://www.nfl.com. When the NFL home page appears, print it.

Based on your understanding of URLs and the above two examples, load the home page of the National Hockey League using either the Open dialog box or the Address text box to enter the URL. When the NHL home page appears, print it. Close the Internet Explorer application, and disconnect from your ISP connection.

PROBLEM 3

Connect to your ISP, open the Word application, and display the Web toolbar. Search the Web for a list of Web pages related to a personal hobby. Print the list. Close the Internet Explorer application, and disconnect from your ISP connection. Close the Word application.

Access 97

CHAPTER

Access 97

1

Introduction
to Access

"

I coordinate the implementation of ADP's 401(k) plans by tracking and maintaining criteria for thousands of employees for ADP's clients in a computer database.

"

Tamra LaPierre
401(k) implementation specialist

Automatic Data Processing
Houston, TX

ADP provides computerized transaction processing, data communications, and information services worldwide to over 350,000 clients.

Chapter Overview:

This chapter assumes that you have little or no experience with any database software. Before you construct a database in Access, certain concepts must be defined. This chapter provides definitions of general database terminology as well as Access-specific terms and concepts.

SNAPSHOT

In this chapter you will learn to:

> Open the Access application

> Identify the components of the Access window

> Define general and Access database terms

> Identify the components of an Access table

> Identify the components of an Access query

> Identify the components of an Access form

> Identify the components of an Access report

> Define an Access macro

> Define an Access module

> Close the Access application

IN THIS BOOK

The next several chapters assume that you have little or no knowledge of Access. However, it is assumed that you have read Chapters 1–3 of the Office unit and that you are familiar with Windows 95 concepts, the Shortcut Bar, and common elements of Office 97 applications.

1.a Opening the Access Application

As discussed in Chapter 1 in the Office unit, Microsoft recommends that your computer have at least 12 MB of RAM to run Access 97. If you are running Office Professional on a computer that has only 8 MB, you may want to close all other Office applications before opening the Access application.

To open Access:

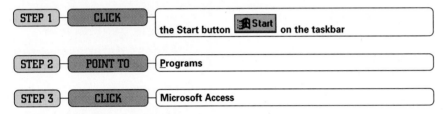

STEP 1 — CLICK — the Start button on the taskbar

STEP 2 — POINT TO — Programs

STEP 3 — CLICK — Microsoft Access

The Microsoft Access application and dialog box open and, as with other Office applications, the Office Assistant may appear. With options in this dialog box, you can open an existing database, create a new blank database, or create a database by using a Database Wizard.

To cancel the Access dialog box and leave the Access application window open:

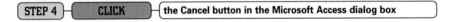

STEP 4 — CLICK — the Cancel button in the Microsoft Access dialog box

QUICK TIP

Remember, you can use the Shortcut bar to quickly start the Access application and open a blank database or an existing database.

CAUTION

A Database Wizard may not perform optimally with less than 12 MB of memory.

Your screen should look like Figure 1-1.

FIGURE 1-1

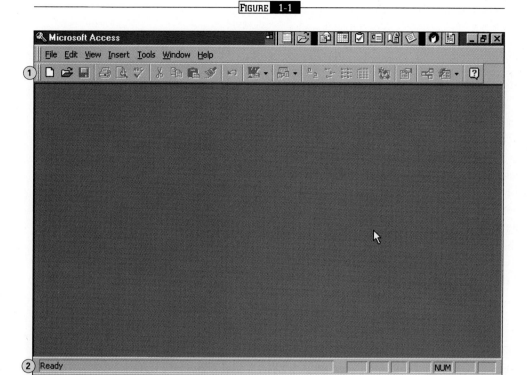

1. Database toolbar
2. Status bar

1.b Identifying the Components of the Access Window

Figure 1-1 identifies the components of the Access window. Elements common to other applications were described in Chapter 1 in the Office unit. Because no database file is open, most of the buttons on the toolbar are not available for immediate use.

TOOLBAR

The default Access toolbar, the Database toolbar, appears below the menu bar. The Database toolbar changes according to the type of information you are showing on your screen.

STATUS BAR

Compared to other Office 97 applications, the Access status bar is abbreviated. The extreme left edge of the status bar indicates the current state of the Access window, such as Ready. Other areas of the status bar indicate such features as NUM LOCK, or CAPS LOCK.

1.c Defining General and Access Database Terms

Before you start working with a database application, it is important to learn the vocabulary that accompanies it. In addition to studying general database terminology, you should also learn Access-specific terms.

GENERAL DATABASE TERMS

Some database terms are common to all database applications, such as database, record, and field.

A **database** is a collection of related information. You probably use several databases in the course of a normal day. A phone book and a personal address book are common examples of databases. Some other examples of databases that might not be as common in everyday use include a price list, a student registration list, and an inventory

Table 1-1 below identifies the components of a database. Notice that each column of the table contains the same type of information and each row contains a separate set of information. In database terms, the columns are called **fields** and the rows are called **records**.

TABLE 1-1

LAST NAME	INITIAL	REGION	ADDRESS	CITY	STATE	POSTAL CODE
Krantz	M	Southwest	8715 Post Oak Blvd.	Houston	TX	77057-5541
Preston	A	West	1504 Rodeo Dr.	Beverly Hills	CA	90222-1134
Singh	S	Midwest	22417 Elm St.	Chicago	IL	60603-2279
Garcia	J	Southeast	1900 Piedmont	Atlanta	GA	30324-0024

ACCESS DATABASE OBJECTS

Access contains its own vocabulary of database terms. In Access, the actual data is only part of the database. An Access database also contains the following **objects** that relate to the data:

- Table
- Query
- Form
- Report
- Macro
- Module

Each of these objects is discussed in more detail in later sections of this chapter.

ACCESS DATABASE VIEWS

In addition to the variety of objects within an Access database, each object also has several different views, or ways of viewing data:

1. Datasheet view
2. Design view
3. Print Preview
4. Layout Preview

Datasheet view presents data in a way similar to an Excel spreadsheet. Multiple records are shown in a column and row format. Datasheet view is available when you work with tables, queries, and forms.

Design view is used to build and modify database objects and also to create new queries. Design view is available in all database object windows.

Print Preview shows the appearance and layout of a report, table, or form in order to confirm what will be printed.

Layout Preview examines a small portion or sample of your data in a report before printing it.

1.d Identifying the Components of an Access Table

An Access **table** contains data in columns and rows. This layout is called a **datasheet**. Each column represents a field, and each row represents a record. Entering records into a table in Access is similar to creating a spreadsheet in Excel.

To begin, open the PETSTORE RECORDS database located on the student disk. To open the PETSTORE RECORDS database:

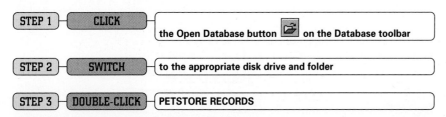

STEP 1 — CLICK — the Open Database button 📂 on the Database toolbar

STEP 2 — SWITCH — to the appropriate disk drive and folder

STEP 3 — DOUBLE-CLICK — PETSTORE RECORDS

The PETSTORE RECORDS database window appears. Click the Tables tab in the database window, if necessary. Your screen should look like Figure 1-2.

FIGURE 1-2

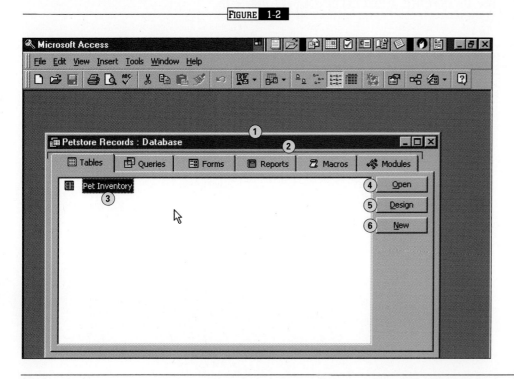

1. Database title bar
2. Database object tabs
3. Table object
4. Open button
5. Design button
6. New button

Figure 1-2 identifies the components of an Access database.

DATABASE TITLE BAR

The **database title bar** indicates the name of the current database file.

NEW BUTTON

You can click the <u>N</u>**ew button** to create a new database object, such as a form or a table.

OPEN BUTTON

You can select a database object and click the **Open button** to view it.

DESIGN BUTTON

You can select a database object and click the <u>D</u>**esign button** to examine its design.

DATABASE OBJECT TABS

The **database object tabs** look like folder tabs across the top of the database window. Each of these tabs provides information about the current database. For example, you can click the Table database object tab to see a list of all the tables in the database.

DATABASE OBJECTS

The **database objects** appear in the window of each object tab. Pet Inventory is a table object in the PETSTORE RECORDS database file.

To examine an Access table:

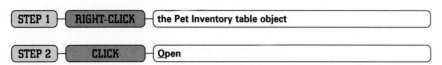

| STEP 1 | RIGHT-CLICK | the Pet Inventory table object |

| STEP 2 | CLICK | <u>O</u>pen |

The Pet Inventory table in the PETSTORE RECORDS database opens in Datasheet view.

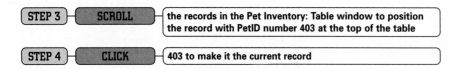

| STEP 3 | SCROLL | the records in the Pet Inventory: Table window to position the record with PetID number 403 at the top of the table |

| STEP 4 | CLICK | 403 to make it the current record |

Your screen should look similar to Figure 1-3.

FIGURE 1-3

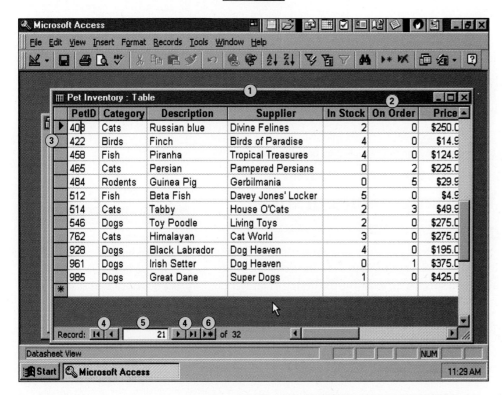

1. Table title bar
2. Field name
3. Record Selector button
4. Navigation buttons
5. Specific Record box
6. New Record button

Figure 1-3 identifies the components of an Access table. Notice that the toolbar is now the Table Datasheet toolbar and contains tools specific to an Access table. The status bar indicates that you are in Datasheet view. Notice also that you can still see a portion of the database window behind the table window. Although Access does not allow you to open more than one database file at a time, you can open more than one database object at a time.

TABLE TITLE BAR

The **table title bar** indicates the name of the current table.

FIELD NAME

The top row of the table indicates each **field name**.

RECORD SELECTOR

You can select or highlight an entire record in the table by clicking the **record selector button**.

RECORD SELECTOR SYMBOLS

The **record selector symbols** are: (1) a triangle which points to the current record, (2) an asterisk ✳ which indicates a new, blank record, (3) a drawing pen 🖋 which indicates you are editing a record, and (4) a null symbol ⊘ which indicates the record is locked and cannot be changed.

NAVIGATION BUTTONS

The four **navigation buttons** allow you to move from one record to the next. The middle two buttons move one record at a time in the direction of each arrow. The first button on the left moves to the first record in the table. The fourth button on the right moves the insertion point to the last record.

QUICK TIP

To verify the toolbar currently shown, right-click the toolbar. The name of the toolbar is listed with a check mark. You can also view a list of toolbars with the Toolbars command on the View menu.

MENU TIP

You can click the Close command on the File menu to close an object.

NEW RECORD BUTTON

The **New Record button** adds a new, blank record to the table.

SPECIFIC RECORD BOX

The **Specific Record box** indicates the ordinal value of the current record as related to the rest of the records in the table.

To conserve your computer's resources, after you have examined the table, you should close it before moving on to other database objects.

To close the Pet Inventory table:

| STEP 1 | CLICK | the Close button ☒ on the Pet Inventory table title bar |

MOUSE TIP

You can also click the Close button on the object title bar or double-click the Control-menu icon on the object title bar to close an object.

1.e Identifying the Components of an Access Query

An Access **query** allows you to ask questions about your data and generate a subset of information that matches criteria you specify. To examine the design of an Access query:

| STEP 1 | CLICK | the Queries object tab |

| STEP 2 | VERIFY | Pet Inventory Query is selected |

| STEP 3 | CLICK | the Design button in the database window |

Your screen should look like Figure 1-4.

QUICK TIP

If you double-click a query object to open it, you open the results of the query. To examine the design of a query, you must click the Design button.

FIGURE 1-4

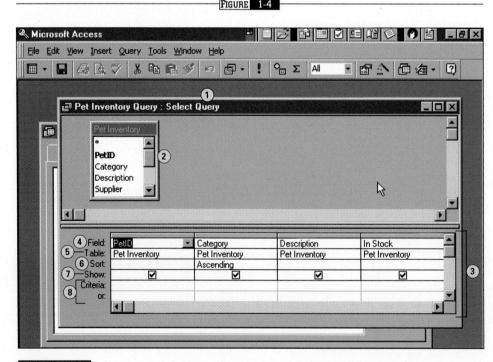

1. Query title bar
2. Field list
3. Design grid
4. Field row
5. Table row
6. Sort row
7. Show check box
8. Criteria rows

QUICK TIP

You can size both panes by dragging the split bar between the panes with the mouse pointer.

Figure 1-4 identifies the components of a query. Notice that the toolbar is the Query Design toolbar and contains tools specific to an Access query. The status bar indicates that Access is in the Read0y mode. The query is in Design view.

QUERY TITLE BAR

The query title bar indicates the name and type of query. The title bar of the Pet Inventory query indicates that this is a select query. Use select queries when you want to view a set of records for examination or modification. The **select query** is the default query type.

FIELD LIST

The **field list** contains all the fields from the table or query being used in the query. You may use as many fields in your query as you wish. You do not have to use every field from a table in a query, however.

DESIGN GRID

The **Design grid** resembles a table and contains the criteria used in the query.

FIELD ROW

The **Field row** is the top row of the Design grid and contains fields that are used in the query.

TABLE ROW

The **Table row** indicates the name of the underlying table that contains the query field.

SORT ROW

The **Sort row** indicates the sort order of a particular field.

SHOW CHECK BOX

The **Show check box** indicates whether or not a particular field will be shown in the query results. If you remove the check mark from the Show check box, the corresponding field does not appear in the query results. This is useful if you want to query on a certain field but do not need to show that field.

CRITERIA ROWS

The **Criteria rows** are used to determine which records will appear in the query results. You can enter specific criteria that the corresponding field must match in order for its record to appear in the query results. The top criteria row is used for exclusive criteria or AND conditions. The bottom criteria rows are used for OR conditions.

To examine the query results:

STEP 1 — CLICK — the View button [icon] list arrow on the toolbar

The drop-down grid of view options appears.

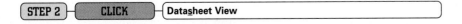
STEP 2 — CLICK — Datasheet View

QUICK TIP

When viewing a query in Design view, the button portion of the View button shows the Datasheet View option. When viewing a query in Datasheet view, the button portion of the View button shows the Design View option. You can click the button portion of the View button to quickly switch between these two views.

The results of the query appear. Your screen should look like Figure 1-5.

FIGURE 1-5

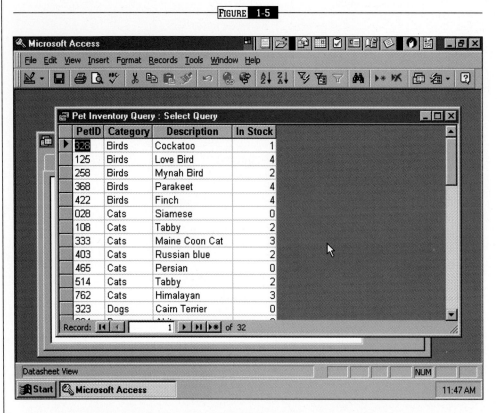

The animals are listed in alphabetical order according to category. Only the Pet ID, Category, Description, and In Stock fields appear. After examining the query, you can close it before moving on to other database objects. To close the Pet Inventory query:

STEP 3 — CLICK —
the Close button ☒ on the Pet Inventory Query title bar

1.f Identifying the Components of an Access Form

Forms can show the data from your table in a variety of ways. You can use a form to input new data, update or correct old data, or simply search and review your data. To examine an Access form:

STEP 1 — CLICK — the Forms object tab

STEP 2 — DOUBLE-CLICK — Pet Inventory Form

Your screen should look similar to Figure 1-6. You may have to size the Pet Inventory Form window slightly smaller or move it upward to view the entire window on your screen.

FIGURE 1-6

1. Form title bar
2. Labels
3. Values
4. Record
5. Navigation buttons
6. Specific Record box
7. New Record button

Figure 1-6 identifies the components of a form. Notice that the toolbar is now the Forms View toolbar and contains tools specific to an Access form. The status bar indicates that you are in Form view.

FORM TITLE BAR

The **title bar** of a form indicates its title. Access uses the name you entered in the Form Wizard, which is discussed later in this unit, until the form is saved with a new name.

LABELS

The field names on a form are referred to as **labels**. These are the same fields found in the table or query that was used to generate the form.

VALUES

Each item of data that corresponds to a label in a form is called a **value**. Together, the values compose a **record**.

NAVIGATION BUTTONS

The **navigation buttons** allow you to move from one record to the next. The single triangle buttons move one record at a time backward or forward. The first button on the left moves to the first record in the form. The fourth button on the right moves to the last record in the form. The last button with the triangle and the asterisk moves the insertion point to the first field in a new record.

SPECIFIC RECORD BOX

The **Specific Record box** indicates the ordinal value of the current record as related to the rest of the records in the form.

NEW RECORD BUTTON

The **New Record button** shows a blank record form for data entry.

After you have examined the form, close it before moving on to other database objects. To close the Pet Inventory form:

| STEP 1 | CLICK | the Close button ☒ on the Pet Inventory Form title bar |

1.g Identifying the Components of an Access Report

Reports are used to organize your data for a printed presentation. You can use reports to manipulate your data into groups and subtotals based on certain fields, such as department or region. Reports can also be based on queries so that only the data that meets your criteria is printed. To open the Pet Inventory Report:

| STEP 1 | CLICK | the Reports object tab |

| STEP 2 | DOUBLE-CLICK | Pet Inventory Report |

After dragging the Report window upward slightly, your screen should look similar to Figure 1-7.

────────────── FIGURE 1-7 ──────────────

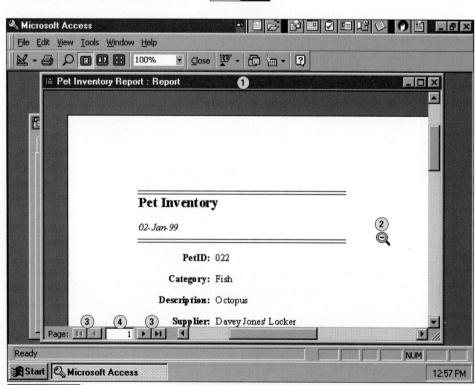

1. Report title bar
2. Magnifier mouse pointer
3. Navigation buttons
4. Specific Page box

Figure 1-7 identifies the components of a report. Notice that the toolbar is now the Print Preview toolbar and contains tools specific to an Access report. The mouse pointer is in the shape of a magnifying glass when placed anywhere on the report. The status bar indicates that Access is in the Ready mode. The report is in Print Preview.

REPORT TITLE BAR

The **title bar** of a report indicates the name of the report. Access provides a default name, which is replaced when you save the report.

MAGNIFIER

The **magnifier** is the shape the mouse pointer assumes when it is placed anywhere on the report. You can use the magnifier to zoom into a particular area of the report and examine it closely.

NAVIGATION BUTTONS

The **navigation buttons** enable you to move from one page to the next. The single triangle buttons move one page at a time backward or forward. The first button on the left moves to the first page in the report. The fourth button on the right moves to the last page in the report.

SPECIFIC PAGE BOX

The **Specific Page box** indicates the ordinal value of the current page as related to the rest of the pages in the report. After you have examined the report, close it before moving on to other database objects. To close the Pet Inventory report:

| STEP 3 | CLICK | the Close button ☒ on the Pet Inventory Report title bar |

1.h Defining an Access Macro

Macros offer a selection of commands that you can use to automate repetitive tasks in the database. For more information about macros, see Access online Help.

1.i Defining an Access Module

Modules are programs written in Visual Basic language that allow for extensive customizing and automation of Access tasks. Modules and macros can be used to create custom applications based on Access databases. For more information about modules, see Access online Help.

1.j Closing the Access application

To close Access:

| STEP 1 | CLICK | the application Close button ☒ on the title bar |

QUICK TIP

You can use keyboard shortcut keys in Access. For a complete listing of these shortcuts, see Access online Help.

You can view help for a selected menu command, dialog box option, or property by pressing the F1 key. You can also get context-sensitive help by pressing the SHIFT+F1 keys to change the mouse pointer to a help pointer. Move the help pointer to the window item you want help on, like a toolbar button, and click.

Summary

SCANS

> A database is a collection of related information. One example of a database is a personal address book.

> A field in a database contains the same type of information. For example, in a personal address book, an individual's name could be in one field, the street address in a second field, and so forth.

> A record in a database contains all the fields for one item. For example, in a personal address book, a record would include all the fields for any individual.

> In addition to the actual data, in Access you work with objects like tables, queries, forms, and reports that relate to the data.

> You can view each database object in different views.

> As you open different objects, Access automatically shows the appropriate toolbar for working with that object.

> An Access table contains data in columns and rows called a datasheet.

> An Access query allows you to ask questions about your data and generate a subset of information that matches criteria you specify.

> Access forms are used to input new data, update existing data, or search for and review data.

> Access reports are used to organize your data for a printed presentation.

> Macros and modules are advanced topics that you can use to customize and automate tasks.

Commands Review

ACTION	MENU BAR	SHORTCUT MENU	MOUSE	KEYBOARD
Open an existing database from inside Access	File, Open Database		📁	ALT+F, O CTRL+O
Open an object		Right-click object, click Open	Select object, click the Open button	
Get help	Help		❓ Press SHIFT + F1 and click the item	F1
Close an object	File, Close		Click the Close button ✖ on the object's title bar or double-click the Control-menu icon on the object's title bar	ALT+F, C

Concepts Review

1. Which of the following is not an Access database object?
[a] table.
[b] form.
[c] query.
[d] datasheet.
[e] module.

2. The navigation buttons enable you to:
[a] move from record to record in a table or form.
[b] move from page to page in a report.
[c] move from object to object in a database window.
[d] a and b.
[e] a, b, and c.

3. Modules are:
[a] a selection of commands used to automate repetitive tasks.
[b] programs written in Visual Basic.
[c] object tabs.
[d] a group of records.
[e] none of the above.

4. When you double-click a query object, you open:
[a] the object in Design view.
[b] the object in Print Preview.
[c] the results of the query.
[d] the underlying table on which the query is based.
[e] none of the above.

5. You can switch back and forth between Design and Datasheet view by clicking the:
[a] Queries object tab.
[b] Switch command on the View menu.
[c] View button.
[d] select query title bar.

Circle ⊤ if the statement is true or ⓕ if the statement is false.

1. ⊤ ⓕ A database is a collection of related information.

2. ⊤ ⓕ You can open more than one database file at a time in Access.

3. ⊤ ⓕ An inventory is an example of a database.

4. ⊤ ⓕ Access automatically opens a blank database for you when the program is loaded via the Start button on the taskbar.

5. ⊤ ⓕ Access toolbars change automatically according to the type of object on the screen.

6. ⊤ ⓕ Layout view shows a small portion of data in a report.

7. ⊤ ⓕ The magnifier allows you to zoom a particular area in Design view.

Identify the components of the Access window indicated in Figure 1-8.

FIGURE 1-8

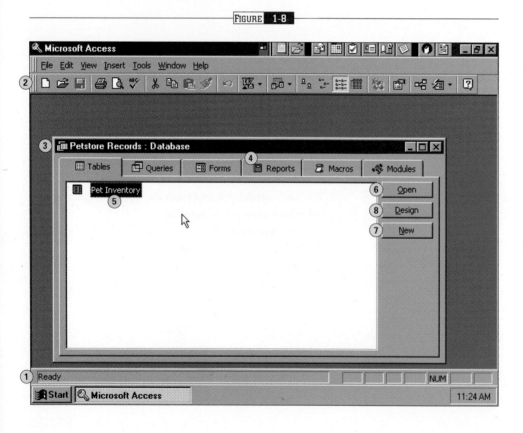

SCANS

Case Problems

PROBLEM 1

Create a Word document and define in your own words the following general and Access terms. Type a separate paragraph for each term. Save and print the document.

1. database
2. record
3. field
4. query

5. table
6. form
7. report
8. Datasheet view
9. Design view

PROBLEM 2

Open the PETSTORE RECORDS database. Using online Help, the F1 key, and the SHIFT+F1 context-sensitive Help pointer review different methods of getting Help while working in Access.

PROBLEM 3

Using the Office Assistant, review using shortcut keys that are global in Microsoft Access. Print the Help topic.

PROBLEM 4

Connect to your ISP and, using the Microsoft on the Web command on the Help menu, link to the Frequently Asked Questions page and research questions about Access. Print at least two Web pages.

CHAPTER 2

Quick Start for Access

> *Accessing and analyzing data from the Multiple Listing Database, a database shared among real estate companies in the area, is an essential function of our business.*

Mark Lippolt
senior vice president

*Coldwell Banker Hunneman & Company
Boston, MA*

*Hunneman and Company—Coldwell Banker,
the residential division of Hunneman Real Estate
Corporation, is the largest homeseller in
Massachusetts.*

Chapter Overview:

In Chapter 1, you learned new database terms as well as some specific terms for the Access application. Access offers a variety of methods to construct and manipulate databases. In this chapter, you will create a new database and then use the Table Wizard to create a table, AutoForm to create a form, AutoReport to create a report, and the Simple Query Wizard to create a query.

SNAPSHOT

In this chapter you will learn to:

> **Create a new database**

> **Create a table using the Table Wizard**

> **Create a form using AutoForm**

> **Create a report using AutoReport**

> **Create a query using the Simple Query Wizard**

2.a Creating a New Database

Planning a Database

Suppose your company owns several furniture stores across the United States. Each store is called a branch, and the stores from several states are grouped by region. In this exercise, you will create a database named BRANCH that can contain data about each store and each region (all the stores from several states). For this illustration, the BRANCH database will contain information about each regional manager. You will begin by creating a regional managers address list.

To start Access and create a new database:

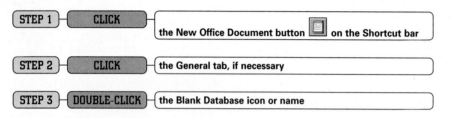

STEP 1	CLICK	the New Office Document button 🗐 on the Shortcut bar
STEP 2	CLICK	the General tab, if necessary
STEP 3	DOUBLE-CLICK	the Blank Database icon or name

In a few seconds, the File New Database dialog box opens. You must give the new database a name and then create it. To name and create a new database:

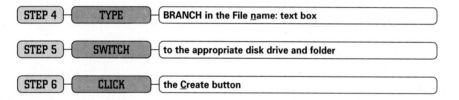

STEP 4	TYPE	BRANCH in the File name: text box
STEP 5	SWITCH	to the appropriate disk drive and folder
STEP 6	CLICK	the Create button

The Branch: Database window opens. Notice that most of the buttons on the Database toolbar are now available. You are ready to create a table object and enter each regional manager's data.

MENU TIP

From inside Access, you can create a new database by clicking the New Database command on the File menu.

MOUSE TIP

From inside Access, you can create a new database by clicking the New Database button on the Database toolbar.

2.b Creating a Table with the Table Wizard

A table is the framework for storing data in a database. You can create a blank, empty table and then enter the data. You can also create a table from an existing external data source. In this chapter you will create a blank table using the Table Wizard. The Table Wizard is an Access feature that allows you to create a table by choosing from a selection of commonly used table templates. After the table is created, you can then enter the data. Designing tables and creating tables without assistance from the Table Wizard is discussed in more detail in Chapter 3.

CREATING A NEW TABLE

To create a table:

| STEP 1 | CLICK | the Tables object tab, if necessary |

There are no tables in the database, so the Tables object list is empty.

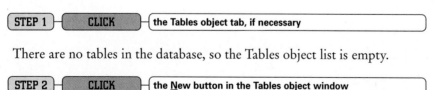

| STEP 2 | CLICK | the New button in the Tables object window |

The New Table dialog box opens. Your screen should look similar to Figure 2-1.

FIGURE 2-1

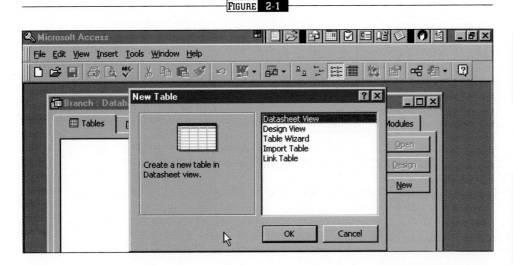

MENU TIP

You can create a new table by clicking the Table command on the Insert menu.

MOUSE TIP

You can create a new table by clicking the New button in the Tables object window or by clicking the New Object button list arrow on the Database toolbar and then clicking Table.

There are five methods to create a table listed in this dialog box. For this exercise, you will use the Table Wizard.

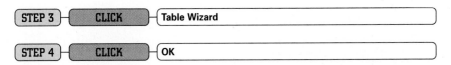

| STEP 3 | CLICK | Table Wizard |

| STEP 4 | CLICK | OK |

In a few seconds, the first Table Wizard dialog box opens. This dialog box contains a list of sample tables with predesigned fields. To create a table, you will select a sample table and then select the sample fields from that table to be included in your new table. By default, the first sample table named Mailing List is selected.

| STEP 5 | OBSERVE | the sample tables in the Sample Tables: list box and the sample fields from the Mailing List table in the Sample Fields: list box |

Each field in the Sample Fields: list box represents the type of information you might have in a mailing list database. To select a sample table and examine the sample fields in that table:

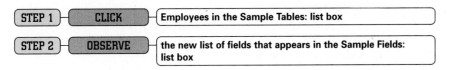

| STEP 1 | CLICK | Employees in the Sample Tables: list box |

| STEP 2 | OBSERVE | the new list of fields that appears in the Sample Fields: list box |

These fields include information you might have in an employee database. The sample tables currently shown are for business-related databases. Notice the Business and Personal option buttons under the Sample Tables: list box. The Business option is selected. In addition to creating business-related database tables, you can also use the Table Wizard to create database tables of personal interest. To examine the sample tables in the personal database category:

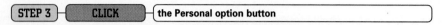

A list of personal-style tables appears in the Sample Table: list box. Examples of the personal tables are: Household Inventory, Plants, and Wine List. To return to the business category of databases:

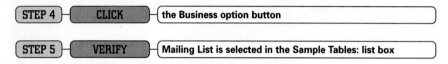

You are now ready to begin adding fields to your table. To add a field to your table:

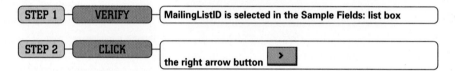

The MailingListID field is added to the Fields in my new table: list box. This is only one way to add a field to your table. To add the next field using an alternate method:

The LastName field is added to the Fields in my new table: list box.

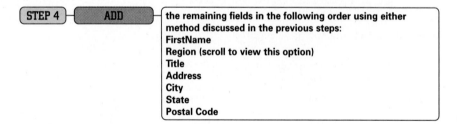

After entering the remaining fields:

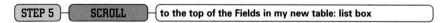

If you have added a field that you do not wish to use in the table, you can remove it from the list. To remove the Title field from the Fields in my new table: list box:

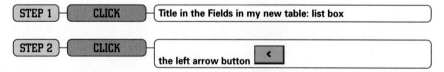

The Title sample field is removed. Your screen should look similar to Figure 2-2.

FIGURE 2-2

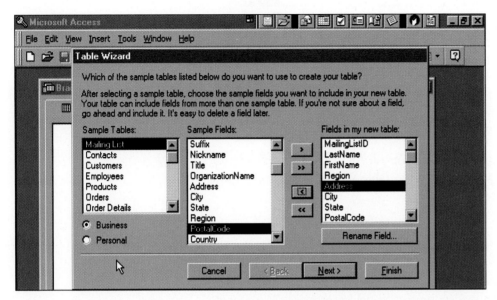

You can rename a field if the sample field name is not appropriate. For example, suppose you plan to enter each manager's first initial rather than first name. To rename the FirstName field:

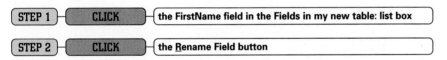

STEP 1 — **CLICK** — the FirstName field in the Fields in my new table: list box

STEP 2 — **CLICK** — the Rename Field button

The Rename field dialog box opens. To enter the new field name:

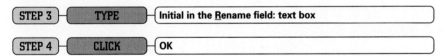

STEP 3 — **TYPE** — Initial in the Rename field: text box

STEP 4 — **CLICK** — OK

The FirstName field is now the Initial field. Now that you have added the fields to your table, proceed to the next step of the Table Wizard.

STEP 5 — **CLICK** — the Next> button [Next >]

The second Table Wizard dialog box opens. At this point, the Table Wizard asks you to name your table. Object names may have any combination of 64 letters, numbers, spaces, and special characters, except for the following:

1. Leading spaces
2. Periods (.)
3. Brackets ([ ])
4. Exclamation Points (!)
5. Backquotes (accent grave) (`)
6. Control characters (ASCII values 0 through 31)

Notice that the default table name is selected for you, indicating that you may begin typing immediately to replace it with a name of your choice. To give the table a new name:

QUICK TIP

To add all the sample fields for a particular sample table to your table quickly, click the double right arrow button. To remove all the sample fields from your table quickly, click the double left arrow button.

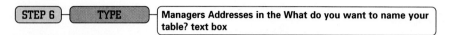

STEP 6 — TYPE — Managers Addresses in the What do you want to name your table? text box

In the lower half of the Table Wizard window, Access presents the options for setting the primary key for the table. Access uses the **primary key** to identify each record in the database as a unique record. For the purposes of this exercise, you should accept the default, and let Access set the primary key for you. To accept the default and go to the next Table Wizard step:

STEP 7 — CLICK — the Next> button [Next >]

You have reached the final step of the Table Wizard. All that remains is to decide what you want to do with your table now that the Table Wizard has created it. The Table Wizard offers the following three choices:

1. Modify the table design.
2. Enter data directly into the table.
3. Enter data into the table using a form the Wizard creates.

If you choose to modify the table design, Access opens the table in Design view and allows you to change field names, data types, and field properties. These topics will be covered in the next chapter. If you choose to enter data directly into the table, Access opens the table in Datasheet view and allows you to enter data as you would into an Excel worksheet. You can choose to have Access create a data entry form for you. To accept the default option to enter data directly into the table:

STEP 8 — CLICK — the Finish button [Finish]

In a few seconds, the Managers Addresses table object is created and appears in Datasheet view. Your screen should look similar to Figure 2-3.

FIGURE 2-3

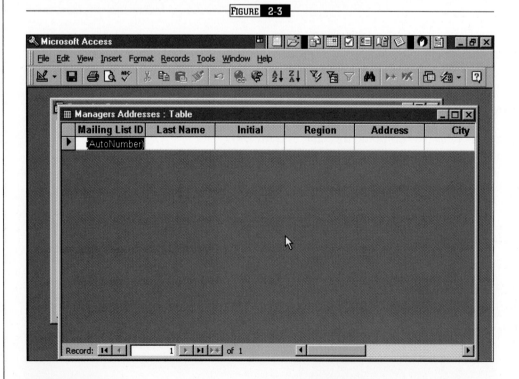

ENTERING RECORDS INTO A TABLE

Datasheet view resembles an Excel worksheet. You can move the insertion point to a new field by clicking the field or by using the keyboard. Table 2-1 below indicates how to move the insertion point in a table using the keyboard.

TABLE 2-1

KEYSTROKE	MOVEMENT
RIGHT ARROW	One field to the right
LEFT ARROW	One field to the left
UP ARROW	One record above
DOWN ARROW	One record below
TAB	One field to the right
SHIFT+TAB	One field to the left
ENTER	One field to the right

Moving from a record, including pressing the ENTER key at the end of a record, not only moves your insertion point, it also saves any changes to the current record.

Notice that the first field of the table: Mailing List ID, is selected. The word (AutoNumber) appears in this field because the Table Wizard set this field as the (AutoNumber) data type. Field data types will be discussed in more detail in Chapter 3. You cannot enter any data in this field. Access uses this field to insert a unique number that identifies the record. To move the insertion point to the Last Name field:

STEP 1 — PRESS — the Tab key (TAB)

To begin entering the data for your first record:

STEP 2 — TYPE — King

Notice the MailingListID field for the first record now contains the number 1. The edit symbol (pencil) on the Record Selector button indicates that data is being added or changed in the current record. Notice that as soon as you type a character in the Last Name field, a blank row is added to the table.

STEP 3 — PRESS — (TAB) to move the insertion point to the Initial field

STEP 4 — TYPE — M

STEP 5 — PRESS — (TAB) to move the insertion point to the Region field

STEP 6 — TYPE — Southwest

STEP 7 — PRESS — (TAB) to move the insertion point to the Address field

STEP 8 — TYPE — 8715 Post Oak

STEP 9 — PRESS — (TAB) to move the insertion point to the City field

STEP 10 — TYPE — Houston

STEP 11 — PRESS — (TAB) to move the insertion point to the State field

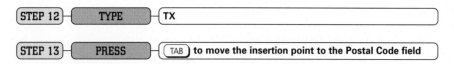

| STEP 12 | TYPE | TX |

| STEP 13 | PRESS | TAB to move the insertion point to the Postal Code field |

The Postal Code field is a special field in this table. Access automatically inserts a hyphen and allows you to enter the four-digit extension at the end of the five-digit number. When entering the Postal Code, you will not have to type the hyphen before you enter the four-digit extension. The Postal Code field is not a required field. You may enter just the five-digit code and leave the four-digit extension blank or you may leave the entire field blank. Setting field properties to require data entry is discussed in Chapter 3. To enter the Postal Code:

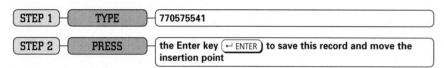

| STEP 1 | TYPE | 770575541 |

| STEP 2 | PRESS | the Enter key ↵ ENTER to save this record and move the insertion point |

The Mailing List ID field in the second record is selected. Your screen should look similar to Figure 2-4.

FIGURE 2-4

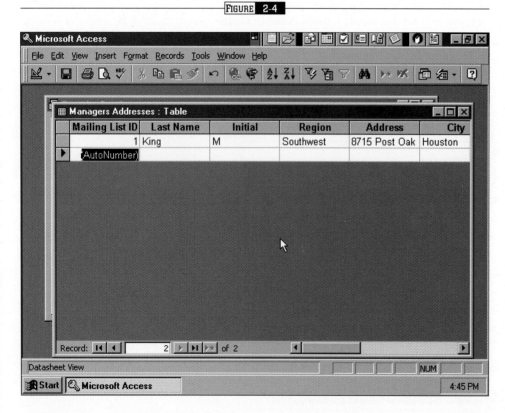

There might be a delay before your insertion point moves to the second record. This depends on the speed of your PC. Access saves the record after you have pressed the ENTER key; the time it takes to do this will vary.

Table 2-2 below provides the data for the second record.

TABLE 2-2

| Preston | A | West | 1504 Rodeo Dr. | Beverly Hills | CA | 902221137 |

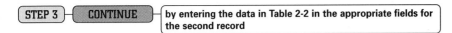

| STEP 3 | CONTINUE | by entering the data in Table 2-2 in the appropriate fields for the second record |

Once you enter the data, be sure to press the ENTER key to save the new record into the database.

EDITING RECORDS IN A TABLE

So far, you have learned that pressing the ENTER key will save a record into a database, but you still can return to a record and change its data. To change the last name in the first record:

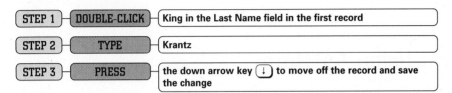

STEP 1	DOUBLE-CLICK	King in the Last Name field in the first record
STEP 2	TYPE	Krantz
STEP 3	PRESS	the down arrow key (↓) to move off the record and save the change

In addition to replacing the contents of a field, you can also change portions of the data. To correct the last digit of the ZIP code in the second record:

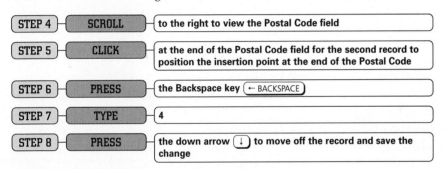

STEP 4	SCROLL	to the right to view the Postal Code field
STEP 5	CLICK	at the end of the Postal Code field for the second record to position the insertion point at the end of the Postal Code
STEP 6	PRESS	the Backspace key (← BACKSPACE)
STEP 7	TYPE	4
STEP 8	PRESS	the down arrow (↓) to move off the record and save the change

SORTING RECORDS IN A TABLE

After entering the records in a table, you may want to change the order in which they appear. For example, you might want to list your managers in alphabetical order by state. To sort the table by state:

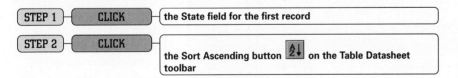

| STEP 1 | CLICK | the State field for the first record |
| STEP 2 | CLICK | the Sort Ascending button [A↓Z] on the Table Datasheet toolbar |

The records are sorted by state in ascending alphabetical order. Your screen should look similar to Figure 2-5.

─── FIGURE 2-5 ───

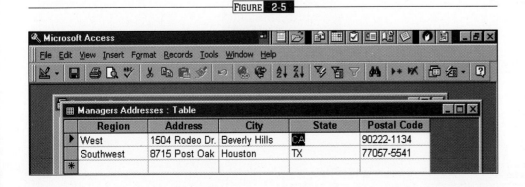

MENU TIP

You can sort records in a table by clicking the field you wish to sort by and then clicking the Sort Ascending or Sort Descending subcommands under the Sort command on the Records menu or you can click Sort Ascending or Sort Descending on a shortcut menu.

MOUSE TIP

You can click the field you wish to sort by and then click the Sort Ascending or Sort Descending button on the Table Datasheet toolbar.

REVERSING A SORT

It is possible to reverse the effects of a sort and show the data in its original order. You can click the Remove Filter/Sort command on the Records menu or shortcut menu to show the data in their original order. To reverse the sort by state:

| STEP 3 | RIGHT-CLICK | the table |

| STEP 4 | CLICK | Remove Filter/Sort |

The records appear in their original order. Close the Managers Addresses table without saving changes.

2.c Creating a Form Using Autoform

You may prefer to create a form for data entry rather than using a table to enter the data into your database. If you have already created a table in your database, you can have Access create a default data entry form quickly using AutoForm.

CREATING A NEW FORM

To create a form with AutoForm:

| STEP 1 | VERIFY | the Managers Addresses table is selected in the Tables object list |

| STEP 2 | CLICK | the New Object button [icon] list arrow on the Database toolbar |

A list of new object options appears. Your screen should look similar to Figure 2-6.

FIGURE 2-6

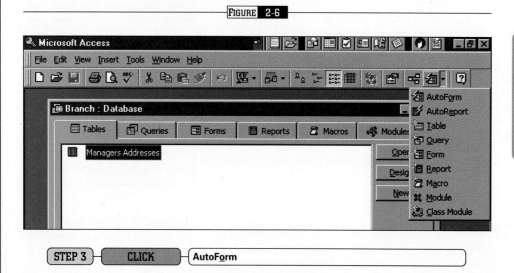

| STEP 3 | CLICK | AutoForm |

The Managers Addresses data entry form window opens. The AutoForm feature has created a default form containing all the fields in the selected table. Your screen should look similar to Figure 2-7.

MENU TIP

You can create a new form by clicking the Form or AutoForm commands on the Insert menu.

MOUSE TIP

You can create a new form by clicking the New button in the Forms object window or by clicking the New Object button list arrow on the Database toolbar and clicking AutoForm or Form.

FIGURE 2-7

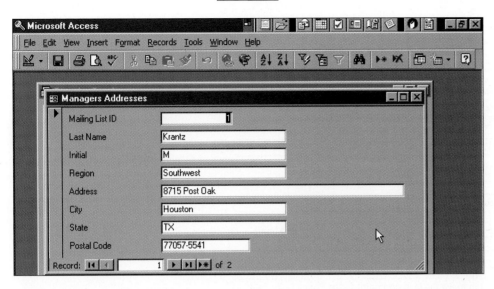

NAVIGATING AND ENTERING RECORDS IN A FORM

When you are working in a form, you may need to move from field to field as well as from record to record. Table 2-3 below indicates how to navigate within the fields of a form using the keyboard.

TABLE 2-3

ACTION	KEYSTROKE
Next field	DOWN ARROW
	RIGHT ARROW
	TAB
	ENTER
Previous field	UP ARROW
	LEFT ARROW
	SHIFT+TAB

Once you have entered records via a form, you can use the form to examine the existing records with the back, forward, first, or last record navigation buttons, or by typing a specific record number in the Specific Record box. You can also enter data for a new record in the form by clicking the New Record button to the right of the navigation buttons.

To add a new record:

STEP 1 — CLICK — the New Record navigation button ▶✳

A blank data entry form appears with (AutoNumber) in the Mailing List ID text box. To enter a new record in a form:

STEP 2 — PRESS — the down arrow key ↓ to move the insertion point to the Last Name text box

STEP 3 — TYPE — Singh

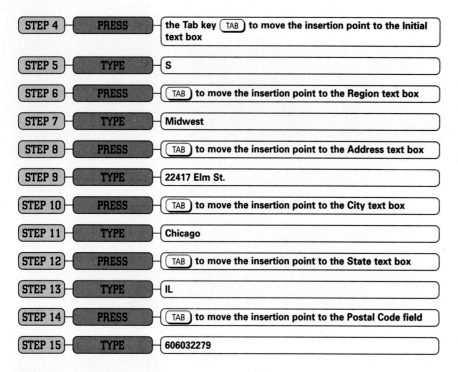

STEP 4 — PRESS — the Tab key TAB to move the insertion point to the Initial text box

STEP 5 — TYPE — S

STEP 6 — PRESS — TAB to move the insertion point to the Region text box

STEP 7 — TYPE — Midwest

STEP 8 — PRESS — TAB to move the insertion point to the Address text box

STEP 9 — TYPE — 22417 Elm St.

STEP 10 — PRESS — TAB to move the insertion point to the City text box

STEP 11 — TYPE — Chicago

STEP 12 — PRESS — TAB to move the insertion point to the State text box

STEP 13 — TYPE — IL

STEP 14 — PRESS — TAB to move the insertion point to the Postal Code field

STEP 15 — TYPE — 606032279

When you press the TAB key after entering the last data value on a form, a blank record appears. If you wish to move to another field within the same record, click with the mouse or use the arrow keys on the keyboard. To move to a blank record:

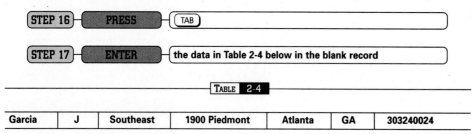

STEP 16 — PRESS — TAB

STEP 17 — ENTER — the data in Table 2-4 below in the blank record

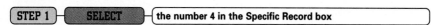

TABLE 2-4

| Garcia | J | Southeast | 1900 Piedmont | Atlanta | GA | 303240024 |

Do not press the TAB key after entering the data. To move to the second record in the database:

STEP 1 — SELECT — the number 4 in the Specific Record box

Notice that the status bar indicates that you may enter a new value.

STEP 2 — TYPE — 2

STEP 3 — PRESS — the Enter key ↵ ENTER

The record for A Preston appears on your screen.

SAVING A FORM

Once you have created a form, save it with a unique name that will enable you to identify its contents. To move to the first record and save the form:

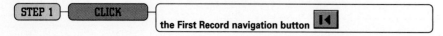

STEP 1 — CLICK — the First Record navigation button ◄|

STEP 2 — CLICK — File

STEP 3 — CLICK — Save As/Export

The Save As dialog box opens. To save the form within the current database and with the default name "Managers Addresses":

STEP 4 — CLICK — OK

The form is saved as Managers Addresses. Close the form window. To view the form in the Forms object list:

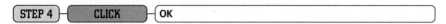

STEP 1 — CLICK — the Forms object tab

The Managers Addresses form object appears in the Forms object list.

Suppose you now want to change the name of the Managers Addresses form object. To change the object name:

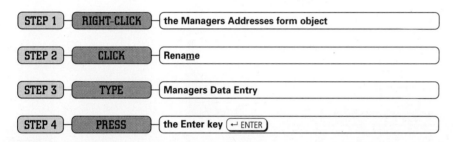

STEP 1 — RIGHT-CLICK — the Managers Addresses form object

STEP 2 — CLICK — Rename

STEP 3 — TYPE — Managers Data Entry

STEP 4 — PRESS — the Enter key (↵ ENTER)

The form object is renamed.

2.d Creating a Report Using AutoReport

Once you have entered all of your data via a table or form, you may want to create a printed presentation of the records called a report. You cannot add data to a report. If you want to include all fields in the report, you can use AutoReport.

CREATING A NEW REPORT

To use AutoReport and have Access generate a simple report for you:

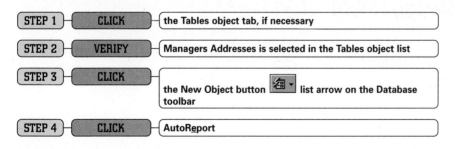

STEP 1 — CLICK — the Tables object tab, if necessary

STEP 2 — VERIFY — Managers Addresses is selected in the Tables object list

STEP 3 — CLICK — the New Object button list arrow on the Database toolbar

STEP 4 — CLICK — AutoReport

MENU TIP

You can create a new report by clicking the Report or AutoReport commands on the Insert menu.

MOUSE TIP

You can create a new report by clicking the New button in the Reports object window or by clicking the New Object button list arrow on the Database toolbar and clicking AutoReport or Report.

Access generates a simple default report which appears in Print Preview. Your screen should look similar to Figure 2-8.

FIGURE 2-8

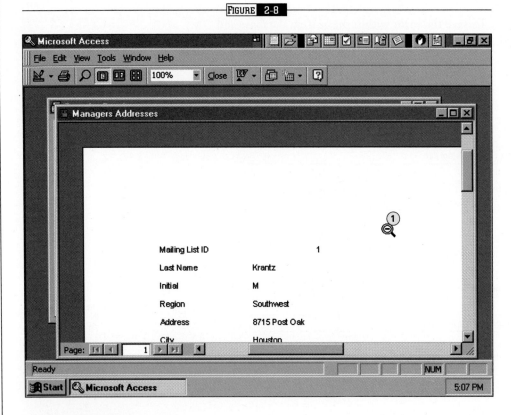

1. Mouse pointer

EXAMINING AND PRINTING A REPORT

Notice that when you move the mouse onto the report area, it appears as a magnifying glass. The magnifying glass allows you to decrease or increase the zoom ratio of the report. To examine the report as it appears on the whole page, you can decrease the zoom ratio on your screen. To decrease the zoom:

STEP 1 — MOVE — the mouse pointer onto the report, if necessary

STEP 2 — CLICK — the report

To set the zoom back to normal and examine a portion more closely:

STEP 3 — MOVE — the mouse pointer to the portion of the report you wish to examine

STEP 4 — CLICK — the report

To view different parts of the report:

STEP 5 — CLICK — the vertical or horizontal scroll bar arrow in the direction you wish to examine

Once you have determined that the report is acceptable, you might want to print it. To print the report:

STEP 6 — CLICK — the Print button 🖨 on the Print Preview toolbar

SAVING A REPORT

Once you have created a report, you can save it with a unique name. To save the report:

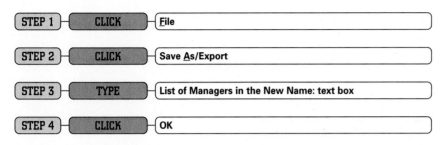

| STEP 1 | CLICK | File |

| STEP 2 | CLICK | Save As/Export |

| STEP 3 | TYPE | List of Managers in the New Name: text box |

| STEP 4 | CLICK | OK |

Close the Report window. To view the report in the Reports object list:

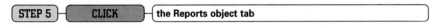

| STEP 5 | CLICK | the Reports object tab |

The List of Managers report appears in the Reports object list.

2.e Creating a Query Using the Simple Query Wizard

A query allows you to examine a subset of the data in your database. You can limit the fields and/or set specific criteria that will determine which fields and records appear in the subset. You cannot add data to a query.

CREATING A NEW QUERY

To create a simple query:

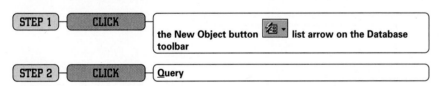

| STEP 1 | CLICK | the New Object button list arrow on the Database toolbar |

| STEP 2 | CLICK | Query |

The New Query dialog box opens. Your screen should look similar to Figure 2-9.

MENU TIP

You can create a new query by clicking the Query command on the Insert menu.

MOUSE TIP

You can create a new query by clicking the New button in the Query object window, or by clicking the New Object button list arrow on the Database toolbar, and then clicking Query.

FIGURE 2-9

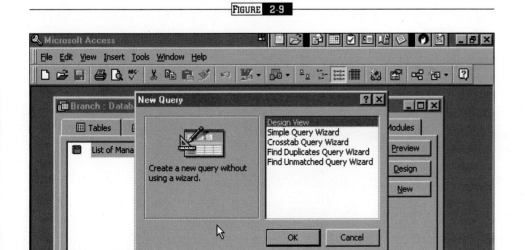

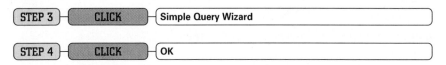

The first Simple Query Wizard dialog box opens. You can select a table and the pertinent fields from that table for your query in this dialog box.

| STEP 1 | VERIFY | Table: Managers Addresses is shown in the Tables/Queries: list box |

While you can use fields from more than one table, in this exercise you will use fields and data from only the Managers Addresses table for your query.

To create a query, you must add the pertinent fields from the selected table(s) to your query. Add those fields that contain data you wish to show in your query results. You do not have to add every field to the query. For example, you might wish to see only the State, Last Name, Initial, and Region fields in your query. To add the Last Name, Initial, Region, and State fields to the query:

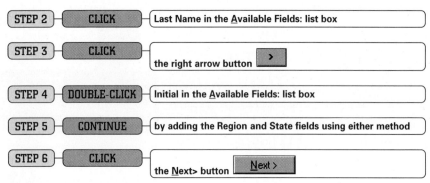

The second Simple Query Wizard dialog box opens. You can title your query and then open it for viewing in this dialog box. To title and open the query:

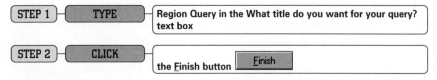

The Region Query: Select Query window opens containing the records from the Managers Addresses table with the fields you specified for the query. Your screen should look similar to Figure 2-10.

FIGURE 2-10

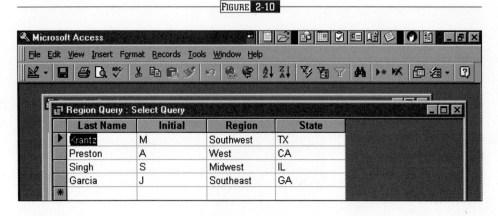

Close the query window. The Region Query object is saved in the database and appears in the Queries object list.

Sorting a Query

The query shows the Managers Addresses records in the same order as they appear in the table, form, and report. The only difference is that you do not see every field. If you wish to change the order in which the records appear, you can sort the query by a particular field. To view the Region Query results and sort the records alphabetically by state:

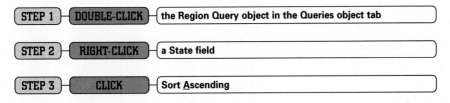

STEP 1	DOUBLE-CLICK	the Region Query object in the Queries object tab
STEP 2	RIGHT-CLICK	a State field
STEP 3	CLICK	Sort Ascending

The records are now sorted and shown in ascending order by State. After you modify a query, you can save it with the changes you have made. To save the query:

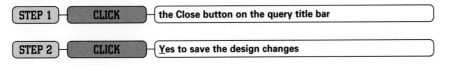

| STEP 1 | CLICK | the Close button on the query title bar |
| STEP 2 | CLICK | Yes to save the design changes |

Close the BRANCH database.

QUICK TIP

You can delete an object by selecting it in the database window and pressing the DELETE key, by clicking the Delete command on the Edit menu, or Delete on the shortcut menu.

Summary

> Access provides the AutoForm and AutoReport features to create simple default forms and reports quickly.

> Access Wizards are step-by-step processes to help you create tables, forms, reports, and queries.

> The framework for storing data in a database is a table. You can create a blank, empty table and then enter the data or you can create a table from an existing external data source.

> The Table Wizard provides a list of sample tables with sample fields defined for each table. You can use these sample tables and fields to create a business or personal database.

> Access object names may have any combination of 64 letters, numbers, spaces, and special characters except leading spaces, periods, brackets, exclamation points, backquotes, and ASCII control characters 0–31.

> After you create a table, you can view it in Datasheet view and enter data much like entering data in an Excel worksheet.

> You can create a data entry form quickly by selecting a table and using the AutoForm feature.

> You can print your data in a report by using the AutoReport feature to create a simple default report quickly.

> A query allows you to examine a subset of the data in your database. The Simple Query Wizard allows you to quickly create a simple query.

Commands Review

ACTION	MENU BAR	SHORTCUT MENU	MOUSE	KEYBOARD
Create a new database	File, New Database			CTRL+N ALT+F, N
Open an existing database	File, Open Database			CTRL+O ALT+F, O
Create a new table, form, report, or query			New button in the object tab	
Rename a selected object	Edit, Rename	Right-click object, click Rename		ALT+E, M
Delete a selected object	Edit, Delete	Right-click object, click Delete		ALT+E, D DELETE
Sort records in a table or query	Records, Sort, Sort Ascending or Sort Descending	Right-click field, click Sort Ascending or Sort Descending		ALT+R, S, A or C
View different records using a form	Edit, Go To, First, Last, Next, Previous, New Record		Navigation buttons	ALT+E, G, F, L, N, P, W

Concepts Review

Circle the correct answer.

1. The framework for storing records in a database is a:
[a] form.
[b] report.
[c] query.
[d] table.
[e] none of the above.

2. The Table Wizard:
[a] quickly creates a default report.
[b] displays a subset of the data in a database.
[c] contains sample tables and fields you can use to create a table.
[d] automatically edits your data as you enter it.
[e] none of the above.

3. You can enter data in a table in:
[a] Design view.
[b] Datasheet view.
[c] Format view.
[d] a and c.
[e] b and c.

4. AutoReport allows you to:
[a] view a subset of your data.
[b] create a simple report.
[c] create a data entry form.
[d] enter records.
[e] all of the above.

5. **AutoForm allows you to:**
   [a] view a subset of your data.
   [b] create a simple report.
   [c] create a data entry form.
   [d] enter records.
   [e] none of the above.

Circle ⊤ if the statement is true or ⨍ if the statement is false.

1. ⊤ ⨍ The Table Wizard will assist you in the creation of business-related tables only.

2. ⊤ ⨍ Object names can be up to 64 characters long.

3. ⊤ ⨍ You must manually save a table after you have added records to it.

4. ⊤ ⨍ Pressing the TAB key after entering a record in a form opens a blank record.

5. ⊤ ⨍ You cannot add data to a report.

6. ⊤ ⨍ The Postal Code field automatically inserts a hyphen when you enter the five-digit Postal Code plus the four-digit extension.

7. ⊤ ⨍ AutoNumber automatically numbers the records in a table.

8. ⊤ ⨍ You must add sample fields to your table one at a time.

IN THIS BOOK

Files created in exercises in other units were saved with filenames that included the chapter and exercise number. For the Access unit of this book, the database exercises are saved with text filenames because the same databases are used in multiple exercises and you cannot save a database with a different name for each exercise.

Because the database exercises used in this unit are modified in subsequent chapters, it will be necessary to complete all exercises at the end of each chapter before going on to the exercises for the next chapter.

Skills Review

EXERCISE 1

1. Create a new database called VANCOUVER LUMBER.
2. Use the Table Wizard to create a table. Use the Employees sample table and select the Region, FirstName, LastName, and DateHired sample fields in that order.
3. Change the FirstName field to Initial.
4. Save the table as Regional Managers. Let Access set a primary key.
5. Enter the data shown in Table 2-5 directly into the table in Datasheet view.

TABLE 2-5

REGION	INITIAL	LAST NAME	DATE HIRED
North	M	Huang	10/19/95
South	A	Kaplan	11/15/96
East	L	Ramirez	09/27/96
West	E	Jackson	12/01/97

6. Print the Regional Managers table. (*Hint:* use the Print button on the Database toolbar.)

7. Close the VANCOUVER LUMBER database.

EXERCISE 2

1. Open the VANCOUVER LUMBER database created in Exercise 1 in this chapter.

2. Open the Regional Managers table created in Exercise 1.

3. Sort the records in ascending order by Region.

4. Print the Regional Managers table.

5. Close the Regional Managers table without saving any changes.

6. Close the VANCOUVER LUMBER database.

EXERCISE 3

1. Open the VANCOUVER LUMBER database modified in Exercise 2 in this chapter.

2. Create a data entry form using AutoForm.

3. Enter the data in Table 2-6 below using the data entry form.

TABLE 2-6

REGION	INITIAL	LAST NAME	DATE HIRED
Northwest	B	Smithson	03/25/98
Corporate	D	Horner	09/13/97

4. Save the form as Data Entry Form.

5. Close the form window.

6. Use AutoReport to create a default report of the records in the table.

7. Save the report as Managers List.

8. Print the Managers List report.

9. Close the report window.

10. Close the VANCOUVER LUMBER database.

Case Problems

PROBLEM 1

Use the Database Properties command on the File menu to find a list of all the objects in the PETSTORE RECORDS, BRANCH, and VANCOUVER LUMBER databases. Create a Word document listing the objects in each database. Save and print the document.

PROBLEM 2

Using the Office Assistant, look up and review the topic "What is a database?". Create a new Word document containing at least three paragraphs describing a database including business and personal examples of a database. Save and print the document.

PROBLEM 3

If your computer has sufficient memory, create a new database using a Database Wizard of your choice. (*Hint:* if Access is open, click the New Database button on the Database toolbar, click the Databases tab, and double-click a Wizard.) Include sample data. Note that it may take several minutes for the Wizard to create all the database objects. After the database is created, open and review the database table, query, form, and report objects.

PROBLEM 4   INTERNET

Connect to your ISP. Using the Microsoft on the Web command on the Help menu, load the Microsoft home page and then link to pages that provide information on the Access 97 application. Print at least two Web pages. Disconnect from your ISP.

Designing and Creating an Access Table

Chapter Overview:

In Chapter 2, you learned the basics of creating a database table, query, form, and report using Access wizards. This chapter shows you how to manually create and design an Access table. You will create fields based on the different types of data available in a table and examine and change the properties of those fields. Finally, you will input and edit data and modify the table design.

SNAPSHOT

In this chapter you will learn to:

> **Design a table**

> **Identify Access data types and properties**

> **Create a table**

> **Add fields to a table**

> **Enter data in a table**

> **Modify the design of a table**

3.a Designing a Table

Before you design a table, you should have an idea of the type of data that you want to include. It is a good plan to make a pencil-and-paper list of the fields you will include in each record. You should also consider how the data in each record will appear. For example, it is wise to have a separate field for Last Name and First Name or Initial, so that you can sort your records using either field. This allows you to list persons with the same last name in correct alphabetical order by taking into account each person's first name or initial.

You should also consider what type of information will appear in each field. For example, will the field contain numbers or text? If the field is going to contain a number, will it be a value you already know, or will you have to perform a calculation to arrive at that value? Should an Employee ID number be considered as a numeric data type even though you will not use it as a value?

Furthermore, you may also want to consider how you could control the data that is entered into the table. You may want to control the number of decimal places in values entered into the database. Once you have a good idea of what type of information your table will include, you can examine the different options Access gives you for presenting the data.

3.b Identifying Access Data Types and Properties

Access offers different data types so that you can make your fields as unique and descriptive as possible. These data types are AutoNumber, Text, Memo, Number, Currency, Date/Time, Yes/No, OLE Object, Hyperlink, and Lookup Wizard.

AUTONUMBER

The **AutoNumber** field is a counter field that automatically displays a unique identifying number for a record. Once this unique number is automatically created, it cannot be changed or deleted.

TEXT

Text fields can contain any combination of letters, numbers, or special characters. The size limit of a Text field is 255 characters. The default length of a Text field is 50 characters. Some examples of a Text field type are:

1. Names
2. Street addresses (alphanumeric)
3. ID numbers

MEMO

Use a **Memo** field if you need to include a lengthy description in a record. The size limit of a Memo field is 64,000 characters. You cannot sort using the Memo field.

NUMBER

Use a **Number** field for integers or decimal numbers that can be non-monetary values used in calculations.

CURRENCY

Use a **Currency** field whenever you want to show a monetary value or to maintain the accuracy of calculations up to 15 digits to the left of the decimal point.

DATE/TIME

Use a **Date/Time** field whenever you want to express a date or time that can be sorted and updated automatically when changes are made to the Regional Settings in the Windows 95 Control Panel.

YES/NO

Yes/No fields contain one character and are used for a Yes/No, On/Off, or True/False response. Some examples of a Yes/No field type are:

1. Item Discontinued (Yes/No)
2. Health Insurance Offered (Yes/No)

OLE OBJECT

Use an **OLE object** when you want to store a document or picture created in another application in a field (for example, an employee's photograph).

HYPERLINK

Use a **hyperlink** to store a Web page URL or the path and filename of a file stored on your computer, another computer, or an FTP site. (Web pages and URLs are discussed in Chapter 3 of the Office unit.)

LOOKUP WIZARD

The Lookup Wizard allows you to choose a value for a field from another table or list. For more detailed information on data types, see Access online <u>H</u>elp.

3.c Creating a Table

Now that you understand some options for field data types, you can create a table and begin adding fields. In the following exercise, you will create a new table in the BRANCH database you created in Chapter 2. First, open the BRANCH database. To manually create a table that includes information about the Southwest Region's employees:

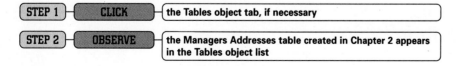

| STEP 1 | CLICK | the Tables object tab, if necessary |
| STEP 2 | OBSERVE | the Managers Addresses table created in Chapter 2 appears in the Tables object list |

To create a second table in the BRANCH database:

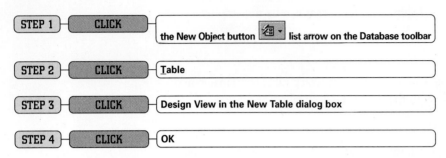

STEP 1 — CLICK — the New Object button [icon] ▾ list arrow on the Database toolbar

STEP 2 — CLICK — Table

STEP 3 — CLICK — Design View in the New Table dialog box

STEP 4 — CLICK — OK

The new table Table1: Table window opens in Design view. Your screen should look similar to Figure 3-1.

FIGURE 3-1

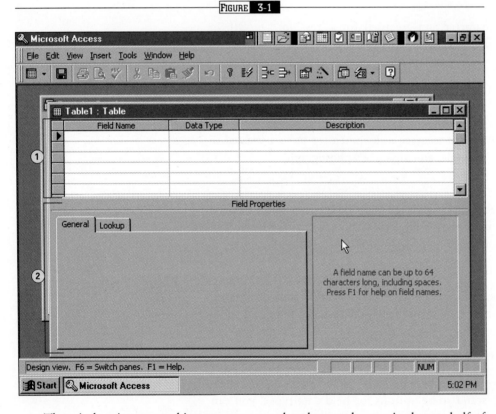

1. Top pane
2. Field Properties pane

The window is separated into two panes: a datasheet-style pane in the top half of the window and the Field Properties pane in the bottom half of the window. You will add field names and data type information in the top pane and then set individual field properties in the bottom pane.

3.d Adding Fields to a Table

You are now ready to specify the fields in your new table. You can move the insertion point from column to column in the top pane just as you would in Datasheet view, using the TAB key or arrow keys. Observe the Help box in the right side of the bottom pane. This box displays Help text for the column in which your insertion point is located. To begin adding fields to the table:

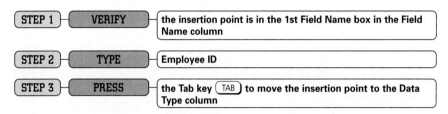

STEP 1 — VERIFY — the insertion point is in the 1st Field Name box in the Field Name column

STEP 2 — TYPE — Employee ID

STEP 3 — PRESS — the Tab key (TAB) to move the insertion point to the Data Type column

Your screen should look similar to Figure 3-2.

FIGURE 3-2

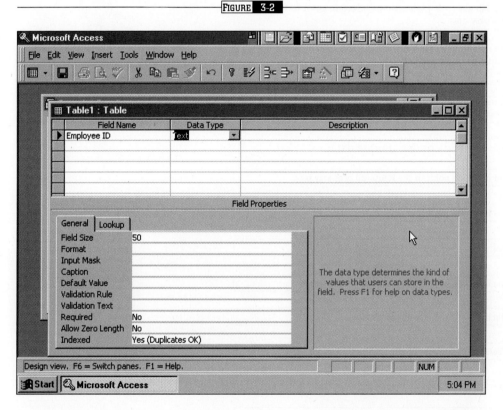

The Text data type appears in the Data Type column because it is the default data type. You can select a different data type from a list box, when necessary, by clicking the Data Type list arrow to view the data type options. The Employee ID field is a Text data type field, therefore no change is necessary. The contents of the Help box now define the term "data type."

Observe the General tab in the left portion of the Field Properties pane. You can move the insertion point into the Field Properties pane by pressing the F6 key. Press the Up Arrow, Down Arrow, TAB, or SHIFT+TAB keys to move between property boxes in the pane. As you move the insertion point to a different property box, the Help box displays Help text for the property.

You can customize the properties for a field in the Field Properties pane. For example, the default size for a Text field is 50 characters. Also, the Required property box indicates this field is not required to contain data. The Indexed property box indicates duplicate Employee ID numbers can exist in the table.

Suppose you want the field size to be 4 and to require unique data to be entered into the field. To modify the Employee ID field properties:

STEP 1 — PRESS — the F6 key (F6) to move the insertion point to the Field Properties pane

The Field Size property box is selected. Notice the new Help text in the Help box.

STEP 2 — TYPE — 4 in the Field Size property box

To review the Help box text for the remaining properties:

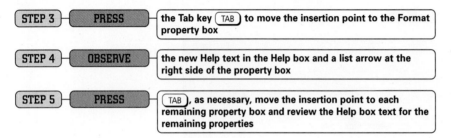

STEP 3 — PRESS — the Tab key (TAB) to move the insertion point to the Format property box

STEP 4 — OBSERVE — the new Help text in the Help box and a list arrow at the right side of the property box

STEP 5 — PRESS — (TAB), as necessary, move the insertion point to each remaining property box and review the Help box text for the remaining properties

QUICK TIP

Press the F1 key when the insertion point is in a field property box to get online Help for that property.

To require that the Employee ID field contain unique data:

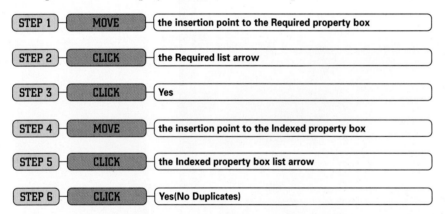

STEP 1 — MOVE — the insertion point to the Required property box

STEP 2 — CLICK — the Required list arrow

STEP 3 — CLICK — Yes

STEP 4 — MOVE — the insertion point to the Indexed property box

STEP 5 — CLICK — the Indexed property box list arrow

STEP 6 — CLICK — Yes(No Duplicates)

To move the insertion point back to the Data Type column and add a field description:

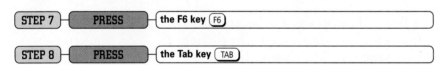

STEP 7 — PRESS — the F6 key (F6)

STEP 8 — PRESS — the Tab key (TAB)

The insertion point is in the Employee ID field Description box and the text in the Help box now defines a field description. The **field description** is optional information for a text field. Field descriptions appear on the status bar when the field is selected and data is being entered in a form or table. To enter a field description for the Employee ID field and create the next field:

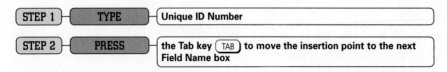

STEP 1 — TYPE — Unique ID Number

STEP 2 — PRESS — the Tab key (TAB) to move the insertion point to the next Field Name box

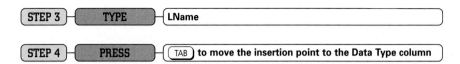

STEP 3	TYPE	LName

STEP 4	PRESS	TAB to move the insertion point to the Data Type column

The LName field is a 25-character, required Text field that will contain an employee's last name. The field name or label you see in Datasheet view and on reports does not have to be the same as the field name you assign in Design view. For example, you may want the field name or label used for Datasheet view and for reports to be "Last Name," which is more descriptive than LName. To change Last Name field properties:

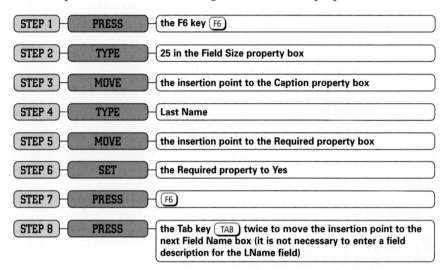

STEP 1	PRESS	the F6 key F6
STEP 2	TYPE	25 in the Field Size property box
STEP 3	MOVE	the insertion point to the Caption property box
STEP 4	TYPE	Last Name
STEP 5	MOVE	the insertion point to the Required property box
STEP 6	SET	the Required property to Yes
STEP 7	PRESS	F6
STEP 8	PRESS	the Tab key TAB twice to move the insertion point to the next Field Name box (it is not necessary to enter a field description for the LName field)

Table 3-1 below describes the next four fields and their description, data type, and modified properties.

TABLE 3-1

FIELD NAME	DATA TYPE	MODIFIED PROPERTIES	DESCRIPTION
Initial	Text	Field size: 2 Caption: First Initial Required: Yes	None
Address	Text	Field size: 30	None
City	Text	Field size: 25	None
State	Text	Field size: 2	None

Continue by adding a Field Name, selecting a data type for the field, and modifying the properties for the Initial, Address, City, and State fields based on the data in Table 3-1. After these fields have been added, move the insertion point to the next Field Name box.

You are now ready to add the Postal Code field which will include an input mask to assure that the 5-digit plus 4-digit code is properly entered. You will use the Input Mask Wizard to create the input mask.

CAUTION

To complete the activities in this section, you must have a complete installation of Access including the Advanced Wizards. For more information on installing Access, see online Help.

To create the Postal Code field:

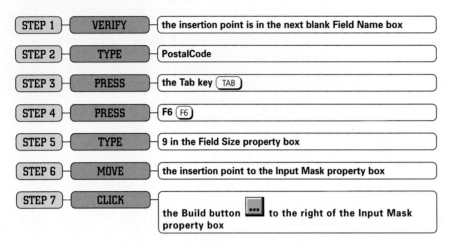

STEP 1	VERIFY	the insertion point is in the next blank Field Name box
STEP 2	TYPE	PostalCode
STEP 3	PRESS	the Tab key (TAB)
STEP 4	PRESS	F6 (F6)
STEP 5	TYPE	9 in the Field Size property box
STEP 6	MOVE	the insertion point to the Input Mask property box
STEP 7	CLICK	the Build button ... to the right of the Input Mask property box

Access takes a few seconds to set up the wizards. You are asked to save the table and set a primary key before you continue. Save the table as **Southwest Staff**. Do not set a primary key at this time.

In a few seconds, the first Input Mask Wizard dialog box opens. You will select an input mask format in this dialog box. Your screen should look similar to Figure 3-3.

FIGURE 3-3

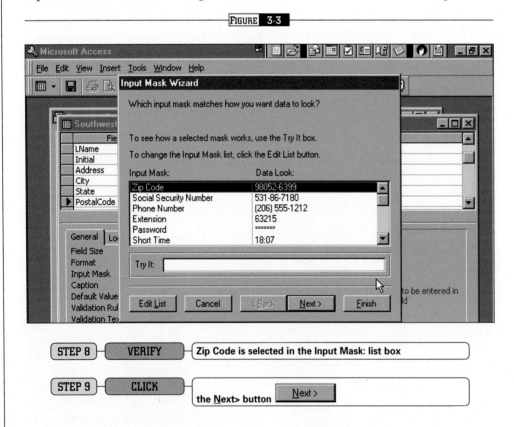

| STEP 8 | VERIFY | Zip Code is selected in the Input Mask: list box |

| STEP 9 | CLICK | the Next> button [Next >] |

The second Input Mask Wizard dialog box opens. You will accept the default place-holder setup for the Zip Code input mask.

STEP 10 — CLICK — the <u>N</u>ext> button   Next >

The third Input Mask Wizard dialog box opens. You will accept the default data storage option and complete the Input Wizard process.

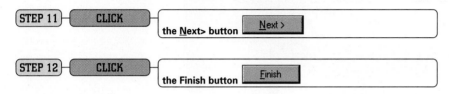

STEP 11 — CLICK — the <u>N</u>ext> button   Next >

STEP 12 — CLICK — the Finish button   <u>F</u>inish

The input mask for the Postal Code is created.

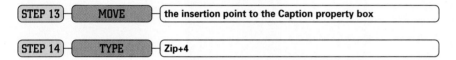

STEP 13 — MOVE — the insertion point to the Caption property box

STEP 14 — TYPE — Zip+4

To create the remaining two fields: Region and Salary (review Table 3-1, if necessary):

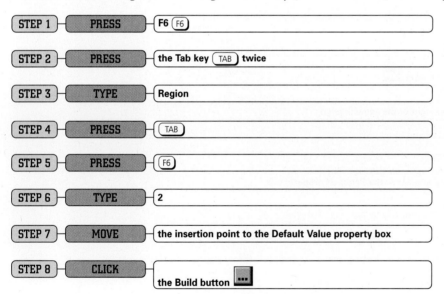

STEP 1 — PRESS — F6 [F6]

STEP 2 — PRESS — the Tab key [TAB] twice

STEP 3 — TYPE — Region

STEP 4 — PRESS — [TAB]

STEP 5 — PRESS — [F6]

STEP 6 — TYPE — 2

STEP 7 — MOVE — the insertion point to the Default Value property box

STEP 8 — CLICK — the Build button [...]

The Expression Builder dialog box opens. Your screen should look similar to Figure 3-4.

FIGURE 3-4

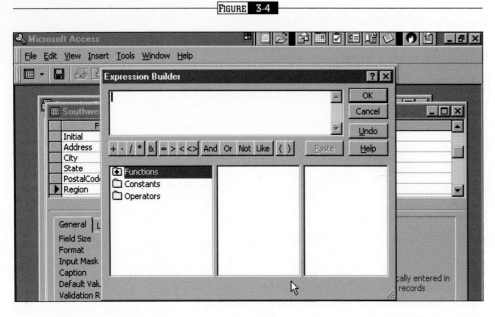

You will set the default value to =SW for the Southwest region. Access will then automatically enter this value for each record.

STEP 9	CLICK	the Equal button =
STEP 10	TYPE	SW to the right of the equal (=) sign
STEP 11	CLICK	OK
STEP 12	MOVE	the insertion point to the Required property box
STEP 13	SET	the Required property to Yes
STEP 14	PRESS	F6

To create the Salary field:

STEP 1	MOVE	the insertion point to the next Field Name box
STEP 2	TYPE	Salary
STEP 3	PRESS	the Tab key TAB
STEP 4	CLICK	the Data Type list arrow

The list of data type options appears. Your screen should look similar to Figure 3-5.

FIGURE 3-5

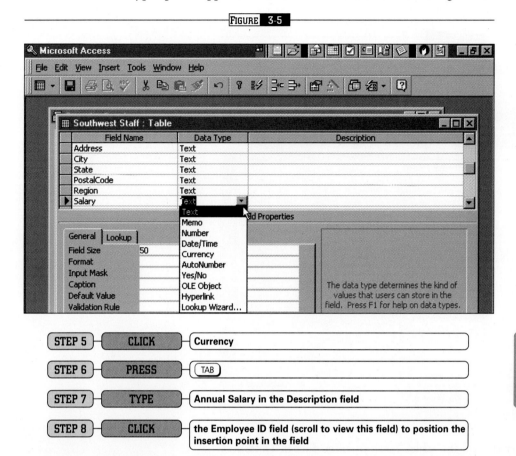

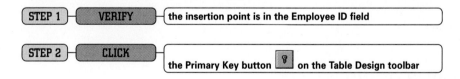

| STEP 5 | CLICK | Currency |

| STEP 6 | PRESS | TAB |

| STEP 7 | TYPE | Annual Salary in the Description field |

| STEP 8 | CLICK | the Employee ID field (scroll to view this field) to position the insertion point in the field |

SETTING THE PRIMARY KEY

After entering all the field names, data types, and modified properties, you should set a **primary key** that Access can use to identify each record as unique. In addition, Access will sort the records by this key. If your table does not have a primary key, Access has no way to keep track of unique records.

To set Employee ID as the primary key:

| STEP 1 | VERIFY | the insertion point is in the Employee ID field |

| STEP 2 | CLICK | the Primary Key button [🔑] on the Table Design toolbar |

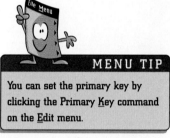

MENU TIP

You can set the primary key by clicking the Primary Key command on the Edit menu.

MOUSE TIP

You can set the primary key with the Primary Key button on the Table Design toolbar.

Notice the Primary Key icon on the field selector button for the Employee ID field. Your screen should look similar to Figure 3-6.

FIGURE 3-6

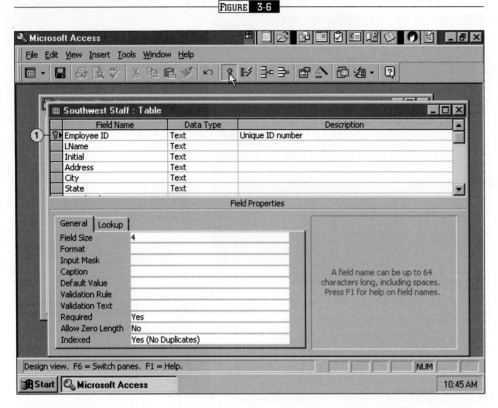

1. Primary Key icon

Now you are ready to enter data in the table. You can enter data in Datasheet view, but before you can switch to Datasheet view you must save the changes to the table. To switch to Datasheet view:

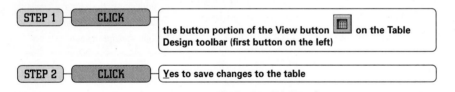

| STEP 1 | CLICK | the button portion of the View button 🔲 on the Table Design toolbar (first button on the left) |
| STEP 2 | CLICK | Yes to save changes to the table |

An empty table appears in Datasheet view.

3.e Entering Data in a Table

Now that you have created and saved your table, you are ready to enter data. The insertion point is in the Employee ID field for the first record. Observe the field description "Unique ID number" for the Employee ID field in the status bar. To enter the first record in the table:

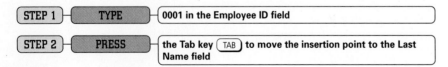

| STEP 1 | TYPE | 0001 in the Employee ID field |
| STEP 2 | PRESS | the Tab key (TAB) to move the insertion point to the Last Name field |

Notice that the leading zeroes remain in place after the Employee ID number. This is because you used a text data type. If you had used a number data type, the leading zeroes would not appear. Continue entering the first record:

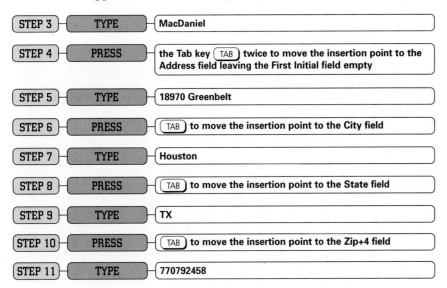

STEP 3	TYPE	MacDaniel
STEP 4	PRESS	the Tab key (TAB) twice to move the insertion point to the Address field leaving the First Initial field empty
STEP 5	TYPE	18970 Greenbelt
STEP 6	PRESS	(TAB) to move the insertion point to the City field
STEP 7	TYPE	Houston
STEP 8	PRESS	(TAB) to move the insertion point to the State field
STEP 9	TYPE	TX
STEP 10	PRESS	(TAB) to move the insertion point to the Zip+4 field
STEP 11	TYPE	770792458

The hyphen between the five-digit code and four-digit extension is added automatically. Notice that the Region field automatically contains SW to indicate the Southwest region.

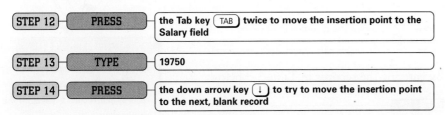

STEP 12	PRESS	the Tab key (TAB) twice to move the insertion point to the Salary field
STEP 13	TYPE	19750
STEP 14	PRESS	the down arrow key (↓) to try to move the insertion point to the next, blank record

Because you did not enter data in the First Initial field, a dialog box opens advising you that the First Initial field cannot contain a "null value." This means you are required to enter data in the First Initial field.

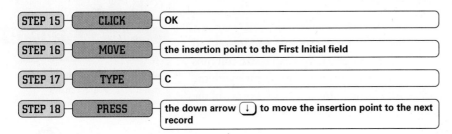

STEP 15	CLICK	OK
STEP 16	MOVE	the insertion point to the First Initial field
STEP 17	TYPE	C
STEP 18	PRESS	the down arrow (↓) to move the insertion point to the next record

Scroll to view the Salary field for the first record. Notice that you did not have to type the dollar sign, the comma, the decimal point, or the decimal places in the Salary field. To begin entering the remaining records:

STEP 1	MOVE	the insertion point to the Employee ID field for the second record
STEP 2	ENTER	the record in Table 3-2 below

TABLE 3-2

0001	Jerez	A	14555 Sycamore	Dallas	TX	752282203	18500

When you attempt to move the insertion point to the next blank record, you are advised that there is a duplicate value in an index. The Employee ID number you entered for the second record "0001" was previously used for the first record. Remember, each Employee ID number must be unique.

STEP 3	CLICK	OK
STEP 4	MOVE	the insertion point to the Employee ID field for the second record
STEP 5	REMOVE	0001
STEP 6	TYPE	0002
STEP 7	PRESS	the down arrow ↓ to accept the record and move the insertion point to the next record

The record is accepted. Continue by entering the records in Table 3-3 below.

TABLE 3-3

0003	Smith	P	9801 Woodvine	Houston	TX	770579801	19350
0004	Costello	N	13583 Juniper	Albuquerque	NM	871071095	21000
0005	Larson	M	2201 Nelson	Tucson	AZ	857133753	22000

RESIZING COLUMNS

Notice that the Address column is not wide enough to see the complete addresses and the State and Region fields are too wide for a two-character entry. You can resize columns in Datasheet view like you resize columns in Excel by first selecting the columns with the mouse, the keyboard shortcut keys, or the Select All button in the upper-left corner of the datasheet. You can select a column by clicking the field name column header or select multiple columns by dragging across multiple field name column headers.

To automatically resize all the columns:

STEP 1	SELECT	all the columns
STEP 2	MOVE	the mouse pointer to the vertical boundary between two field name column headers until the mouse pointer becomes a vertical line with arrows pointing left and right ↔
STEP 3	DOUBLE-CLICK	the boundary

QUICK TIP

Remember that as soon as you remove the insertion point from a record, that record is saved to the database.

MENU TIP

You can resize selected columns with commands on the Format menu or a shortcut menu.

MOUSE TIP

You can resize columns by dragging the field name boundary or by double-clicking the boundary to have Access automatically size the column to the largest entry.

Click anywhere in the table to deselect the columns and scroll to view the leftmost columns. The column widths of all the columns are adjusted to the longest entry in the column including the field name. Your screen should look similar to Figure 3-7.

FIGURE 3-7

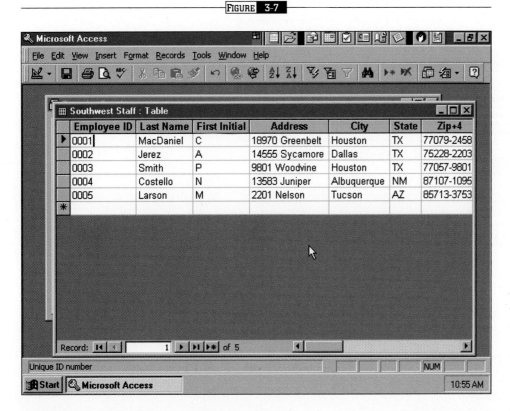

Close the table and save the layout changes.

3.f Modifying Table Design

After you have created a table and entered records in it, you still can change aspects of the table design. For example, you may wish to add another field to the table or change the name of an existing field. You must return to Design view to modify the table.

> **IN THIS BOOK**
>
> Previously, when necessary to switch to Design view or Datasheet view, you were given specific instructions on how to do so. In the remaining chapters of this unit, you will be instructed to switch to Design or Datasheet view. Review the specific steps presented earlier in this chapter, if necessary.

ADDING A FIELD TO A TABLE

To add the 25-character Text field "Department" to the Southwest Staff table:

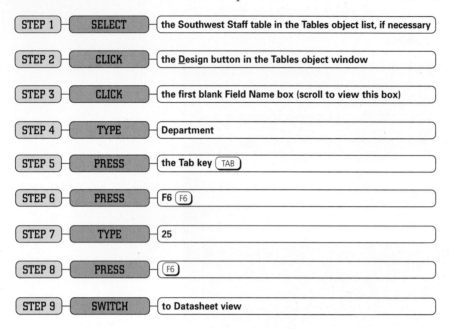

STEP 1	SELECT	the Southwest Staff table in the Tables object list, if necessary
STEP 2	CLICK	the Design button in the Tables object window
STEP 3	CLICK	the first blank Field Name box (scroll to view this box)
STEP 4	TYPE	Department
STEP 5	PRESS	the Tab key (TAB)
STEP 6	PRESS	F6 (F6)
STEP 7	TYPE	25
STEP 8	PRESS	(F6)
STEP 9	SWITCH	to Datasheet view

A dialog box opens on your screen, alerting you that you did not save the table design before attempting to switch to Datasheet view. To save the table:

| STEP 10 | CLICK | the Yes button |

To see the new field in the table:

| STEP 11 | SCROLL | to the right to display the Department field which was added as the last field |

Your screen should look similar to Figure 3-8.

FIGURE 3-8

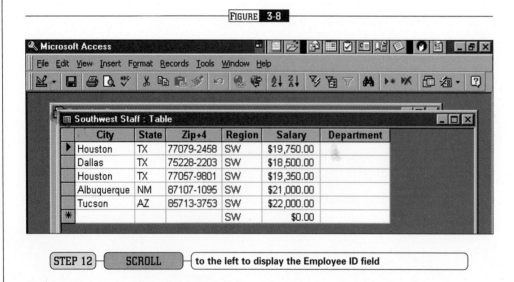

| STEP 12 | SCROLL | to the left to display the Employee ID field |

MOVING A FIELD

By default, the Department field, which was added last, appears in the rightmost column of the table. Suppose you want to place it before the Address field. To do this you must first select the Department field in Design view and then drag the field to its new location. To move the Department field:

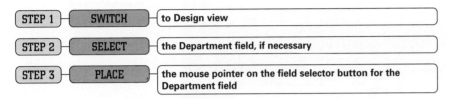

STEP 1 — SWITCH — to Design view

STEP 2 — SELECT — the Department field, if necessary

STEP 3 — PLACE — the mouse pointer on the field selector button for the Department field

The mouse pointer should be a left-pointing mouse pointer. Your screen should look similar to Figure 3-9.

FIGURE 3-9

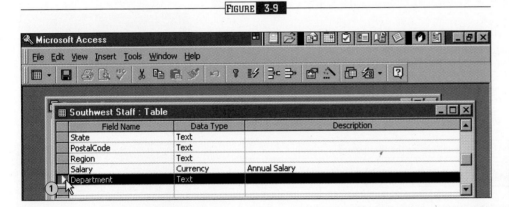

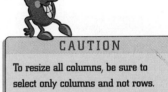

1. Selected record and mouse pointer

CAUTION

To resize all columns, be sure to select only columns and not rows.

To move the Department field:

STEP 4 — DRAG — the Department field upward, releasing the mouse button when a dark horizontal line appears below the Initial field

Click in the table to deselect the Department field, if necessary. The Department field is moved. Your screen should look similar to Figure 3-10.

FIGURE 3-10

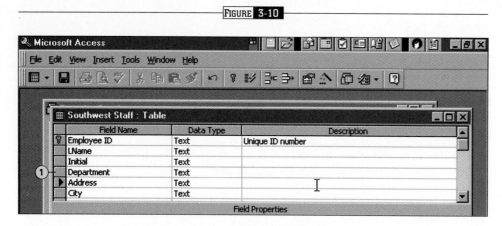

1. New position for the Department field

After modifying the design of a table, you must save it.
To save the change and return to Datasheet view:

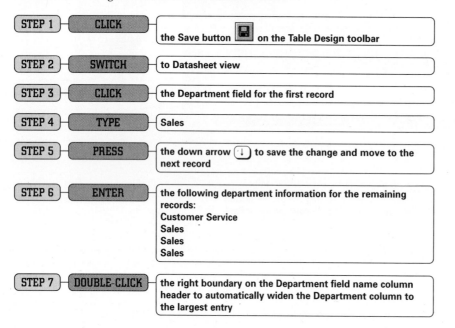

STEP 1 — CLICK — the Save button 💾 on the Table Design toolbar

STEP 2 — SWITCH — to Datasheet view

STEP 3 — CLICK — the Department field for the first record

STEP 4 — TYPE — Sales

STEP 5 — PRESS — the down arrow ⬇ to save the change and move to the next record

STEP 6 — ENTER — the following department information for the remaining records:
Customer Service
Sales
Sales
Sales

STEP 7 — DOUBLE-CLICK — the right boundary on the Department field name column header to automatically widen the Department column to the largest entry

MENU TIP
You can click the Save command on the File menu to save the table.

MOUSE TIP
You can click the Save button on the Table Design toolbar to save the table.

Close the Southwest Staff table and save the changes if necessary. Close the BRANCH database. For more information on designing and creating tables, see Access online Help.

Summary

> The first step in designing a table is to consider what fields you will include in each record, how the fields in each record will be arranged, and what type of information will appear in each field.

> Access offers several different field data types to help make the fields in a table as unique and descriptive as possible.

> Each field in a table has properties like the field size that can be customized to meet specific needs. You can control data entry by modifying field properties. For example, you can require that fields contain data, that the data in a field be unique to that record, that a default value appear in a field, and that the field name or label that appears in Datasheet view or on reports be different than the field name assigned to a field in Design view.

> Table fields are created and properties modified in Design view, and data is entered in a table in Datasheet view.

> You should set a primary key in a table that Access can use to identify each unique record.

> Columns can be selected and resized in Datasheet view just like the columns on an Excel worksheet.

> After you have created a table and entered data, you can still modify the table by adding new fields or changing the name of existing fields.

Commands Review

ACTION	MENU BAR	SHORTCUT MENU	MOUSE	KEYBOARD
Create a new table			New button in the Tables object window	
Switch between panes in Design view			Click in the pane	F6
Set a primary key	Edit, Primary Key		🔑	ALT+E, K
Resize columns in Datasheet view	Format, Column Width	Right-click column, click Column Width	Drag column boundary, or double-click column boundary	ALT+O, C

SCANS

ACCESS UNIT

Concepts Review

Circle the correct answer.

1. Which of the following is not a data type?
[a] Text.
[b] Currency.
[c] Date/Time.
[d] Number.
[e] Hyperlink.
[f] all are data types.

2. To move the insertion point in Design view, you can:
[a] press the TAB key.
[b] press an arrow key.
[c] click a field box.
[d] press the SHIFT+TAB keys.
[e] all of the above.

3. You can change a field's properties in the:
[a] Datasheet View pane.
[b] Table pane.
[c] Query pane.
[d] Design pane.
[e] none of the above.

4. Which key can you press in Design view to get online Help for a field property?
[a] F6.
[b] SHIFT+F6.
[c] F1.
[d] the ENTER key.
[e] the BACKSPACE key.

5. The Input Mask field property controls:
[a] the number of characters in a field.
[b] the default value of a field.
[c] the label for a field that you see on a report.
[d] whether or not data is required for a field.
[e] none of the above.

Circle T if the statement is true or F if the statement is false.

1. T F An employee identification number must be a Number field.

2. T F After entering field names and modifying properties, you should set a primary key for a table.

3. T F The default field size for a Text field is 30 characters.

4. T F You cannot change the position of a field in a table once the table has been saved.

5. T F If a field's Required property is set to "Yes," you can skip that field when entering data.

6. T F The Counter data type automatically displays a unique identifying number for a record.

7. T F You must use a Number field for integers or decimal numbers that can be values in calculations.

8. T F You cannot add a new field to a table once it has been saved.

Skills Review

EXERCISE 1

1. Create a new database named PROSPECT.
2. Create a new table in Design view using the criteria in Table 3-4.

TABLE 3-4

FIELD NAME	DATA TYPE	FIELD SIZE	OTHER CRITERIA
Client ID	Text	4	Unique value; required data
Initial	Text	2	Required data
LName	Text	30	Use Last Name for the Caption for Datasheet View and reports; required data
Address	Text	25	
City	Text	25	
State	Text	2	Default value "CA"
Postal Code	Text	9	Input Mask for five-digit code plus four-digit extension

3. Save the table as Prospective Clients.
4. Set Client ID as the primary key.
5. Change to Datasheet view and input the data from Table 3-5 below:

TABLE 3-5

CLIENT ID	INITIAL	LNAME	ADDRESS	CITY	POSTAL CODE
0001	M	Roberts	1589 Longview Drive	Bakersfield	933121258
0002	R	Johnson	9803 Sagora Way	Chino	917099803
0003	E	Barrett	1219 Woodrow Ave.	Fresno	937032569
0004	J	Ramirez	899 Lawndale Street	Los Angeles	900041358

6. Print the Prospective Clients table.
7. Close the Prospective Clients table.
8. Close the PROSPECT database.

EXERCISE 2

1. Open the PROSPECT database created in Exercise 1 in this chapter.
2. Open the Prospective Clients table in Design view.
3. Add a new 15-character Text field named field Sales Rep.
4. Position the Sales Rep field before the Initial field.
5. Add the following sales representatives for each record:
   Record 1   Wilson
   Record 2   Howard
   Record 3   Nguyen
   Record 4   Dominguez
6. Resize all the column widths to accommodate the longest entry in each column.
7. Print the Prospective Clients table.
8. Close the Prospective Clients table and save changes. Close the PROSPECT database.

EXERCISE 3

1. Open the VANCOUVER LUMBER database modified in Chapter 2, Exercise 3.
2. Open the Regional Managers table in Design view.
3. Change the caption of the Region field to Sales Region.
4. Move the Initial field after the LastName field.
5. Save the Regional Managers table.
6. Change to Datasheet view.
7. Resize the Regional ManagersID and Initial columns.
8. Print the Regional Managers table.
9. Close the Regional Managers table and save changes. Close the VANCOUVER LUMBER database.

Case Problems

PROBLEM 1

Create a Word document containing answers to the following questions:

1. How can I require that data be entered in a field?
2. How can I define a value that is automatically entered when I add a new record?
3. How can I control the maximum number of characters I can enter in a field?
4. How can I select a predefined input mask for a field?
5. How can I see a different field name in Datasheet view and on a report?

Use the Office Assistant, if necessary, to research answers to the questions. Save and print the document.

PROBLEM 2

You are the secretary to the sales manager for a retail electronics firm with several stores in the city. She has asked you to create an Access database with a table containing information on the sales staff for all the stores. The table should include the following fields:

1. An employee identification number.
2. The employee's first and last names.
3. The employee's street address and telephone number.
4. The store number where the employee works.
5. Whether the employee is paid based on salary or commission.

Create the database and table using appropriate field names. Modify the field properties as desired. Enter at least five records using fictitious data. Print the table.

PROBLEM 3 INTERNET

Using Office Assistant, review how to create a Hyperlink field and how to enter a hyperlink address in Form or Design view. Create a Word document containing at least five paragraphs describing the processes of creating and using a hyperlink field. Save and print the document.

Using Queries and Filters

Robert Goodman
president

Pinnacle Enterprises
Everett, MA

Pinnacle Enterprises is a customized travel promotion company that designs travel-related promotional programs for businesses.

> " Computers are an invaluable business management tool for me. I use software applications for organizing my databases, conducting mailings, producing documents, and accounting. "

Chapter Overview:

In Chapter 3, you learned how to create a table in Design view. After you create a table, it is often necessary to rearrange the records in a different order or to show only those records that meet specific criteria. You can accomplish this by either sorting the records or filtering the records. This chapter discusses two methods of sorting records: sorting a table in Datasheet view and creating a query to sort records. Creating queries to show records that meet specific criteria is described, and filtering a table to show specific records is demonstrated.

S N A P S H O T

In this chapter you will learn to:

> **Analyze an inventory database table**

> **Sort a table in Datasheet view**

> **Use queries to sort records**

> **Use queries to select records**

> **Use filters to select records**

4.a Analyzing an Inventory Database Table

In order for you to be able to see the results of the sorts and queries you are going to perform, you should work with a larger database file than the samples you have created up to this point. In this chapter, you will use the PETSTORE RECORDS database located on the student disk.

First, open the PETSTORE RECORDS database. To examine the Pet Inventory table:

STEP 1 — CLICK — the Tables object tab, if necessary

STEP 2 — DOUBLE-CLICK — Pet Inventory

The Pet Inventory table opens in Datasheet view. Observe the fields in the table. The table includes inventory information about the animals at a pet store. There are 32 records in order by identification number in the PetID field. To observe the design of the table:

STEP 3 — SWITCH — to Design view

Review the data type and properties for each field. Notice that the PetID field is the primary key.

4.b Sorting a Table in Datasheet View

By default, the Pet Inventory table is sorted according to the primary key, the PetID field. If you want to see all animals grouped together by category, you can sort the records by category.

STEP 1 — SWITCH — to Datasheet view

To sort the table by category:

STEP 2 — MOVE — the insertion point to the Category field for any record

STEP 3 — CLICK — the Sort Ascending button on the Table Datasheet toolbar

The records are sorted in ascending order by category. You can save the new layout of a sorted table by clicking the Save button on the Table Datasheet toolbar. To save the table with this layout:

STEP 1 — CLICK — the Save button on the Table Datasheet toolbar

Close the Pet Inventory table. You will now open the Pet Inventory table in Datasheet view and return the records to their original order. To return the Pet Inventory table records to their original order:

STEP 2 — DOUBLE-CLICK — Pet Inventory in the Tables object list

Observe that the records are in ascending order by category.

Access does not allow you to have more than one database open at the same time. If you have a database file open and click to open another one, Access automatically closes the current database.

Sorting Records

MENU TIP
You can sort records in a table in Datasheet view by clicking the Sort Ascending or Sort Descending subcommand under the Sort command on the Records menu or with a shortcut menu.

MOUSE TIP
You can sort records in a table in Datasheet view by clicking the Sort Ascending or Sort Descending buttons on the Table Datasheet toolbar.

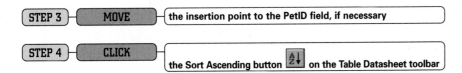

STEP 3 — MOVE — the insertion point to the PetID field, if necessary

STEP 4 — CLICK — the Sort Ascending button on the Table Datasheet toolbar

The records are returned to their original order. Save and close the table.

4.c Using Queries to Sort Records

Suppose you want to keep a table in its original order by primary key, but maintain several different sort orders for the records. You can create and save queries to sort records. To create a sort query:

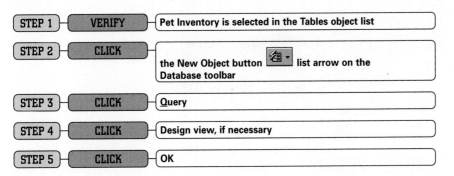

STEP 1 — VERIFY — Pet Inventory is selected in the Tables object list

STEP 2 — CLICK — the New Object button list arrow on the Database toolbar

STEP 3 — CLICK — Query

STEP 4 — CLICK — Design view, if necessary

STEP 5 — CLICK — OK

The Query1 : Select Query window opens. Your screen should look similar to Figure 4-1.

FIGURE 4-1

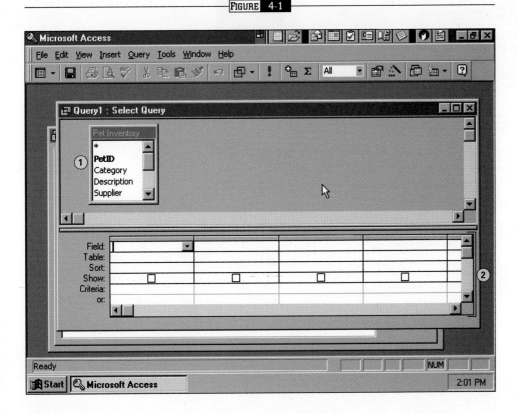

1. Field list
2. Design grid

The top half of the window contains a field list for the selected table, Pet Inventory. The bottom half of the window is the Design grid. In order to see a field in the query results, you will have to add it to the Design grid. To add the first field:

STEP 1 — DOUBLE-CLICK — PetID in the Pet Inventory field list box

The PetID field is added to the Design grid. Your screen should look similar to Figure 4-2.

FIGURE 4-2

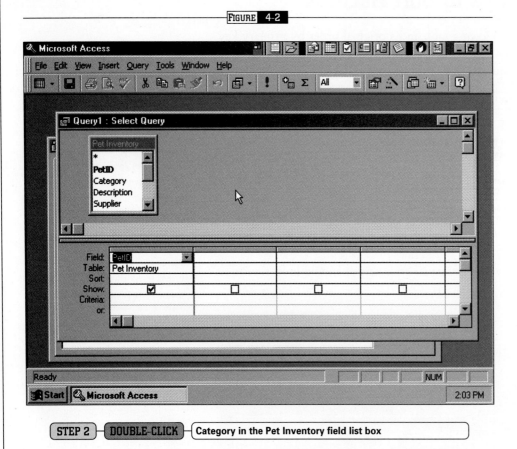

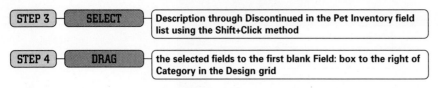

STEP 2 — DOUBLE-CLICK — Category in the Pet Inventory field list box

The Category field is added to the right of the PetID field. To add a group of contiguous fields to the Design grid at one time, you can use the SHIFT+Click method to select multiple fields. Then drag the selected fields to the Design grid. Use the CTRL+Click method to select noncontiguous fields.

STEP 3 — SELECT — Description through Discontinued in the Pet Inventory field list using the Shift+Click method

STEP 4 — DRAG — the selected fields to the first blank Field: box to the right of Category in the Design grid

Notice the mouse pointer becomes a multiple fields pointer when in the Design grid. When you release the mouse button, the remaining fields are added to the Design grid. Scroll to view the added fields. After you have scrolled completely to the left, the Design grid should look like Figure 4-3.

FIGURE 4-3

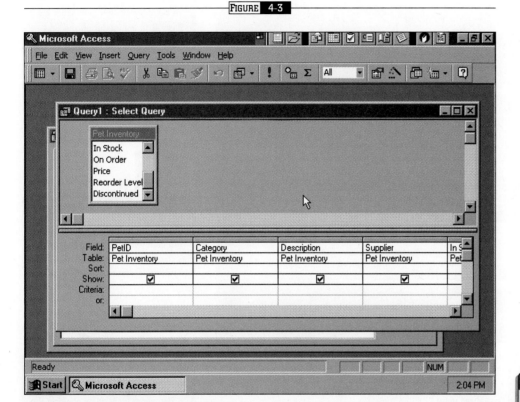

Once the fields have been added to the Design grid, you can determine the field by which you want to sort. In this case, you want to see animals grouped by category, so you will sort by the Category field. To sort by the Category field:

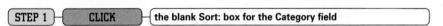

STEP 1 ├─ CLICK ─┤ the blank Sort: box for the Category field

A list arrow appears at the right edge of the box, indicating a list of sort options that are available. To show the list and select an option:

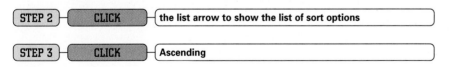

STEP 2 ├─ CLICK ─┤ the list arrow to show the list of sort options

STEP 3 ├─ CLICK ─┤ Ascending

QUICK TIP

You can use fields from multiple tables or queries in a query. To add a table or query field list, click the Show Table command on the Query menu. Then click the Tables, Queries, or Both tab, and double-click the desired table or query in the list. You can also add additional field lists with a shortcut menu.

To remove a field list, right-click the list and then click Remove Table.

Your screen should look similar to Figure 4-4.

FIGURE 4-4

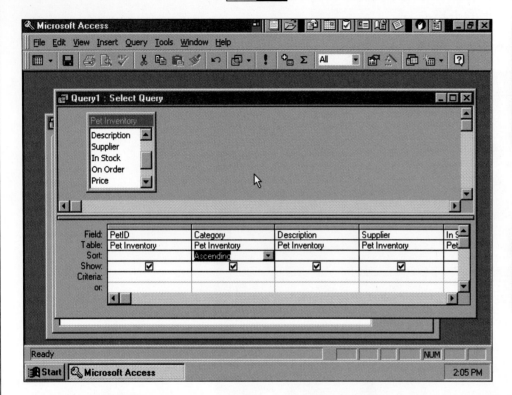

To run the sort query:

STEP 1 SWITCH to Datasheet view

The records appear in ascending order by category in Datasheet view. Your screen should look similar to Figure 4-5.

FIGURE 4-5

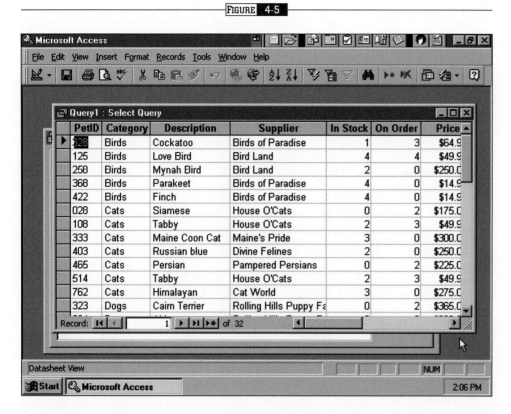

Scroll and examine the records in the query. All 32 records are listed by category, but the suppliers are not in order within each category. It is possible to sort by more than one field at a time. If you want to sort according to category and supplier, to better organize your records, you can add the Supplier field to the sort. The records will be sorted by each sort key in the Design grid in order from left to right. To add the Supplier field to the sort query:

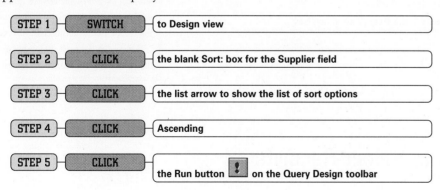

STEP 1 — SWITCH — to Design view

STEP 2 — CLICK — the blank Sort: box for the Supplier field

STEP 3 — CLICK — the list arrow to show the list of sort options

STEP 4 — CLICK — Ascending

STEP 5 — CLICK — the Run button [!] on the Query Design toolbar

The suppliers are now sorted in ascending order within each category. Your screen should look similar to Figure 4-6.

FIGURE 4-6

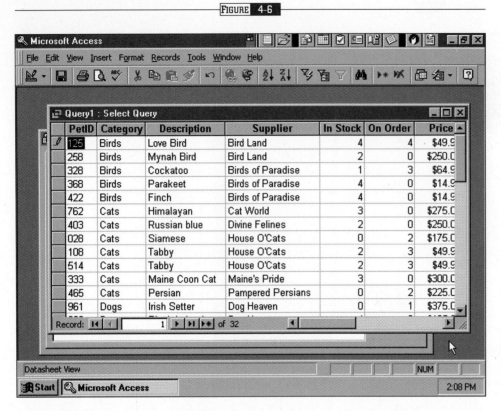

MENU TIP

You can save a query for the first time with the Save As/Export command on the File menu.

Once you have the records sorted as you want them, you should save the query so that you can refer back to it.

To save and close the query:

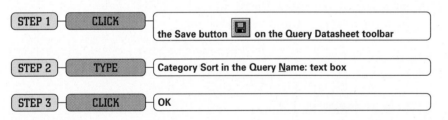

STEP 1	CLICK	the Save button 🖫 on the Query Datasheet toolbar
STEP 2	TYPE	Category Sort in the Query Name: text box
STEP 3	CLICK	OK

Close the query window. Once you have created and saved a query on a particular database table, you can continue to use and modify that query.

MOUSE TIP

You can save a query for the first time by clicking the Save button on the Query Datasheet toolbar. Access will open the Save As dialog box by default so you can name the query.

4.d Using Queries to Select Records

The size of a database naturally increases as you add records. Eventually, it is no longer feasible to look for certain records in the database by clicking the navigation buttons. This would be particularly cumbersome if you were looking for more than one record at a time. For example, you may wish to see a whole group of records that share a certain value in common. You can create a query that will show each record which shares that common value.

SELECTING RECORDS BY FIELD VALUE

When you execute a simple sort query, Access includes every record in the query results. You can limit the results of the query so that they include only those records that meet specific criteria. For example, suppose you want to see only those records for animals that will be discontinued after the current stock is sold. These records contain the word "Yes" in the Discontinued field. To select records containing the word "Yes" in the Discontinued field:

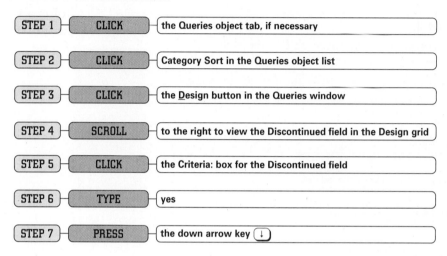

STEP 1	CLICK	the Queries object tab, if necessary
STEP 2	CLICK	Category Sort in the Queries object list
STEP 3	CLICK	the Design button in the Queries window
STEP 4	SCROLL	to the right to view the Discontinued field in the Design grid
STEP 5	CLICK	the Criteria: box for the Discontinued field
STEP 6	TYPE	yes
STEP 7	PRESS	the down arrow key (↓)

Notice that once you move the insertion point out of the box, the word "yes" appears with a capital "Y" and with the rest of the letters in lowercase. To run the query:

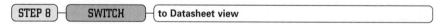

| STEP 8 | SWITCH | to Datasheet view |

Four records meet the criterion. Scroll to the right to see that each record contains a "Yes" in the Discontinued field. Your screen should look similar to Figure 4-7.

FIGURE **4-7**

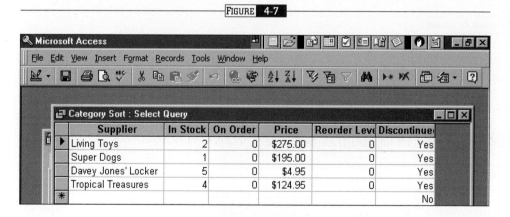

This is the list of products that will no longer be carried after the current stock is sold. You may now save this query with a new name, even though you based it on the Category Sort query. To save the query with a new name:

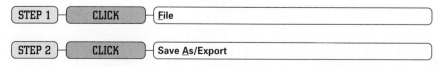

| STEP 1 | CLICK | File |
| STEP 2 | CLICK | Save As/Export |

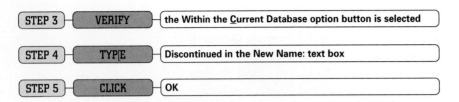

STEP 3	VERIFY	the Within the Current Database option button is selected
STEP 4	TYP[E	Discontinued in the New Name: text box
STEP 5	CLICK	OK

You do not have to close a query before using it as the foundation for another query.

SELECTING RECORDS WITHIN A RANGE OF VALUES

You may have a large number of pet suppliers and not be able to remember the name of one, although you know it begins with the letter "d." You can design a query that will select each record whose Supplier field starts with a "d." Access can use a wildcard character to perform this query. To design a query that will list each record whose Supplier field begins with a "d":

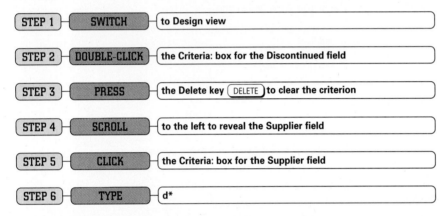

STEP 1	SWITCH	to Design view
STEP 2	DOUBLE-CLICK	the Criteria: box for the Discontinued field
STEP 3	PRESS	the Delete key (DELETE) to clear the criterion
STEP 4	SCROLL	to the left to reveal the Supplier field
STEP 5	CLICK	the Criteria: box for the Supplier field
STEP 6	TYPE	d*

The asterisk is a **wildcard character** that indicates Access should look for any combination of characters in the Supplier field preceded by a "d." The query is not case-sensitive; you can use an uppercase or a lowercase "d." To enter the wildcard formula:

| STEP 7 | PRESS | the down arrow key (↓) |

Access replaces your entry with a formula. Like "d*" is how Access identifies a wildcard formula. Your screen should look similar to Figure 4-8.

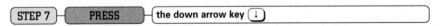

FIGURE 4-8

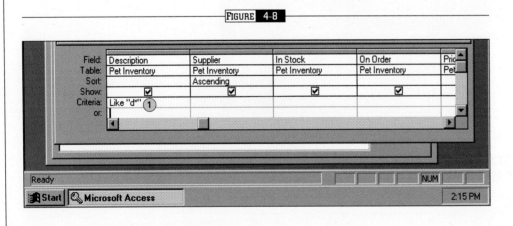

1. Wildcard formula

To run the query:

STEP 8 — SWITCH — to Datasheet view

Seven records match the criterion. All the suppliers listed begin with "d." Notice also that the records are still sorted by category and supplier because you did not change those criteria. Your screen should look similar to Figure 4-9.

FIGURE 4-9

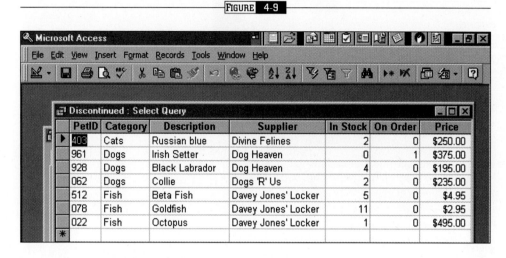

Discontinued : Select Query

PetID	Category	Description	Supplier	In Stock	On Order	Price
403	Cats	Russian blue	Divine Felines	2	0	$250.00
961	Dogs	Irish Setter	Dog Heaven	0	1	$375.00
928	Dogs	Black Labrador	Dog Heaven	4	0	$195.00
062	Dogs	Collie	Dogs 'R' Us	2	0	$235.00
512	Fish	Beta Fish	Davey Jones' Locker	5	0	$4.95
078	Fish	Goldfish	Davey Jones' Locker	11	0	$2.95
022	Fish	Octopus	Davey Jones' Locker	1	0	$495.00

To save the current query with a new name:

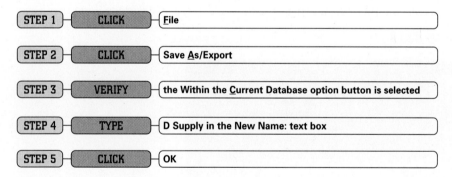

STEP 1 — CLICK — File

STEP 2 — CLICK — Save As/Export

STEP 3 — VERIFY — the Within the Current Database option button is selected

STEP 4 — TYPE — D Supply in the New Name: text box

STEP 5 — CLICK — OK

In addition to selecting records within a range of text values, you can also design a query to select records within a range of numeric values. To select all the animals whose price is greater than $250.00:

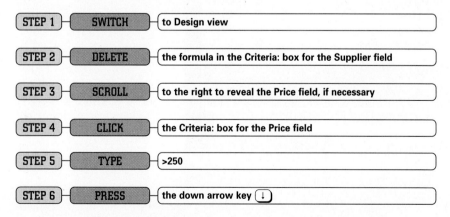

STEP 1 — SWITCH — to Design view

STEP 2 — DELETE — the formula in the Criteria: box for the Supplier field

STEP 3 — SCROLL — to the right to reveal the Price field, if necessary

STEP 4 — CLICK — the Criteria: box for the Price field

STEP 5 — TYPE — >250

STEP 6 — PRESS — the down arrow key (↓)

Access does not change your entry. The greater-than symbol is recognized as a query operator. Your screen should look similar to Figure 4-10.

FIGURE 4-10

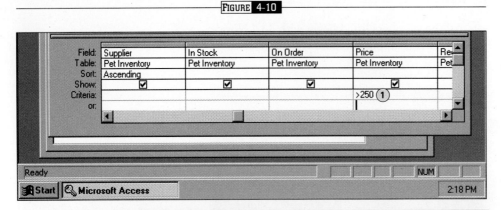

1. Query operator

IN THIS BOOK

Previously in this unit you have been given the specific instructions to run a query by switching to Datasheet view or by clicking the Run button on the Query Design toolbar. In the remaining chapters of this book you will be instructed to run the query using either method.

STEP 7 — RUN — the query

Nine records match the current criterion. Scroll to view the Price column. All records have a price greater than $250.00. Your screen should look similar to Figure 4-11.

FIGURE 4-11

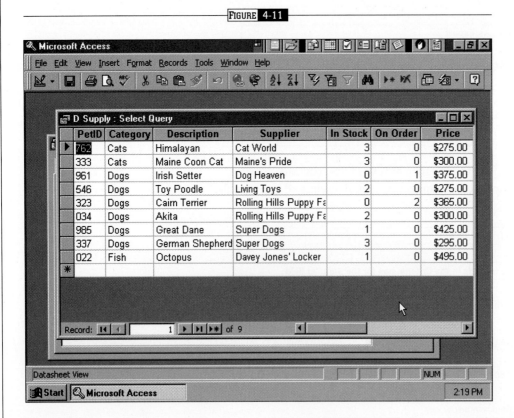

Save the query as Expensive.

SELECTING RECORDS WITH AND/OR CONDITIONS

Just as you can sort on more than one field at a time, you can also design queries that take into account data from more than one field. If you want to make your query more specific, you can design it so that each record selected must match a specific value in two or more fields, rather than only one. If you want to make your query broader, you can design it so that each record can match either one value or another value in two or more fields. The two previous examples are referred to as **AND/OR conditions**.

An AND condition will limit the number of possible records in the query results. If you want to select records on a narrow scope, you should use an AND condition. Any conditions on the same row of the Design grid are AND conditions. An OR condition will increase the number of possible records in the query results. If you want to select records on a wide scope, you should use an OR condition. Any conditions on different rows of the Design grid are OR conditions.

To demonstrate using AND/OR conditions, suppose you want to view all of the records for cats that cost more than $250.00. You will create selection criteria for the Category and Price fields. To design a query with an AND condition that will select these records:

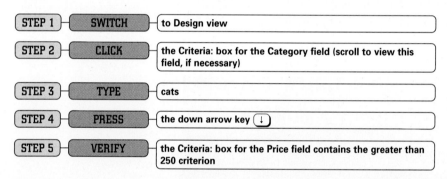

STEP 1	SWITCH	to Design view
STEP 2	CLICK	the Criteria: box for the Category field (scroll to view this field, if necessary)
STEP 3	TYPE	cats
STEP 4	PRESS	the down arrow key (↓)
STEP 5	VERIFY	the Criteria: box for the Price field contains the greater than 250 criterion

After you move the insertion point from the Criteria: box, Access encloses the criterion "cats" in quotation marks. You do not have to type the quotation marks. You may also use uppercase or lowercase letters; criteria are not case-sensitive.

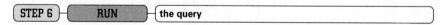

| STEP 6 | RUN | the query |

There are two cats that cost more than $250.00. Your screen should look similar to Figure 4-12.

FIGURE 4-12

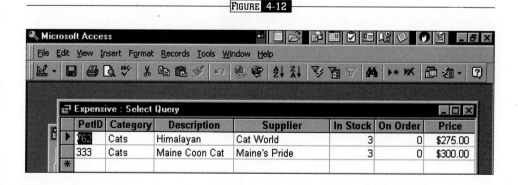

To illustrate the impact of using AND versus OR, you will delete the current criterion and create an OR condition to select records for cats OR any animal that costs more than $250.00. To create an OR condition:

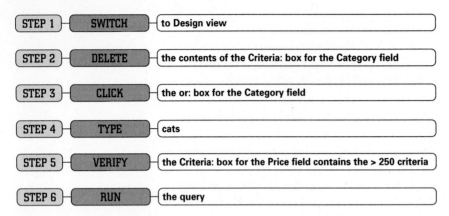

STEP 1 — SWITCH — to Design view

STEP 2 — DELETE — the contents of the Criteria: box for the Category field

STEP 3 — CLICK — the or: box for the Category field

STEP 4 — TYPE — cats

STEP 5 — VERIFY — the Criteria: box for the Price field contains the > 250 criteria

STEP 6 — RUN — the query

Fourteen records match the current criteria. Scroll to confirm that the records viewed are for either cats or any animal whose price is greater than $250.00. After scrolling back to the left, your screen should look similar to Figure 4-13.

FIGURE 4-13

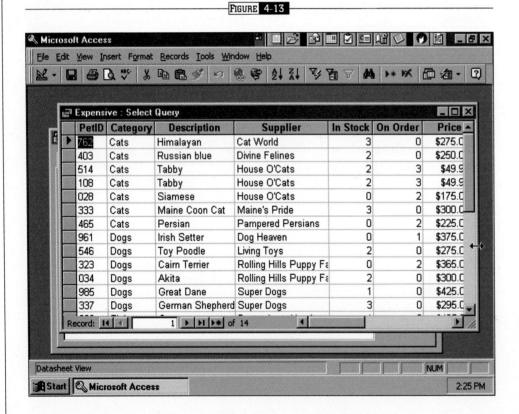

PetID	Category	Description	Supplier	In Stock	On Order	Price
762	Cats	Himalayan	Cat World	3	0	$275.0
403	Cats	Russian blue	Divine Felines	2	0	$250.0
514	Cats	Tabby	House O'Cats	2	3	$49.9
108	Cats	Tabby	House O'Cats	2	3	$49.9
028	Cats	Siamese	House O'Cats	0	2	$175.0
333	Cats	Maine Coon Cat	Maine's Pride	3	0	$300.0
465	Cats	Persian	Pampered Persians	0	2	$225.0
961	Dogs	Irish Setter	Dog Heaven	0	1	$375.0
546	Dogs	Toy Poodle	Living Toys	2	0	$275.0
323	Dogs	Cairn Terrier	Rolling Hills Puppy Fa	0	2	$365.0
034	Dogs	Akita	Rolling Hills Puppy Fa	2	0	$300.0
985	Dogs	Great Dane	Super Dogs	1	0	$425.0
337	Dogs	German Shepherd	Super Dogs	3	0	$295.0

Record: ◄◄ ◄ 1 ► ►► ►* of 14

QUERYING FOR HIGHEST OR LOWEST VALUES

Sometimes you need to view records that meet the highest or lowest value criteria such as the highest salaries or the lowest sales. The Top Values feature in Access allows you to set a highest or lowest criterion in a query.

To demonstrate this feature, you will first create a query to show all records in descending order by price and then modify the query to show only the five highest prices. To query for all records in descending order by price:

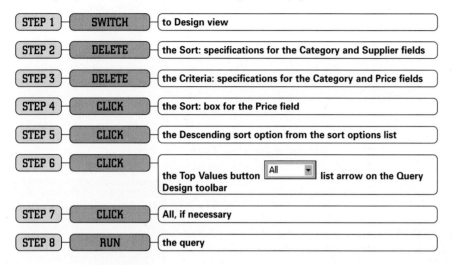

STEP 1	SWITCH	to Design view
STEP 2	DELETE	the Sort: specifications for the Category and Supplier fields
STEP 3	DELETE	the Criteria: specifications for the Category and Price fields
STEP 4	CLICK	the Sort: box for the Price field
STEP 5	CLICK	the Descending sort option from the sort options list
STEP 6	CLICK	the Top Values button [All ▼] list arrow on the Query Design toolbar
STEP 7	CLICK	All, if necessary
STEP 8	RUN	the query

Scroll to view the Price field to confirm that all 32 records are shown in descending order by price. To modify the query to show only the top five prices:

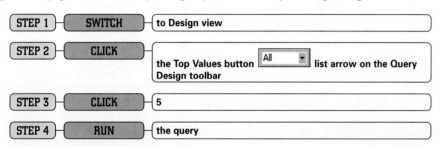

STEP 1	SWITCH	to Design view
STEP 2	CLICK	the Top Values button [All ▼] list arrow on the Query Design toolbar
STEP 3	CLICK	5
STEP 4	RUN	the query

Scroll to view the Price field, if necessary. Notice that although you requested the top five prices, six records meet the Top Values criterion. This is because two of the records, the Akita Dog and the Maine Coon Cat, both have the same price of $300.00, which is one of the top five prices. Your screen should look similar to Figure 4-14.

FIGURE 4-14

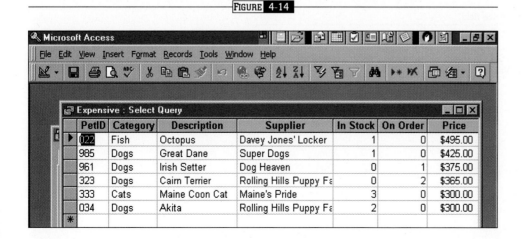

Save the query as Top 5 Prices. Close the query window. The Queries object list now shows six queries for the PETSTORE RECORDS database.

4.e Filtering to Select Records

Filtering Records

You can also select records directly in a table in Datasheet view by filtering the records. Filtering records is a good method to show specific records temporarily. Access has two methods of filtering records: Filter by Selection and Filter by Form.

FILTER BY SELECTION

The Filter by Selection feature allows you to select a field value and then show just the records that match that field. Once the filtered records are shown, you can filter the records again to create a subset of those records.

Suppose you want to show all the records for fish in the Pet Inventory table:

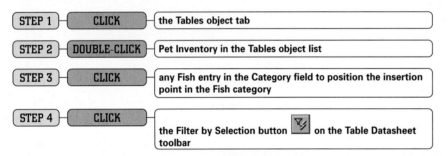

STEP 1	CLICK	the Tables object tab
STEP 2	DOUBLE-CLICK	Pet Inventory in the Tables object list
STEP 3	CLICK	any Fish entry in the Category field to position the insertion point in the Fish category
STEP 4	CLICK	the Filter by Selection button [icon] on the Table Datasheet toolbar

Five records for fish are shown. Now suppose you want to show a subset of these filtered records. To show only those records for the Davey Jones' Locker supplier:

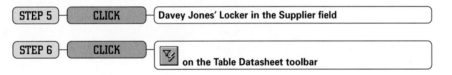

| STEP 5 | CLICK | Davey Jones' Locker in the Supplier field |
| STEP 6 | CLICK | [icon] on the Table Datasheet toolbar |

The three records that meet the criterion appear. To sort the records in descending order by price:

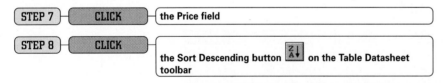

| STEP 7 | CLICK | the Price field |
| STEP 8 | CLICK | the Sort Descending button [icon] on the Table Datasheet toolbar |

The three records appear in descending order by price. Your screen should look similar to Figure 4-15.

FIGURE 4-15

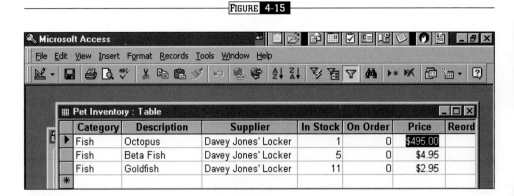

Close the table without saving any changes.

FILTER BY FORM

The Filter by Form feature presents a blank form in which you type the selection criteria or select criteria from a list.

To filter using the Filter by Form feature:

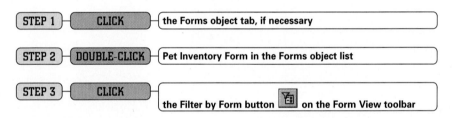

STEP 1 — CLICK — the Forms object tab, if necessary

STEP 2 — DOUBLE-CLICK — Pet Inventory Form in the Forms object list

STEP 3 — CLICK — the Filter by Form button on the Form View toolbar

QUICK TIP

You can remove a filter by clicking the Remove Filter/Sort command on the Records menu or with a shortcut menu.

MENU TIP

You can filter a table by entering the filter criteria in a blank form with the Filter by Form subcommand under the Filter command on the Records menu.

MOUSE TIP

You can filter a table by entering the filter criteria in a blank form with the Filter by Form button on the Table Datasheet toolbar.

The Pet Inventory: Filter by Form window appears. Your screen should look similar to Figure 4-16.

FIGURE 4-16

To filter the table to show all records for the birds in stock:

STEP 4 — CLICK — the Category field

A list arrow appears at the right edge of the field indicating a list of Category options is available.

STEP 5 — CLICK — the list arrow to show the list of Category options

STEP 6 — CLICK — Birds

STEP 7 — CLICK — the In Stock field

STEP 8 — TYPE — >0

STEP 9 — CLICK — the Apply Filter button 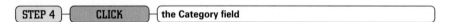 on the Filter/Sort toolbar

Five records meet the filter criteria for birds in stock. You can save a filter with the table, query, or form. To save the filter with the form:

STEP 10 — CLICK — the Save button 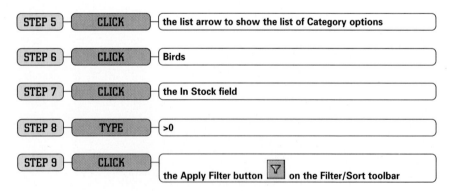 on the Filter/Sort toolbar

Close the form window. To demonstrate that the filter is saved with the form:

STEP 1 — DOUBLE-CLICK — Pet Inventory Form in the Forms object list

The first record of the complete 32-record table appears.

STEP 2 — CLICK — 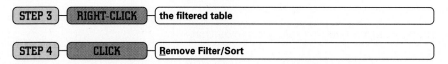 the Apply Filter button ▽ on the Filter/Sort toolbar

The form shows the first of five filtered records for birds in stock. To remove the filter:

STEP 3 — RIGHT-CLICK — the filtered table

STEP 4 — CLICK — Remove Filter/Sort

The form again shows the first of 32 records in the original order by primary key. Close the form window. Close the PETSTORE RECORDS database. For more information on using queries and filtering records, see Access online Help.

Summary

> When working with a large database, it is sometimes necessary to rearrange the records in an order other than by primary key and to show specific records meeting selection criteria.

> You can sort records in a table in Datasheet view or create queries to sort records.

> Queries based on tables or other queries can be used to select records that meet specific criteria.

> Filtering records in a table in Datasheet view or by a form is a quick way to select records temporarily for viewing or editing.

Commands Review

ACTION	MENU BAR	SHORTCUT MENU	MOUSE	KEYBOARD
Save a new table layout			🖫	
Sort records in a table in Datasheet view	Records, Sort, Sort Ascending or Sort Descending	Right-click field, click Sort Ascending or Sort Descending	⬆↓ ⬇↓	ALT+R, S, A or C
Run a query	Query, Run		❗ ▦	ALT+Q, R
Save a query with a new name	File, Save As/Export			ALT+F, A
Query for highest or lowest values			All ▾	
Filter records in a table by selection	Records, Filter, Filter by Selection	Right-click a field, click Filter by Selection	⧩	ALT+R, F, S
Filter records by a blank form or datasheet	Records, Filter, Filter by Form	Right-click a form, click Filter by Form	⧨	ALT+R, F, F

SCANS

Concepts Review

Circle the correct answer.

1. You can view specific records in a database by:
   [a] formatting the records.
   [b] filtering a table in Design view.
   [c] specifying criteria in a query.
   [d] filtering by a form.
   [e] b and c.
   [f] c and d.

2. How many databases can you have open in Access at one time?
   [a] 2.
   [b] 3.
   [c] unlimited.
   [d] 1.
   [e] 4.

3. By default a table is sorted:
   [a] by the Category field.
   [b] in descending order by price.
   [c] by the primary key.
   [d] in ascending order by last name.

4. A select query:
   [a] summarizes data.
   [b] makes changes to many records at one time.
   [c] cannot be saved.
   [d] retrieves data from a table(s) and shows records based on specific criteria.
   [e] none of the above.

5. An AND condition:
   [a] limits the number of possible records in query results.
   [b] increases the number of possible records in query results.
   [c] has no effect on query results.
   [d] must be specified in the Design grid.
   [e] a and d.
   [f] b and d.

Circle T if the statement is true or F if the statement is false.

1. T F The Top Values feature allows you to specify highest or lowest values in a query.

2. T F Filtering records is a good method to view specific records temporarily.

3. T F You cannot control the number of fields used in the query results.

4. T F You can sort by only one field at a time.

5. T F It is possible to design a query that will select records within a range of numeric values.

6. T F When you remove a filter, it is deleted from the table or form.

7. T F The only way to add fields to the Design grid is to drag them to the Design grid.

8. T F Queries must be based on only one table.

9. T F The only way to run a query is by clicking the Run button.

Skills Review

EXERCISE 1

1. Open the PETSTORE RECORDS database modified in this chapter.
2. Open the D Supply query in Design view.
3. Leave the current criterion as it is.
4. Add an AND condition to the Design grid that will look for dogs.
5. Run the query.
6. Save the query using the name D Supply: Dogs.
7. Print the D Supply: Dogs query.
8. Close the query window and close the PETSTORE RECORDS database.

EXERCISE 2

1. Open the PETSTORE RECORDS database modified in Exercise 1 in this chapter.
2. Open the Expensive query in Design view.
3. Leave the current criterion as it is.
4. Add an OR condition to the Design grid that will look for records that have more than four animals in stock.
5. Run the query.
6. Save the query as Expensive Stock/Order.
7. Print the Expensive Stock/Order query.
8. Close the query window and close the PETSTORE RECORDS database.

EXERCISE 3

1. Open the PETSTORE RECORDS database modified in Exercise 2 in this chapter.
2. Open the Pet Inventory table in Datasheet view.
3. Filter the table to show all records for Rodents that are not in stock.
4. Print the filtered table.
5. Remove the filter.
6. Close the table without saving changes.
7. Open the Pet Inventory Form.
8. Filter by form for all records for animals currently on order. (*Hint:* delete any previous filter criteria and filter the On Order: field for greater than zero.)
9. Apply the filter.
10. Save the filter with the form.
11. Print the filtered records in the form.
12. Close the form window and close the PETSTORE RECORDS database.

Case Problems

PROBLEM 1

Using the Office Assistant, review crosstab queries and action queries. Create a Word document with at least four paragraphs briefly describing these query types.

PROBLEM 2

Open an existing database. Sort a table in Datasheet view in any order you choose. Print the table. Create a new query in Design view. Add all the fields to the Design grid and add a sort criterion. Run the query and print the results. Save the query. Modify the query to select specific records of your choice. Run the query. Print the query results. Save the query with a new name. Open a table in Datasheet view and filter the table by selection. Filter the records again to create a subset of records. Print the subset. Close the table without saving any changes.

PROBLEM 3

Using the Office Assistant, review the differences and similarities between select queries and filters. Create a Word document with at least two paragraphs describing these similarities and differences.

PROBLEM 4

Connect to your ISP and display the Web toolbar. Search the WWW for Web pages listing toll-free telephone numbers (1-800 listings). Print at least one Web page.

CHAPTER

5

Using the Form Wizards

Susan Mosher
president

Mosher Associates
East Shodack, NY

Mosher Associates provides management and leadership development training with an emphasis on mutual respect for all work styles.

" *At Mosher Associates we use database, word processing, and spreadsheet applications to collect and organize data, write curricula, and keep track of billing.* "

Chapter Overview:

In Chapter 4, you learned how to create queries to sort records and how to use queries and filters to view specific records. You can also use forms in several ways. For example, forms can be used to provide structure for data entry, to create custom dialog boxes, or to create special forms called "switchboard" forms that list options for opening other forms or reports. In this chapter, you will use the AutoForm Wizards and the Form Wizard to create single-column and tabular forms for data entry. Modifying an existing report in Design view is also illustrated.

SNAPSHOT

In this chapter you will learn to:

> Use the AutoForm Wizards

> Use the Form Wizard

> Modify a form in Design view

5.a Using the Autoform Wizards

Suppose you want to enter data in the Pet Inventory table in the PET-STORE RECORDS database you modified in Chapter 4. The Pet Inventory table contains too many fields to show at one time in Datasheet view. You must scroll to view all the fields. To solve this problem, you can create a form that will show the fields for each record in one column.

First, open the PETSTORE RECORDS database. You will use the AutoForm Wizards to create three different form layouts for entering data in the Pet Inventory table. To create a single-column data entry form:

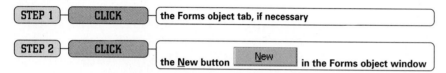

STEP 1 — CLICK — the Forms object tab, if necessary

STEP 2 — CLICK — the New button [New] in the Forms object window

The New Form dialog box appears. Your screen should look similar to Figure 5-1.

FIGURE 5-1

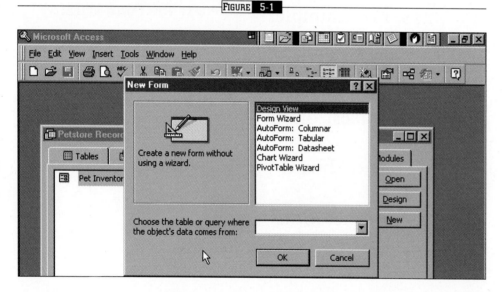

The different Form Wizards are listed in the list box on the right side of the dialog box. When you click a wizard, a brief description of that wizard appears in the box to the left of the list box. First, you select the wizard you want to use, then you select the underlying table or query that contains the data, and finally you begin the step-by-step Form Wizards process. To review the Form Wizards:

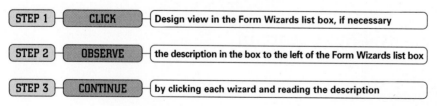

STEP 1 — CLICK — Design view in the Form Wizards list box, if necessary

STEP 2 — OBSERVE — the description in the box to the left of the Form Wizards list box

STEP 3 — CONTINUE — by clicking each wizard and reading the description

CREATING A COLUMNAR FORM

The **AutoForm: Columnar** Wizard creates a single-column form using every field from the table you specify. To use the AutoForm: Columnar Wizard and select the underlying table or query:

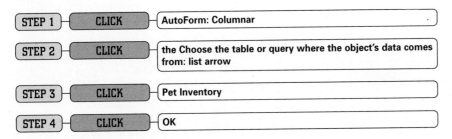

STEP 1	CLICK	AutoForm: Columnar
STEP 2	CLICK	the Choose the table or query where the object's data comes from: list arrow
STEP 3	CLICK	Pet Inventory
STEP 4	CLICK	OK

In a few seconds, the Pet Inventory form window opens in Form view. Notice that all fields from the Pet Inventory table are shown and all 32 records are available for editing. You can also create and delete records in the form. Your screen should look similar to Figure 5-2.

FIGURE 5-2

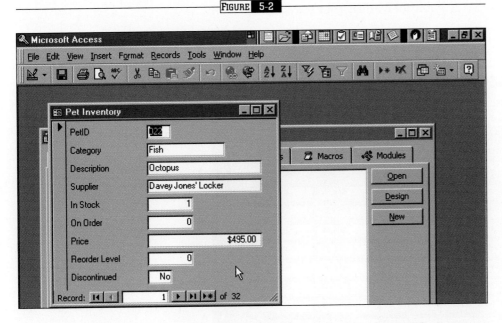

You can add special formatting called **autoformats** to your form. When you use one of the AutoForm Wizards, Access creates the form with the *last* autoformat used. The illustration in this section assumes the Standard autoformat was the last autoformat used. The background of your form may differ, depending upon the autoformat last used. Working with autoformats is discussed in more detail later in this chapter.

Close the form window without saving changes.

CREATING A TABULAR FORM

Sometimes you may want to view several records at one time in a format similar to a Word table. The **AutoForm: Tabular** Wizard shows multiple records in a column-and-row format. To select the AutoForm: Tabular Wizard and the underlying table or query:

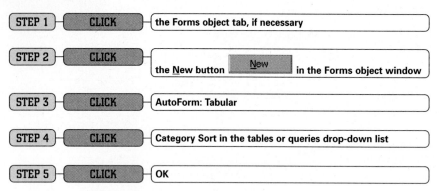

STEP 1 — CLICK — the Forms object tab, if necessary

STEP 2 — CLICK — the New button [New] in the Forms object window

STEP 3 — CLICK — AutoForm: Tabular

STEP 4 — CLICK — Category Sort in the tables or queries drop-down list

STEP 5 — CLICK — OK

QUICK TIP

An alternative way to create a columnar-type form using all fields is to select the appropriate table in the Tables object list, click the New Object button list arrow on the Database toolbar, and click AutoForm. An example of creating a form using this method can be found in Chapter 2.

In a few seconds, all the fields in the Category Sort query are shown in a tabular form and all 32 records in the query are available for editing. Your screen should look similar to Figure 5-3.

FIGURE 5-3

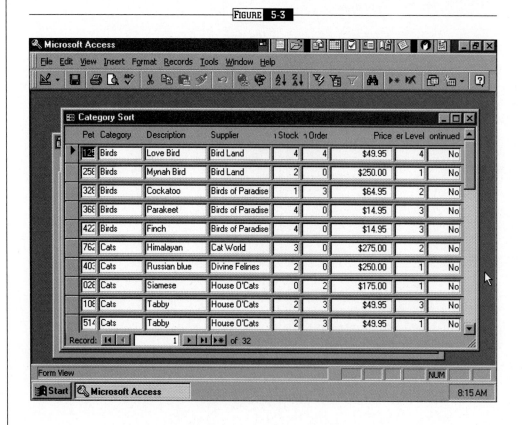

Notice that although you can see all the fields for each record, there is not enough space in the column headers for some of the complete field names or in the PetID column to view the entire identification number. You can modify the size and position of the column header information and details information by switching to Design view. Modifying a form in Design view will be discussed later in this chapter.

Close the form window without saving changes.

CREATING A DATASHEET FORM

Perhaps you would like your data entry form to resemble an Excel worksheet or a datasheet. The **AutoForm: Datasheet** Wizard creates a datasheet form using all the fields in the underlying table or query. To use the AutoForm: Datasheet Wizard and select the underlying table or query:

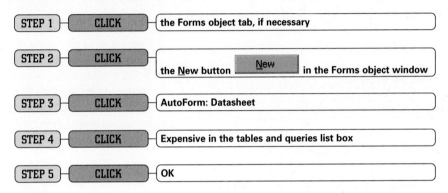

STEP 1	CLICK	the Forms object tab, if necessary
STEP 2	CLICK	the New button [New] in the Forms object window
STEP 3	CLICK	AutoForm: Datasheet
STEP 4	CLICK	Expensive in the tables and queries list box
STEP 5	CLICK	OK

In a few seconds, all the fields and records in the Expensive query are shown in a datasheet-type form. Your screen should look similar to Figure 5-4.

FIGURE 5-4

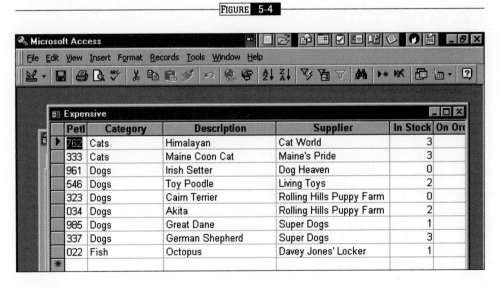

Close the form window without saving changes.

5.b Using the Form Wizard

By default, the AutoForm Wizards automatically select all the fields in the underlying table or query for a form. You can still take advantage of a wizard to speed up the form creation process and, at the same time, select only those fields you want in the form. The Form Wizard is a step-by-step process that allows you to create a form quickly by selecting the fields to be included, picking a layout format, and selecting a built-in style for the form.

The Form Wizard automatically lays out all the labels and controls for your form. **Controls** are graphical objects like command buttons, option buttons, and text boxes you can use to perform a task in the form. **Labels** are the text that identifies the controls. In the data entry form you will create in the next section, the controls are text boxes used to enter or edit field contents and the labels are the field names that identify each text box.

To select the Form Wizard and desired table or query:

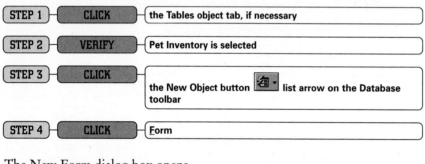

STEP 1	CLICK	the Tables object tab, if necessary
STEP 2	VERIFY	Pet Inventory is selected
STEP 3	CLICK	the New Object button [icon] list arrow on the Database toolbar
STEP 4	CLICK	Form

The New Form dialog box opens.

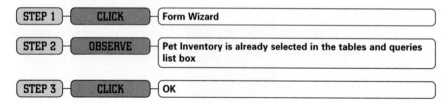

STEP 1	CLICK	Form Wizard
STEP 2	OBSERVE	Pet Inventory is already selected in the tables and queries list box
STEP 3	CLICK	OK

In a few seconds, the first Form Wizard dialog box opens. You will select the fields you want and their order in your form in this dialog box. To add the Category field first and then the PetID field:

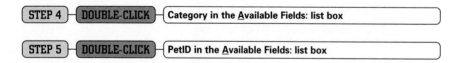

| STEP 4 | DOUBLE-CLICK | Category in the Available Fields: list box |
| STEP 5 | DOUBLE-CLICK | PetID in the Available Fields: list box |

The Category and PetID fields are added to the <u>S</u>elected Fields in: list box in that order. Notice that Description is now the first field in the <u>A</u>vailable Fields: list and it is selected. To add some of the remaining fields in their default order:

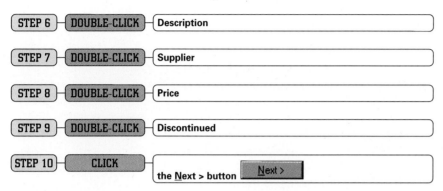

STEP 6	DOUBLE-CLICK	Description
STEP 7	DOUBLE-CLICK	Supplier
STEP 8	DOUBLE-CLICK	Price
STEP 9	DOUBLE-CLICK	Discontinued
STEP 10	CLICK	the <u>N</u>ext > button [Next >]

The second Form Wizard dialog box opens. In this dialog box you select a Columnar, Tabular, or Datasheet layout for your form. The Form Wizard shows a preview of the selected layout on the left side of the dialog box. To select a layout:

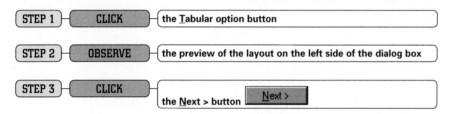

STEP 1	CLICK	the <u>T</u>abular option button
STEP 2	OBSERVE	the preview of the layout on the left side of the dialog box
STEP 3	CLICK	the <u>N</u>ext > button [Next >]

In a few seconds, the third Form Wizard dialog box opens. You can select a style for your form in this dialog box. When you click a style in the style list box, a preview of that style appears to the left of the style list box. To review the built-in form styles:

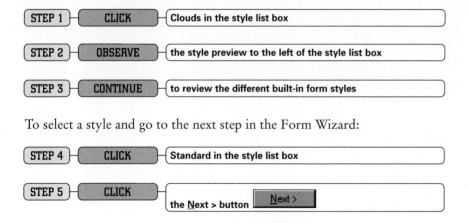

STEP 1	CLICK	Clouds in the style list box
STEP 2	OBSERVE	the style preview to the left of the style list box
STEP 3	CONTINUE	to review the different built-in form styles

To select a style and go to the next step in the Form Wizard:

| STEP 4 | CLICK | Standard in the style list box |
| STEP 5 | CLICK | the <u>N</u>ext > button [Next >] |

CAUTION

Once a style is selected it remains selected for all new forms until a new style is selected in the third Form Wizard screen or with the AutoFormat command on the F<u>o</u>rmat menu in Design view.

QUICK TIP

You can also apply these built-in styles to an existing form by switching to Design view and clicking the AutoFormat command on the F<u>o</u>rmat menu or the Auto-Format button on the Form Design toolbar.

The fourth Form Wizard dialog box opens. You are ready to give the form a title. The title appears in the title bar of the form and in the Forms object list. To give the form a title:

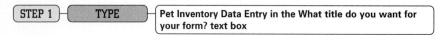
STEP 1 — TYPE — Pet Inventory Data Entry in the What title do you want for your form? text box

Notice that the "Open the form to view or enter information." option button is selected. To complete the steps of the Form Wizard and open the Pet Inventory Data Entry form:

STEP 2 — CLICK — the Finish button [Finish]

In a few seconds, the completed form appears in Form view. Leave the form open to continue working in the next section.

5.c Modifying a Form in Design View

You can modify the form to make it more attractive and easier to read. For example, suppose you want to center all labels, abbreviate the Discontinued label, and change the size of the PetID and Description labels. To modify the form:

STEP 1 — SWITCH — to Design view

The form appears in Design view. Your screen should look similar to Figure 5-5.

FIGURE 5-5

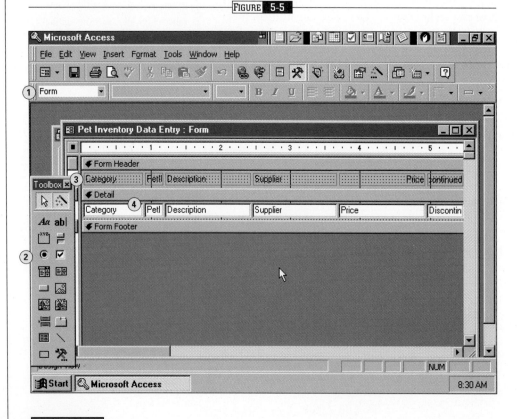

1. Formatting toolbar
2. Toolbox
3. Label controls
4. Field controls

Notice that two additional toolbars are now visible: the Formatting (Form/Report Design) toolbar, anchored below the Form Design toolbar, and the Toolbox, floating on the left side of your screen. Use the What's This? command on the Help menu to review the buttons on these two additional toolbars. Notice that some of the buttons on the Formatting toolbar are not available at this time. These buttons will become available when a column label or detail object is selected.

You will not need the Toolbox for this exercise. To hide the Toolbox if it is visible:

STEP 2 — **CLICK** — the Toolbox button 🛠 on the Form Design toolbar

The form design is composed of objects called controls. Each label and field is a **control**. You can move, resize, and delete the label and field controls. To select the Category label control:

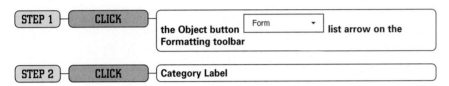

STEP 1 — **CLICK** — the Object button [Form ▾] list arrow on the Formatting toolbar

STEP 2 — **CLICK** — Category Label

The Category Label control is selected. Notice the selection or sizing handles on the control boundaries and that the Formatting toolbar buttons are now available. Your screen should look similar to Figure 5-6.

──────── **FIGURE 5-6** ────────

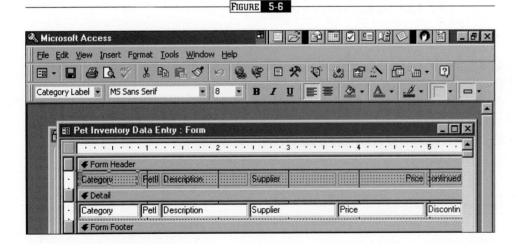

To center the Category label inside the control:

STEP 3 — **CLICK** — the Center button ≡ on the Formatting toolbar

The Category label is centered in the control object. You can also select a control by clicking it. To select and center the PetID label:

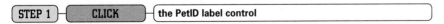

STEP 1 — **CLICK** — the PetID label control

The Category label control is deselected and the PetID label control is selected. Notice the selection or sizing handles on the boundaries of the PetID label control.

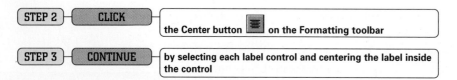

| STEP 2 | CLICK | the Center button ⬛ on the Formatting toolbar |
| STEP 3 | CONTINUE | by selecting each label control and centering the label inside the control |

The label "Discontinued" is too long to fit inside the control. To abbreviate the Discontinued label:

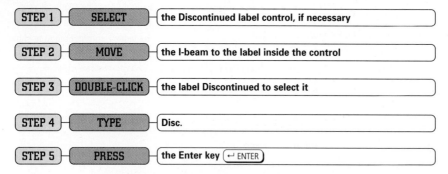

STEP 1	SELECT	the Discontinued label control, if necessary
STEP 2	MOVE	the I-beam to the label inside the control
STEP 3	DOUBLE-CLICK	the label Discontinued to select it
STEP 4	TYPE	Disc.
STEP 5	PRESS	the Enter key (↵ ENTER)

Click in the form area below the form Footer to deselect the Discontinued label control. To change the size of the Description and PetID label controls:

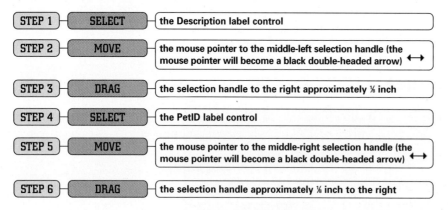

STEP 1	SELECT	the Description label control
STEP 2	MOVE	the mouse pointer to the middle-left selection handle (the mouse pointer will become a black double-headed arrow) ↔
STEP 3	DRAG	the selection handle to the right approximately ⅛ inch
STEP 4	SELECT	the PetID label control
STEP 5	MOVE	the mouse pointer to the middle-right selection handle (the mouse pointer will become a black double-headed arrow) ↔
STEP 6	DRAG	the selection handle approximately ⅛ inch to the right

Deselect the PetID control. Observe that the width of the two controls is changed and you can now see the entire PetID label text.
To review the form changes:

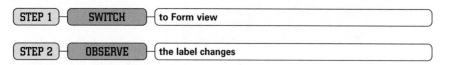

| STEP 1 | SWITCH | to Form view |
| STEP 2 | OBSERVE | the label changes |

Save the modified form as Price List. Close the form window. Close the PET-STORE RECORDS database. For more information on creating different types of Access forms or creating and modifying forms in Design view, see Access online Help.

QUICK TIP

You can move a selected control by moving the mouse pointer to the control. When the mouse pointer changes to a hand shape, drag the control to the new location.

Summary

> Forms can be used for data entry, to create custom dialog boxes, and to create special "switchboard" forms that list options for opening other forms or reports.

> The Form Wizards help you create columnar, tabular, and datasheet-type forms quickly.

> There are several Form Wizards you can use to create an Access form.

> The AutoForm Wizards create a form using all the fields in the underlying table or query.

> To create a form quickly and still select the specific fields to be included in the form, you can use the Form Wizard.

> You can create a form with a wizard, or you can create a form in Design view.

> Forms created with a Form Wizard can be modified in Design view.

SCANS

Commands Review

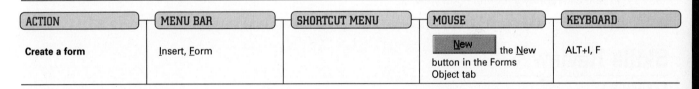

ACTION	MENU BAR	SHORTCUT MENU	MOUSE	KEYBOARD
Create a form	Insert, Form		New the New button in the Forms Object tab	ALT+I, F

Concepts Review

1. **Which of the following is not a Form Wizard?**
   - [a] AutoForm: Chart.
   - [b] AutoForm: Columnar.
   - [c] AutoForm: Tabular.
   - [d] AutoForm: Datasheet.
   - [e] a, b, c, and d are Form Wizards.

2. **Which of the following will create a single-column form using all the fields in the underlying table or query by default?**
   - [a] select the table or query, click the New Object button list arrow, click New Form.
   - [b] select the table or query, click the New Object button list arrow, click AutoForm.
   - [c] click the Forms object tab, click the New button.
   - [d] click the Tables object tab, click the New button.
   - [e] none of the above.

3. **The AutoForm: Datasheet Wizard creates a form that resembles:**
   [a] a Word table.
   [b] an Excel worksheet.
   [c] a PowerPoint chart slide.
   [d] none of the above.

4. **When you use the Form Wizard, you can select:**
   [a] a form layout.
   [b] a built-in style.
   [c] specific fields to be included.
   [d] a and c.

5. **Which of the following toolbars are visible in Form Design view?**
   [a] Formatting.
   [b] Toolbox.
   [c] Form Design.
   [d] Form view.
   [e] a, b, and d.
   [f] a, b, and c.

Circle ⊤ if the statement is true or ⒡ if the statement is false.

1. ⊤ ⒡ You must add fields to a form in the exact order that they appear in the Form Wizards field list boxes.

2. ⊤ ⒡ The objects in a form design are called controls.

3. ⊤ ⒡ Controls in a form design can be sized but not moved.

4. ⊤ ⒡ You can sort in a form.

5. ⊤ ⒡ You can add and delete records in Form Design view.

6. ⊤ ⒡ The built-in form style automatically defaults to the Standard style each time a new form is created.

7. ⊤ ⒡ The built-in form styles can only be applied through the Form Wizard.

8. ⊤ ⒡ The AutoForm: Columnar wizard is a step-by-step process that allows you to select specific fields, the form layout, and the form style.

9. ⊤ ⒡ You can modify a form in Form view.

10. ⊤ ⒡ The Form Wizard automatically lays out all the labels and controls for your form.

Skills Review

EXERCISE 1

1. Open the BRANCH database modified in Chapter 3.
2. Using the Form Wizard, create a form based on the Southwest Staff table.
3. Include all available fields in the form.
4. Use the Columnar layout.
5. Use a style of your choice.
6. Name the form SW Data Entry.
7. Switch to Design view and change the width of the PostalCode field control to view the entire contents of the field.
8. Switch back to Form view. Observe that you can now see all the Zip+4 data.
9. Print the SW Data Entry form.
10. Close the SW Data Entry form and save the changes.
11. Close the BRANCH database.

EXERCISE 2

1. Open the PROSPECT database created and modified in Exercises 1 and 2 in Chapter 3.
2. Using the AutoForm: Tabular wizard, create a form based on the Prospective Clients table.
3. Switch to Design view and make the following changes:
   (a) Change the style to a style of your choice. (*Hint:* click the AutoFormat command on the Format menu.)

(b) Center the labels inside their controls.

(c) Maximize the form window, if necessary.

(d) Size the label and field controls as necessary to view the entire label text or field contents.

(e) Change the Sales Rep label to "Rep" and the Postal Code label to the phrase "Zip+4".

4. Switch back to Form view and observe the label changes. (*Hint:* you can switch between Form view and Design view as you modify the control widths to view each change, if desired.)

5. Save the form as Client Data Entry.

6. Print the Client Data Entry form.

7. Close the Client Data Entry form and the PROSPECT database.

EXERCISE 3

1. Open the VANCOUVER LUMBER database modified in Exercise 3 in Chapter 3.

2. Using the Form Wizard, create a columnar form based on the Regional Managers table.

3. Include only the following fields: Region, Last Name, and Date Hired.

4. Use the Standard style.

5. Name the form "Date Hired".

6. Print the Date Hired form.

7. Close the Date Hired form.

8. Open the Data Entry Form. Because this form was created before you changed the caption property for the Region field to Sales Region, the form still shows the original label "Region."

9. Switch to Design view.

10. Edit the contents of the Region label control to be "Sales Region".

11. Switch back to Form view, verify the change, and save the form.

12. Close the Data Entry Form and the VANCOUVER LUMBER database.

Case Problems

PROBLEM 1

Using the Office Assistant, look up and review how to create and work with subforms and switchboard forms. Create a Word document with at least five paragraphs defining subforms and switchboard forms and how to use them.

PROBLEM 2

Open an existing database. Use the Form Wizards of your choice to create three different forms: columnar, tabular, and datasheet. Use all the fields from the underlying table or query in the columnar and datasheet forms. Select specific fields for the tabular form. Print the forms.

PROBLEM 3

Open an existing database and form. Display the form in Design view. Explore moving, sizing, and deleting controls in the form. Save the modified form with a new name. Print the form.

PROBLEM 4 INTERNET

Connect to your ISP and, using the Microsoft on the <u>W</u>eb command on the <u>H</u>elp menu, connect to the <u>D</u>eveloper Forum Web page. Review the current topics under discussion and print at least two Web pages.

CHAPTER

6

Using the Report Wizards

> *In addition to using my computer for accessing travel information and making reservations, I use word processing applications for building client itineraries.*

Ralph Mancini
travel consultant

Vista Travel
Cambridge, MA

Vista Travel is a provider of efficient and effective methods of managing and processing travel requests while maintaining the highest level of client satisfaction.

Chapter Overview:

In Chapter 5, you learned how to use the various Form Wizards to create forms with different formats and styles. Reports can also be created quickly and easily in several different formats. In this chapter, you will use the AutoReport Wizards and the Report Wizard to create columnar, tabular, and grouped reports. Modifying an existing report in Design view is also illustrated.

SNAPSHOT

In this chapter you will learn to:

> **Use the AutoReport Wizards**

> **Use the Report Wizard**

> **Modify a report in Design view**

6.a Using the AutoReport Wizards

Suppose you want to create an inventory report based on the Pet Inventory table in the PETSTORE RECORDS database you modified in Chapter 5. You can create columnar or tabular reports with the AutoReport Wizards. Like the Auto-Form Wizards discussed in Chapter 5, the AutoReport Wizards include all the fields in the underlying table or query by default.

First, open the PETSTORE RECORDS database. You will use the AutoReport Wizards to create two different report layouts based on the Pet Inventory table. To create a columnar report:

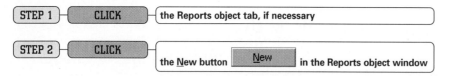

STEP 1 — CLICK — the Reports object tab, if necessary

STEP 2 — CLICK — the New button New in the Reports object window

The New Report dialog box opens. Your screen should look similar to Figure 6-1.

FIGURE 6-1

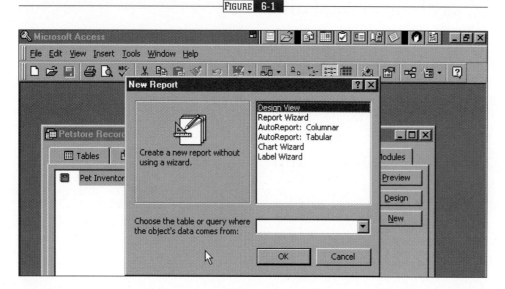

The different Report Wizards are listed on the right side of the dialog box. When you click a wizard, a brief description of that wizard appears in the box to the left of the list box. First, you select the wizard you want to use, then you select the underlying table or query that contains the data, and finally you begin the step-by-step Report Wizards process. To review the Report Wizards:

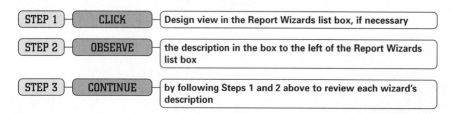

STEP 1 — CLICK — Design view in the Report Wizards list box, if necessary

STEP 2 — OBSERVE — the description in the box to the left of the Report Wizards list box

STEP 3 — CONTINUE — by following Steps 1 and 2 above to review each wizard's description

CREATING A COLUMNAR REPORT

The **AutoReport: Columnar** Wizard creates a single-column report using all the fields from the specified table or query. To select a wizard and the underlying table or query:

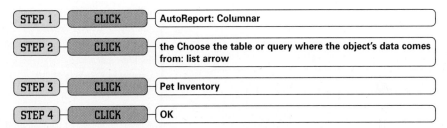

STEP 1	CLICK	AutoReport: Columnar
STEP 2	CLICK	the Choose the table or query where the object's data comes from: list arrow
STEP 3	CLICK	Pet Inventory
STEP 4	CLICK	OK

In a few seconds, the Pet Inventory report window opens in Print Preview. Scroll to view the report. Notice that all fields from the Pet Inventory table are shown and all 32 records are included. After scrolling to view the first record, your screen should look similar to Figure 6-2.

FIGURE 6-2

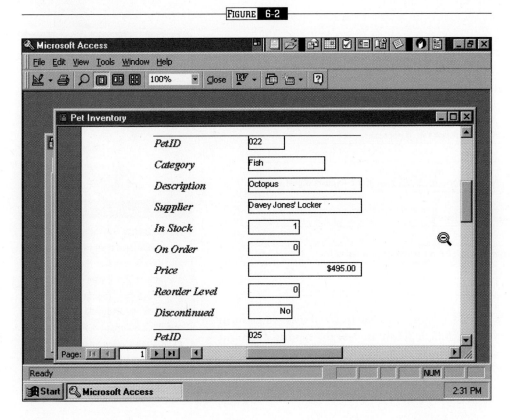

You can print the report with the Print button on the Print Preview toolbar. You can also zoom the report. When the mouse pointer is positioned on the report, it changes to a magnifying glass. You can zoom the report larger or smaller by clicking the report with the magnifying glass mouse pointer. To zoom the report:

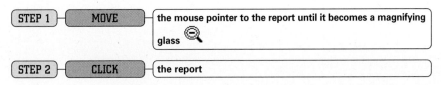

| STEP 1 | MOVE | the mouse pointer to the report until it becomes a magnifying glass |
| STEP 2 | CLICK | the report |

The report is zoomed smaller and the entire page can be viewed. You can view the report in one or two pages. To view the report in two pages:

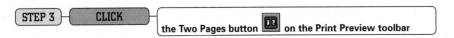

The report is shown in two small pages.
To view the report in one page:

The report is again shown in one page.
To zoom the report:

Close the report window without saving changes.

CREATING A TABULAR REPORT

There may be times when you want to view several records at one time in a report layout similar to a Word table. The **AutoReport: Tabular** Wizard shows multiple records in a column-and-row format. To select the AutoReport: Tabular Wizard and the underlying table or query:

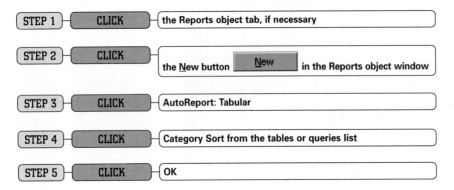

In a few seconds, all the fields in the Category Sort query are shown in a tabular report. All 32 records in the query are included. Scroll to view the report. Zoom the report to one page using the mouse. Your screen should look similar to Figure 6-3.

FIGURE 6-3

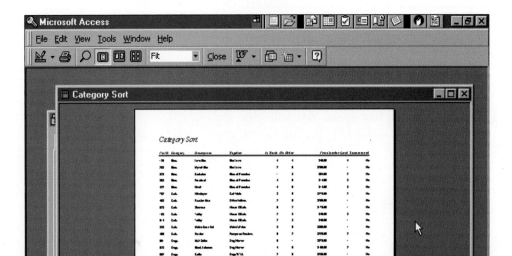

Zoom the report to 100%. Notice that although you can see all the fields for each record, there is not enough space between some of the labels to see the entire label text. You can modify the size and position of the labels and fields by switching to Design view. Modifying a report in Design view will be discussed later in this chapter.

Close the report window without saving changes.

6.b Using the Report Wizard

By default, the AutoReport Wizards automatically select all the fields in the underlying table or query for a report. The Report Wizard, however, allows you to create a report quickly by selecting the fields to be included, selecting grouping levels, choosing sort and summary options, picking a layout format, and selecting a built-in style for the report. To select the Report Wizard and desired table or query:

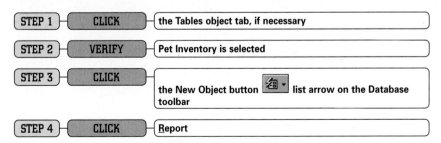

STEP 1	CLICK	the Tables object tab, if necessary
STEP 2	VERIFY	Pet Inventory is selected
STEP 3	CLICK	the New Object button [icon] list arrow on the Database toolbar
STEP 4	CLICK	Report

The New Report dialog box opens.

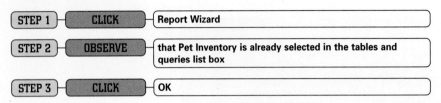

In a few seconds, the first Report Wizard dialog box opens. You will select the fields you want and their order in your report in this dialog box. For this report, you do not want to include the Supplier and Discontinued fields. To add all the fields in their default order:

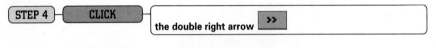

To remove the Supplier and Discontinued fields:

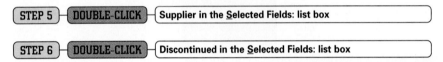

The Supplier and Discontinued fields are removed from the Selected Fields: list box and appear in the Available Fields: list box.

The second Report Wizard dialog box opens. You will select a grouping level for your report in this dialog box. Grouping allows you to have like records shown together on a report. When you select a grouping level from the list box on the left side of the dialog box, a preview of your grouping level is visible in the box on the right side of the dialog box. Suppose you want the records to be grouped by category. To select a grouping level:

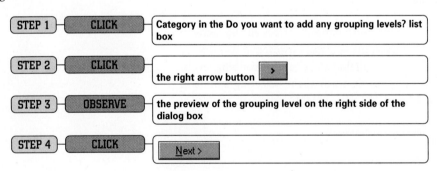

The third Report Wizard dialog box opens. You can select sort and summary options in this dialog box. You need to add a summary total for the In Stock and On Order fields. To view the summary options:

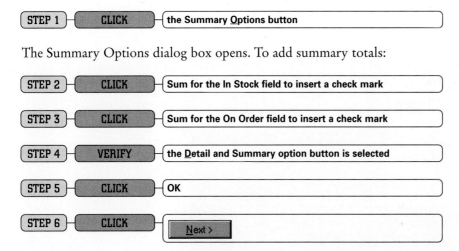

The Summary Options dialog box opens. To add summary totals:

The fourth Report Wizard dialog box opens. You will select a layout and paper orientation in this dialog box. A preview of the selected layout appears at the left side of the dialog box. You want your report to use the Stepped layout, landscape orientation, and you want all the fields adjusted so they print on one page. To select the layout options:

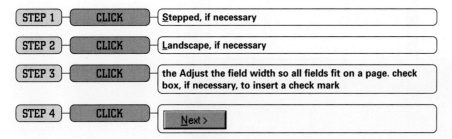

The fifth Report Wizard dialog box opens. You will select a style for your report in this dialog box. When you click a style in the list box on the right side of the dialog box, a preview of the style appears in the box on the left side of the dialog box. To select a style and go to the next step:

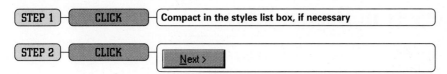

The sixth Report Wizard dialog box opens. You are ready to give the report a title. The title appears in the title bar of the report and in the Reports object list. To give the report a title:

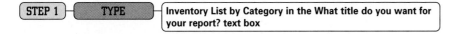

Notice that the "Preview the report" option button is selected. To complete the steps of the Report Wizard and view the Inventory List by Category report in Print Preview:

STEP 2 — CLICK — the Finish button | Finish

In a few seconds, the completed report appears in Print Preview. Scroll to view the report. View the report in two pages. Your screen should look similar to Figure 6-4.

FIGURE 6-4

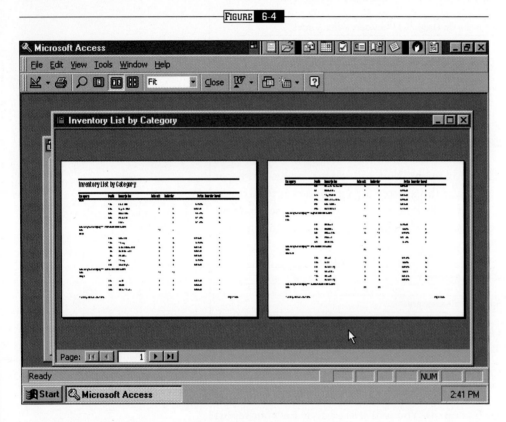

Close the Print Preview window. Click the Reports object tab and verify that the Inventory List by Category report has been added to the Reports object list.

6.c Modifying a Report in Design View

You can modify an existing report in Design view by moving, resizing, or deleting controls. You can also apply a different style, or format the contents of the label controls. To view the report in Design view:

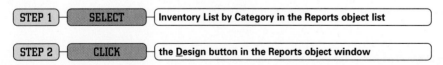

STEP 1 — SELECT — Inventory List by Category in the Reports object list

STEP 2 — CLICK — the Design button in the Reports object window

The report appears in Design view. The Formatting toolbar appears and the Toolbox may appear. Your screen should look similar to Figure 6-5.

FIGURE 6-5

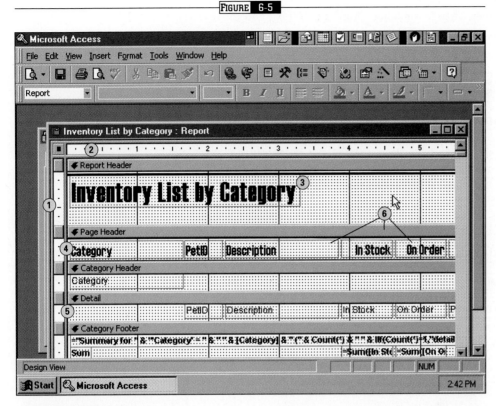

1. Vertical ruler
2. Horizontal ruler
3. Report header
4. Page header
5. Detail section
6. Controls

You will not need the Toolbox for this exercise. To hide the Toolbox if it appears:

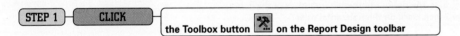

STEP 1 — CLICK — the Toolbox button [icon] on the Report Design toolbar

The report design consists of several components.

RULERS

Use the vertical and horizontal **rulers** when you are moving controls and resizing different sections of the report.

REPORT HEADER AND FOOTER SECTIONS

The **report header** appears at the top of the first page of the report. The **report footer** appears at the end of the report.

PAGE HEADER AND FOOTER SECTIONS

The **page header** appears at the top of each page of the report. The **page footer** appears at the bottom of each page of the report.

DETAIL SECTION

The **detail section** contains the actual records within the report.

CONTROLS

Controls are indicators that locate the position of text and data in the report.

Scroll to view these report components. Suppose you want to remove the summary text at the end of each category, change the label "Sum" to "Total", and move the "Total" label closer to the In Stock and On Order summary total values. To delete the summary text line:

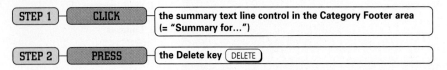

| STEP 1 | CLICK | the summary text line control in the Category Footer area (= "Summary for...") |
| STEP 2 | PRESS | the Delete key (DELETE) |

The summary text line control is deleted. To change the text in the Sum control:

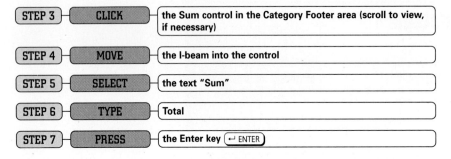

STEP 3	CLICK	the Sum control in the Category Footer area (scroll to view, if necessary)
STEP 4	MOVE	the I-beam into the control
STEP 5	SELECT	the text "Sum"
STEP 6	TYPE	Total
STEP 7	PRESS	the Enter key (↵ ENTER)

The text inside the control is changed. To move the Total control closer to the summary values:

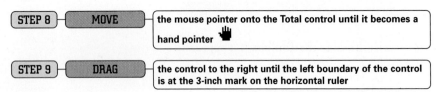

| STEP 8 | MOVE | the mouse pointer onto the Total control until it becomes a hand pointer 🖑 |
| STEP 9 | DRAG | the control to the right until the left boundary of the control is at the 3-inch mark on the horizontal ruler |

Deselect the control by clicking in the report area (not on a control).

Before you print your report, you should preview it again and make sure the changes are acceptable. To save time, you can view the report in Layout Preview, which shows your report with a sample of your data. To view a sample report:

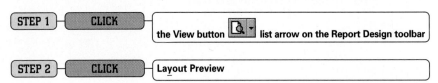

| STEP 1 | CLICK | the View button [icon] list arrow on the Report Design toolbar |
| STEP 2 | CLICK | Layout Preview |

QUICK TIP

You can select multiple controls by first selecting a control and then holding down the SHIFT key and clicking additional controls.

Your report with sample data appears in Layout Preview. Scroll to view the changes made to the In Stock and On Hand summary label. After zooming the report, your screen should look similar to Figure 6-6.

FIGURE 6-6

QUICK TIP

You can click the AutoFormat command on the Format menu to change the style of a report in Design view.

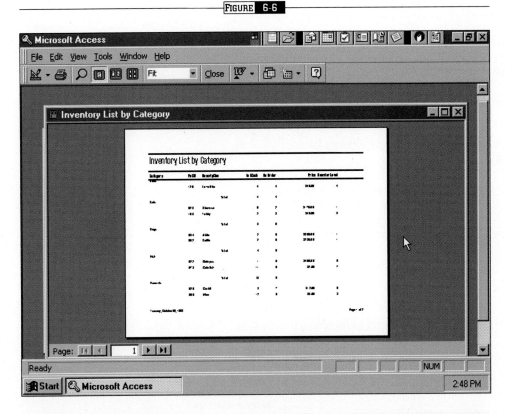

Close the report window and save the changes. Close the PETSTORE RECORDS database. For more information on creating reports with the Report Wizards or from scratch in Design view, see Access online Help.

SCANS

Summary

> Reports can be created quickly and easily using the Report Wizards.

> There are several Report Wizards you can use to create an Access report.

> The AutoReport Wizards create a report using all the fields in the underlying table or query.

> To create a report quickly and select the specific fields to be included in the report, you can use the Report Wizard.

> You can create a report with a wizard, or you can create a report in Design view.

> Reports created with a Report Wizard can be modified in Design view.

Commands Review

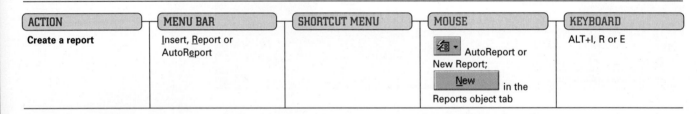

ACTION	MENU BAR	SHORTCUT MENU	MOUSE	KEYBOARD
Create a report	Insert, Report or AutoReport		AutoReport or New Report; New in the Reports object tab	ALT+I, R or E

Concepts Review

1. **Which of the following is not a Report Wizard?**
   [a] Chart Wizard.
   [b] AutoReport: Columnar.
   [c] PivotTable Wizard.
   [d] AutoReport: Tabular.
   [e] a, b, c, and d are Report Wizards.

2. **Which of the following will create a columnar report using all the fields in the underlying table or query by default?**
   [a] select the table or query, click the New Object button, click New Report.
   [b] select the table or query, click the New Object button list arrow, click AutoReport.
   [c] click the Reports object tab, click the New button.
   [d] click the Tables object tab, click the New button.
   [e] none of the above.

3. **The AutoReport: Tabular Wizard creates a report that resembles:**
   [a] a Word table.
   [b] an Excel worksheet.
   [c] a PowerPoint chart slide.
   [d] none of the above.

4. **When you use the Report Wizard, you can select:**
   [a] a report layout.
   [b] a built-in style.
   [c] specific fields to be included.
   [d] layout and paper orientation.
   [e] a, b, and d.
   [f] a, b, c, and d.

5. **When you create a report it is automatically viewed in:**
   [a] Design view.
   [b] Print Preview.
   [c] Layout Preview.
   [d] Table view.
   [e] none of the above.

Circle T if the statement is true or F if the statement is false.

1. T F You must add fields to a report in the exact order that they appear in the Report Wizards field list boxes.
2. T F The objects in a report design are called controls.
3. T F You can select only one control at a time in Design view.
4. T F When you create a report with a Report Wizard, it cannot be modified.
5. T F You can add and delete records in Report Design view.
6. T F Reports can be zoomed in Design view.
7. T F The built-in report styles can only be applied through the Report Wizard.
8. T F The AutoReport: Tabular Wizard is a step-by-step process that allows you to select specific fields, the report layout, and the report style.
9. T F You can show multiple pages in Print Preview.
10. T F You can use the AutoFormat button on the Report Design toolbar to change the layout of your report.

Skills Review

EXERCISE 1

1. Open the BRANCH database that was modified in Chapter 5 in Exercise 1.
2. Use the AutoReport: Tabular Wizard to create a report based on the Southwest Staff table.
3. Observe that some of the labels and field values cannot be seen completely.
4. Switch to Design view.
5. Move and size the Page Header and Detail controls until you can view all the labels and field values completely. (*Hint*: remember that you can select multiple controls with the SHIFT+Click method and then size or move the selected controls at one time.)
6. Save the report as Staff List.
7. Print the Staff List report.
8. Close the report window and the BRANCH database.

EXERCISE 2

1. Open the PROSPECT database modified in Exercise 2 in Chapter 5.
2. Using the Report Wizard create a tabular report in portrait orientation based on the Prospective Clients table.
3. Include the fields Sales Rep, LName, and City.
4. Do not group, sort, or summarize.
5. Select the Bold style.
6. Name the report Clients List.
7. Observe the report.
8. Switch to Design view and make the following changes:
   (a) Change the style to a style of your choice. (*Hint*: click the AutoFormat command on the Format menu.)
   (b) Size and move the controls as desired to create an attractive appearance.
9. Print the report.
10. Close the report and save the changes. Close the PROSPECT database.

EXERCISE 3

1. Open the VANCOUVER LUMBER database that was modified in Exercise 3 in Chapter 5.
2. Use the AutoReport: Columnar Wizard to create a report based on the Regional Managers table.
3. Save the report as Managers Listing.
4. Switch to Design view and delete the Detail controls for the Date Hired field.
5. Print the report.
6. Close the report without saving changes. Close the VANCOUVER LUMBER database.

Case Problems

PROBLEM 1

Using the Office Assistant, look up and review what is new in Access 97 for creating, printing, and previewing reports. Create a Word document with at least three paragraphs listing and describing three new features. Save and print the document.

PROBLEM 2

Open an existing database. Use the Report Wizards of your choice to create three different reports: columnar, tabular, and a grouped report. Include the fields, layout, and style of your choice. Modify the reports in Design view as desired. Print the reports.

PROBLEM 3

Open an existing database and report. View the report in Design view. Explore moving, sizing, and deleting controls in the report. Save the modified report with a new name. Print the report.

PROBLEM 4

Connect to your ISP and, using the Microsoft on the Web command on the Help menu, load the Microsoft Office Home Page and look for information about creating Access reports. Print at least one Web page.

SCANS

Integrating Access Data with Other Office Applications and the Internet

"

At CS we use computers to publish our quarterly journal, to maintain our membership database, and to communicate with our field coordinators and other organizations.

"

Amy Stoll
special projects coordinator

Cultural Survival
Cambridge, MA

Cultural Survival, an international human rights organization, works with and for indigenous peoples as they seek to maintain their cultures and secure control over their land and resource bases.

Chapter Overview:

In the previous chapters of this unit, you learned how to create tables, queries, forms, and reports. After you create a database, you can increase your productivity with office tasks by integrating your Access database objects with other Office applications, or by publishing your Access data to a company intranet or to the Internet. This chapter illustrates some ways you can integrate Access data with the Word and Excel applications and the Internet.

SNAPSHOT

In this chapter you will learn to:

> **Integrate Access data with Word**

> **Integrate Access data with Excel**

> **Create hyperlinks and HTML documents using Access**

7.a Integrating Access Data with Word

You can use data stored in an Access database as a data source for a Word Mail Merge. Datasheets, forms, and reports can be saved as rich-text format (.RTF) files, which maintain font and style formatting and can then be opened in Word. You can copy/paste records from a Word table or text separated by tabs into an Access datasheet or form.

MERGING ACCESS DATA WITH A WORD DOCUMENT

Suppose you have created an interoffice memo in Word and you need to send it to several people in your organization. The names of the recipients are maintained in an Access database. You can merge the names from the Access database with the Word document either by exporting the data to a Word data source file or by selecting the database table or query as a data source during the merge process in the Word application.

You can also merge Access data with a Word document from the Access application. In the following activity, you will use the BRANCH database you modified in Chapter 6. You will merge the Initial, LName, and City fields from the Southwest Staff table with the SOUTHWEST STAFF MEMORANDUM document located on the student disk.

First, open the BRANCH database. It is not necessary to open an object to merge it with a Word document. Simply select the object in the object window and begin the merge process. To begin the merge:

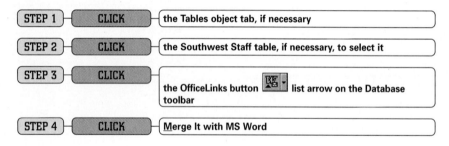

STEP 1	CLICK	the Tables object tab, if necessary
STEP 2	CLICK	the Southwest Staff table, if necessary, to select it
STEP 3	CLICK	the OfficeLinks button 📇 list arrow on the Database toolbar
STEP 4	CLICK	Merge It with MS Word

MENU TIP

You can integrate Access data with Word by pointing to the Office Links command on the Tools menu and then clicking Merge It with MS Word or Publish It with MS Word.

MOUSE TIP

You can integrate Access data with Word by clicking the OfficeLinks button list arrow on the Database toolbar and then clicking Merge It with MS Word or Publish It with MS Word.

The Microsoft Word Mail Merge Wizard dialog box opens. Your screen should look similar to Figure 7-1.

FIGURE 7-1

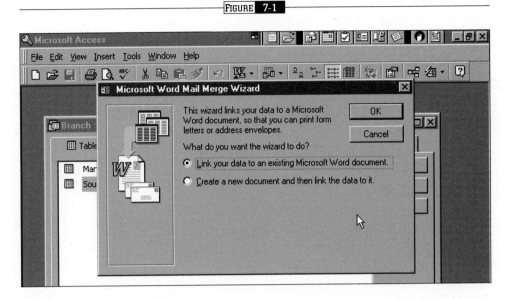

You can merge with an existing Word document or create a new document and then continue the merge process. To merge with SOUTHWEST STAFF MEMORANDUM:

STEP 5	VERIFY	the "Link your data to an existing Microsoft Word document." option button is selected

STEP 6	CLICK	OK

The Select Microsoft Word Document dialog box opens. To select the SOUTH-WEST STAFF MEMORANDUM:

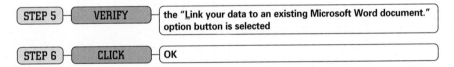

STEP 7	SWITCH	to the appropriate disk drive and folder

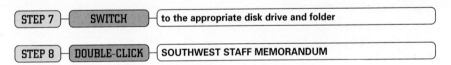

STEP 8	DOUBLE-CLICK	SOUTHWEST STAFF MEMORANDUM

In a few seconds, the Word application and SOUTHWEST STAFF MEMO-RANDUM document open. Maximize the Word window, if necessary. Notice that the Mail Merge toolbar appears. You can proceed with the merge by inserting the date as a field and inserting the merge fields for the initial, last name, and city. To insert the TO: and DATE: fields:

STEP 1	MOVE	the insertion point to the right of the tab character following TO: (display the nonprinting characters, if necessary)

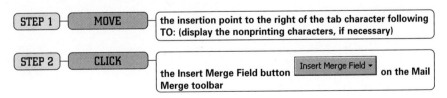

STEP 2	CLICK	the Insert Merge Field button [Insert Merge Field ▼] on the Mail Merge toolbar

The list of fields from the Southwest Staff table appears. To add the Initial and LName fields and the appropriate punctuation:

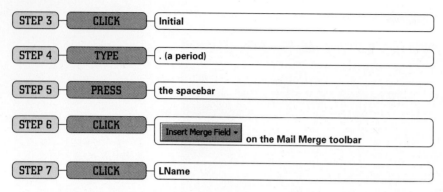

STEP 3	CLICK	Initial
STEP 4	TYPE	. (a period)
STEP 5	PRESS	the spacebar
STEP 6	CLICK	Insert Merge Field ▾ on the Mail Merge toolbar
STEP 7	CLICK	LName

The merge fields and appropriate punctuation and spacing are inserted. Next, you will create a new line for the City. If you press the ENTER key, you will create a new paragraph. Instead of creating a new paragraph, you can position the City field inside the current paragraph and below the Initial and LName fields by inserting a different nonprinting character, the new line character. To create a new line and insert the City merge field:

| STEP 8 | PRESS | the Shift+Enter keys (SHIFT)+(↵ ENTER) to insert a new line character |

A new line character is inserted at the end of the TO: line and the insertion point moves to the left margin. Display the nonprinting characters, if desired, to view the new line character.

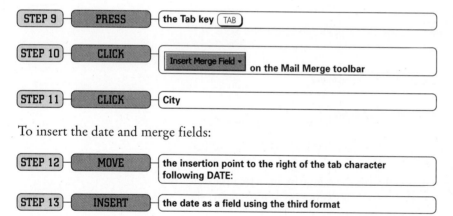

STEP 9	PRESS	the Tab key (TAB)
STEP 10	CLICK	Insert Merge Field ▾ on the Mail Merge toolbar
STEP 11	CLICK	City

To insert the date and merge fields:

| STEP 12 | MOVE | the insertion point to the right of the tab character following DATE: |
| STEP 13 | INSERT | the date as a field using the third format |

For the figures in this chapter, the field shading has been turned off in the Options dialog box. Your screen should look similar to Figure 7-2.

FIGURE 7-2

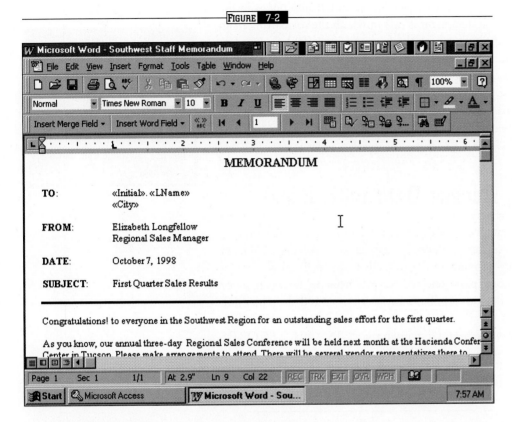

You are now ready to proceed with the merge.
To merge to a new document:

STEP 14 — CLICK the Merge to New Document button on the Mail Merge toolbar

Scroll through the new merged document. Notice that each new section contains the memorandum for a different staff member. Save the merged document as CONFERENCE INVITATION. Save the Word main document as CONFERENCE MERGE MAIN DOCUMENT. Close all Word documents and exit the Word application.

You can also merge Access data with a Word main document from the Word application. During the mail merge process, simply select an Access table or query when prompted for the data source you want to use.

Close the BRANCH database, but leave the Access application open.

EXPORTING ACCESS DATA TO WORD

Sometimes you may want to export an Access query, form, report, or table object to Word by saving it as a rich-text format document that automatically opens in the Word application. (A rich-text format document is one in which the formatting from the source application is converted to agree with the formatting available in the destination application.) The .RTF file is saved in the folder where the Access application is stored. To do this, select the Access table or query and then click the Publish It with MS Word subcommand under the Office Links command on the Tools menu or the OfficeLinks button on the Database toolbar.

For more information on integrating Access data with Word, see Access or Word online Help.

QUICK TIP

You can select and copy data from an Access table datasheet and then paste the data into a Word document with the menu commands, the toolbar buttons, or with the drag-and-drop method just like you would from an Excel worksheet.

7.b Integrating Access Data with Excel

Access data can be integrated with Excel by exporting a table or query to an Excel worksheet. You can convert an Excel worksheet to an Access table from Excel or create an Access table by copying a range of cells from an Excel worksheet to an Access database. You can copy/paste selected records from an Access table or query to Excel using the menu commands, toolbar buttons, or drag-and-drop method.

Suppose you want to export the Discontinued query data in the PETSTORE RECORDS database to an Excel worksheet. First, open the PETSTORE RECORDS database. To export data to Excel:

STEP 1	CLICK	the Discontinued query in the Queries object list to select it
STEP 2	CLICK	File
STEP 3	CLICK	Save As/Export
STEP 4	VERIFY	the To An External File or Database option button is selected
STEP 5	CLICK	OK

The Save Query 'Discontinued' In dialog box opens. To save the query, including the formats and column widths, in an Excel worksheet:

STEP 6	CLICK	Microsoft Excel 97 in the Save as type: list box
STEP 7	CLICK	the Save Formatted check box to insert a check mark
STEP 8	SWITCH	to the appropriate disk drive and folder
STEP 9	CLICK	Export

QUICK TIP

You can also export an Access table or query to an Excel worksheet and automatically open Excel by selecting the table or query and clicking the Office Links command on the Tools menu or the OfficeLinks button on the Database toolbar and then clicking Analyze It with MS Excel.

In a few seconds, the Access data is saved in the specified folder as an Excel workbook named "Discontinued" containing a worksheet also named "Discontinued."

To view the "Discontinued" query data as an Excel worksheet:

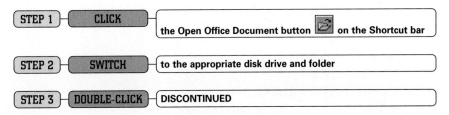

STEP 1	CLICK	the Open Office Document button on the Shortcut bar
STEP 2	SWITCH	to the appropriate disk drive and folder
STEP 3	DOUBLE-CLICK	DISCONTINUED

The DISCONTINUED workbook opens with one worksheet (also named Discontinued) containing the formatted records from the Access query. Close the Excel application and close the DISCONTINUED workbook. Close the PETSTORE RECORDS database and the Access application.

For more information on integrating Access data and Excel, see Access or Excel online <u>H</u>elp.

7.c Creating Hyperlinks and HTML Documents

You can create hyperlinks to link Access data to other Office documents just as you did with Word documents, Excel workbooks, and PowerPoint presentations. You can also use hyperlinks as labels on Access forms and reports to link them to other Office documents, documents on a company intranet, or pages on the Internet. Access tables, queries, forms, and reports can also be published as HTML documents on an intranet or the World Wide Web (WWW).

LINKING ACCESS DATA TO A WORD DOCUMENT WITH A HYPERLINK

Suppose you want to send an interoffice memo to the secretarial staff that contains information about the regional managers. You can type the information in the memo, or you can insert a hyperlink that allows each recipient to open an Access database and review the desired information.

First, open the SOUTHWEST STAFF SECRETARIAL MEMO located on the student disk. This memo advises the secretarial staff to review the new regional managers data maintained in an Access database and specific query. You will create a link to the database in the body of the memo. To create a hyperlink to the BRANCH database:

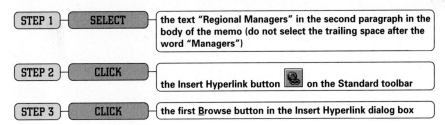

STEP 1	SELECT	the text "Regional Managers" in the second paragraph in the body of the memo (do not select the trailing space after the word "Managers")
STEP 2	CLICK	the Insert Hyperlink button on the Standard toolbar
STEP 3	CLICK	the first <u>B</u>rowse button in the Insert Hyperlink dialog box

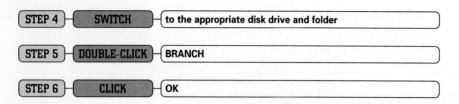

STEP 4	SWITCH	to the appropriate disk drive and folder
STEP 5	DOUBLE-CLICK	BRANCH
STEP 6	CLICK	OK

The words "Regional Manager" are underlined and in a different color indicating a hyperlink.

Save the document as SECRETARIAL MEMO WITH HYPERLINK. You should always test a hyperlink. (Remember to edit hyperlinks if you move the linked file.) To test the hyperlink:

| STEP 7 | CLICK | the **Regional Managers** hyperlink |

The Access application and BRANCH database open. The Word application remains open and minimized; however, the Word document automatically closes when you click the hyperlink. Close the Word application and the BRANCH database, but leave the Access application open to continue working in the next section.

CREATING AN HTML DOCUMENT

Suppose you want to make the information in the Products table of the WORLD-WIDE FOODS CORPORATION database available as an HTML document. You can use the Publish to the Web Wizard to create the HTML document. First, open the WORLDWIDE FOODS CORPORATION database located on the student disk. Click the Tables object tab, if necessary, and verify that the Products table is selected. To save the Products table as an HTML document and start the Publish to the Web Wizard:

CAUTION

When you save the HTML output file, you must save it to a folder. For example, if you want to save it to a floppy disk, you must create a folder on the floppy disk first.

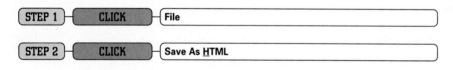

| STEP 1 | CLICK | File |
| STEP 2 | CLICK | Save As **HTML** |

The Publish to the Web Wizard dialog box opens. Your screen should look similar to Figure 7-3.

FIGURE 7-3

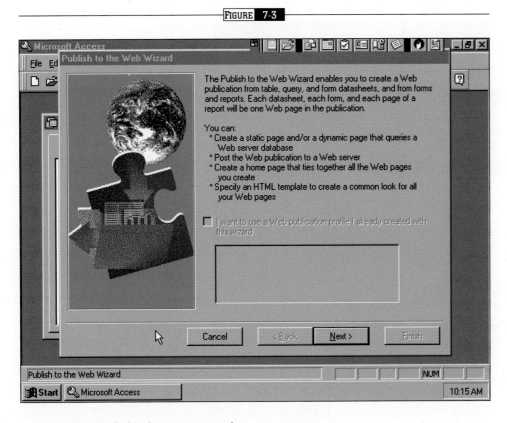

Review the dialog box contents, then:

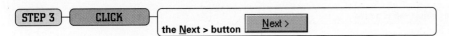

STEP 3 — CLICK — the Next > button   Next >

The second Wizard dialog box opens. Your screen should look similar to Figure 7-4.

FIGURE 7-4

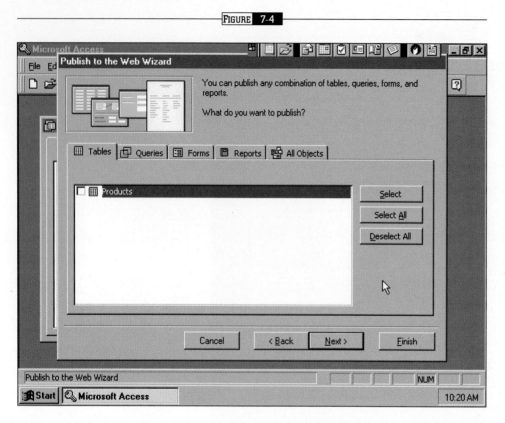

You select the Access object(s) you want to publish to an HTML document in this dialog box. To select the Products table:

STEP 4 — VERIFY — the Tables object tab is active

STEP 5 — CLICK — the Products check box to insert a check mark

STEP 6 — CLICK —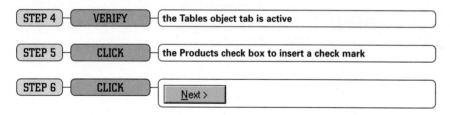

The third Wizard dialog box opens. Your screen should look similar to Figure 7-5.

FIGURE 7-5

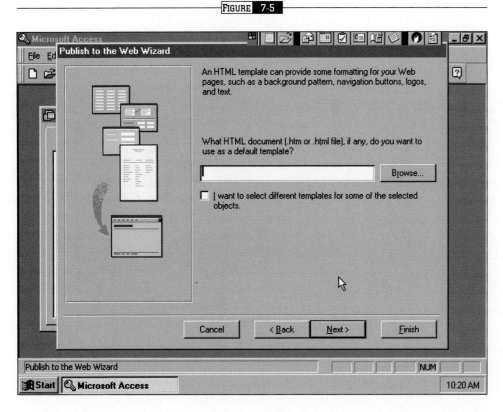

You can select an HTML template to apply to your document in this dialog box. To select a template:

STEP 7 — CLICK — the Browse button

The Select an HTML template dialog box opens.

STEP 8 — DOUBLE-CLICK — Sky in the list of files

The path to the Sky HTML template appears in the Browse text box.

STEP 9 — CLICK — 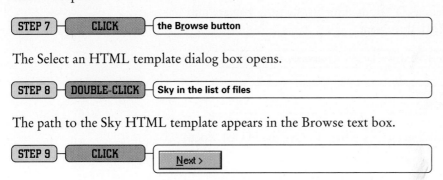 Next >

The fifth Wizard dialog box opens. Your screen should look similar to Figure 7-6.

FIGURE 7-6

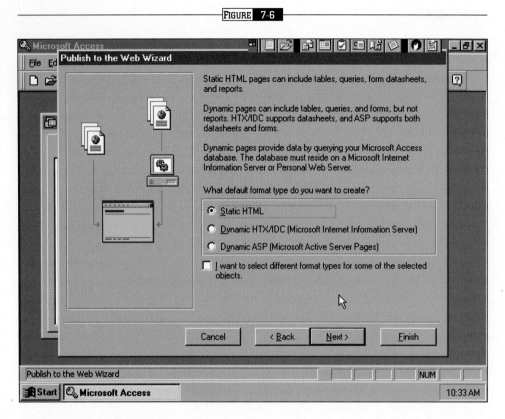

You can specify a static (does not change when the underlying data change) or dynamic (changes with changes in the underlying data) HTML document in this dialog box. Note the restrictions for dynamic HTML documents. Because you are publishing a report, it must be a static HTML document.

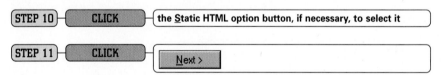

STEP 10 — **CLICK** — the **S**tatic HTML option button, if necessary, to select it

STEP 11 — **CLICK** — Next >

The sixth Wizard dialog box opens. You specify where to save the HTML document in this dialog box.

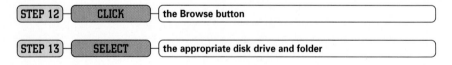

STEP 12 — **CLICK** — the Browse button

STEP 13 — **SELECT** — the appropriate disk drive and folder

The path where the HTML document will be saved is inserted in the Browse text box.

STEP 14 — **CLICK** — Next >

The seventh Wizard dialog box opens. If you were publishing multiple Access objects to HTML documents, you could create a summary-type "home page" in this dialog box that would include links to the individual pages created from the multiple objects. You do not need a "home page" for the HTML document you are creating. To open the next Wizard dialog box:

STEP 15 — **CLICK** — Next >

The final Wizard dialog box opens. You can create a Web publication profile in this dialog box that provides shortcuts to republishing a set of Access objects. You do not need a Web profile for the HTML document you are creating. To complete the Wizard process:

STEP 16 — **CLICK** — the Finish button | Finish

In a few seconds, an HTML document named Products_1 is created. You can review the Products_1 HTML document as a local file by minimizing the Access application and opening the Internet Explorer. Type the path and filename of the Products_1 HTML document in the Address text box or click the Open command on the File menu and use the Browse button to locate and open the HTML document in the Internet Explorer.

For more information on integrating Access objects with the Internet, see Access online Help.

CAUTION

When you use a Web template, Access assumes any .JPG or .GIF graphics files related to the template are located in the same folder as the HTML document you are creating. You may need to copy the necessary files to the output folder. Review using Web templates in Access online Help.

Summary

> Access data can be integrated with the Word application by merging the Access data directly in Word as a data source or by using the Microsoft Mail Merge Wizard from Access.

> Access tables and queries can be saved as rich-text format (.RTF) files and then can be opened in Word.

> You can export an Access table or query to an Excel workbook.

> Access data can be copied and pasted into a Word document or an Excel workbook using the menu commands, toolbar buttons, a shortcut menu or drag-and-drop.

> You can create hyperlinks between Access tables, queries, forms, and reports and other Office documents or HTML documents.

> Access tables, queries, forms, and reports can be published to an HTML document.

Commands Review

ACTION	MENU BAR	SHORTCUT MENU	MOUSE	KEYBOARD
Integrate Access data with Word or Excel	Tools, Office Links			ALT+T, L
Save as an HTML document	File, Save as HTML			ALT+F, H

Concepts Review

1. You can integrate Access data and Word by:

[a] merging the Access data as a data source when using the Word Mail Merge Helper.

[b] using the Microsoft Mail Merge Wizard in Access.

[c] exporting a table or query to a file that can be used as a data source.

[d] a and b.

[e] a, b, and c.

2. Which of the following command(s) allow(s) you to integrate Access data with Word and Excel by automatically opening the Word or Excel application?

[a] Merge It with MS Word.

[b] Publish It with MS Word.

[c] Analyze It with MS Excel.

[d] b and c.

[e] a, b, and c.

3. Which of the following wizards can you use to publish Access objects to HTML documents?

[a] Microsoft Mail Merge Wizard.

[b] Web Template Wizard.

[c] Import Wizard.

[d] Export Wizard.

[e] none of the above.

4. Integrating Access data with other Office applications:

[a] increases productivity.

[b] saves time.

[c] reduces the need for duplicate data entry.

[d] a and c.

[e] a, b, and c.

5. You cannot add hyperlinks to Access objects as:

[a] a field in a form.

[b] a field in a table.

[c] a label in a report.

[d] a label in a form.

Circle Ⓣ if the statement is true or Ⓕ if the statement is false.

1. Ⓣ Ⓕ You can merge data from an Access database directly into a Word document.

2. Ⓣ Ⓕ You must open a table object before you can merge the records into a Word document.

3. Ⓣ Ⓕ You can only merge into an existing Word document.

4. Ⓣ Ⓕ You should insert spaces, blank lines, and punctuation as needed in a merge main document when an Access table or query is your data source.

5. Ⓣ Ⓕ The only way to merge Access data with a Word document is with the Microsoft Mail Merge Wizard.

6. Ⓣ Ⓕ You can copy/paste Access data into a Word document, but you can only export Access data to an Excel workbook.

7. Ⓣ Ⓕ You can export Access data to an Excel workbook with or without maintaining formatting and column widths.

8. Ⓣ Ⓕ To create a hyperlink between an Access object and a Word document, the hyperlink *must* be in the Word document.

9   Ⓣ Ⓕ A range of cells in an Excel worksheet can be copied and pasted into an Access database.

Skills Review

EXERCISE 1

1. Open the PROSPECT database modified in Exercise 1 in Chapter 6.
2. Select the Prospective Clients table and use the Microsoft Mail Merge Wizard in Access to merge it with the CLIENT SALES MEMORANDUM Word document located on the student disk.
3. Use the Sales_Rep, Initial, and LName merge fields.
4. Preview the merge.
5. Merge to a new document.
6. Save the merged document as MERGED SALES MEMOS.
7. Save the main document as SALES MERGE MAIN.
8. Print the MERGED SALES MEMOS document.
9. Close all Word documents and exit the Word application.
10. Close the PROSPECT database and exit the Access application.

EXERCISE 2

1. Open the PETSTORE RECORDS database modified in Chapter 6.
2. Export the Category Sort query to an Excel workbook and automatically open Excel and the workbook. (*Hint*: select the query and click the OfficeLinks button list arrow on the Datasheet toolbar, then click Analyze It with MS Excel.)
3. Rename the Sheet1 tab "Pet Inventory by Category". (*Hint*: use the mouse pointer to drag the split bar located immediately to the left of the left horizontal scroll arrow to show the entire sheet tab.)
4. Print the worksheet in landscape orientation.
5. Close the Excel application and the Category Sort workbook and save changes.
6. Close the PETSTORE RECORDS database and exit the Access application.

EXERCISE 3

1. Open the Word application and a blank document.
2. Open the VANCOUVER LUMBER database and open the Regional Managers table in Datasheet view.
3. Select the Sales Region, Last Name, Initial, and Date Hired columns. (*Hint*: use the mouse to select the columns just as you would in a Word table.)
4. Use the drag-and-drop method to copy the records to the blank Word document. (*Hint*: remember to use the CTRL key to copy; also remember you can drag a selected range to a button on the taskbar to copy the range to a different Office document.)
5. Using commands on the Table menu, center the table between the left and right margins of the Word document.
6. Save the Word document as MANAGERS RECORDS.
7. Print the document.
8. Close the MANAGERS RECORDS document and the Word application.
9. Close the VANCOUVER LUMBER database and the Access application.

SCANS

Case Problems

PROBLEM 1

Using the Office Assistant, review the new Access features for working with other applications. Create a Word document that describes five of these new features. Save and print the document.

PROBLEM 2

Open an existing database.

1. Copy selected records from a table or query to a Word document using both drag-and-drop and the toolbar buttons. Save and print the Word document.

2. Export a table or query to a Word document as an .RTF file that automatically opens Word and the file. Save and print the Word document.

3. Export a table or query to an Excel workbook saving the formatting. Print the Excel worksheet.

4. Use drag-and-drop to copy selected records from a table or query to an Excel worksheet. Save the workbook and print the worksheet.

PROBLEM 3   INTERNET

Using the Office Assistant, research how to create a label on a form or report that is a hyperlink to a Word document. Open an existing database and add a hyperlink label in a report to an existing Word document. Test the hyperlink. Print the report and the Word document.

Introduction to the Windows Explorer

Appendix Overview

The Windows Explorer is an application that provides tools for managing your folders and files. This appendix introduces Explorer options including expanding and collapsing the display of folders, creating new folders, renaming folders and files, deleting folders and files, and formatting a disk.

SNAPSHOT

In this appendix you will learn to:

> Open Explorer

> Review Explorer options

> Create a new folder

> Move and copy folders and files

> Rename folders and files

> Delete folders and files

> Format a disk

A.a Opening Explorer

You can open the Explorer application from the Start menu or from a Shortcut menu.

To open Explorer:

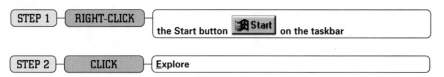

The Explorer window appears. Maximize the Explorer window, if necessary.

If the Explorer toolbar is not displayed, complete the following steps to display the toolbar:

Use ToolTips to review the buttons on the toolbar.

If the Name, Size, Type, and Date Modified buttons are not displayed below the toolbar on the right side of the window:

The Explorer window is divided into two panes: the Tree pane on the left and the Contents pane on the right. The panes are divided by a separator bar that can be dragged to the left or right with the mouse pointer to resize the panes. The Tree pane displays the organizational structure of your computer including listing all desktop objects, My Computer objects, and the folders located at each disk drive. The Contents pane displays all folders and files contained in a folder selected in the Tree pane.

A.b Reviewing Explorer Options

You can display disk drive icons, folders, and files (called objects) for your computer by selecting an item from the Go to a different folder list box on the toolbar. You can display the next level up by clicking the Up One Level button on the toolbar.

To display everything on your computer:

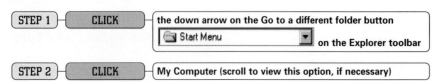

The Contents pane lists all the disk drives and system folders for your computer.

MENU TIP

You can open Explorer by clicking the Start button on the taskbar, pointing to Programs, and then clicking Windows Explorer or you can right-click the Start button on the taskbar and click Explore to open Explorer. You can also right-click some desktop objects and click Explore to open Explorer.

IN THIS BOOK

In the exercises in this appendix, it is assumed that the student disk is in Drive A. If your configuration is different, your instructor may modify the following exercises.

To display the contents of the student disk:

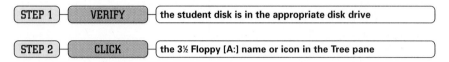

In a few seconds, the Contents pane displays the contents of the student disk.

Notice the small plus sign (+) to the left of the 3½ Floppy [A:] icon. This indicates that there are additional folders at this location that can be displayed in the Tree pane. Displaying these additional folders is called "expanding."

When all the folders are displayed for this location, the plus sign (+) becomes a minus sign (-). The minus sign (-) indicates you can hide or collapse the folders at this location. You can expand or collapse the levels of folders displayed in the Tree pane by clicking the plus or minus sign.

To expand the display of folders for the student disk in the Tree pane:

| STEP 1 | CLICK | the plus sign to the left of the 3½ Floppy [A:] icon |

All the folders located on the student disk are now displayed at the next level below the 3½ Floppy [A:] icon in the Tree pane.

You can display the contents of a folder by clicking the folder in the Tree pane or double-clicking the folder in the Contents pane.

To display the contents of the Word folder:

| STEP 2 | CLICK | the Word folder under the 3½ Floppy [A:] icon in the Tree pane |

The contents of the Word folder on the student disk appear in the Contents pane.

You can arrange the display of folders and files in the Contents pane in Name, Size, Type, or Date Modified order by clicking a button above the list of objects in the Contents pane.

To display the files in the Word folder by size:

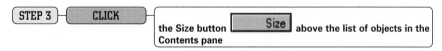

The files are displayed in ascending order by size.

To display the files in order by name:

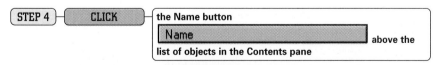

The files are displayed in ascending order by name.

You can display the objects in the Contents pane with large or small icons, in a list without details, or in a list with all details.

To change the display of the objects in the Contents pane:

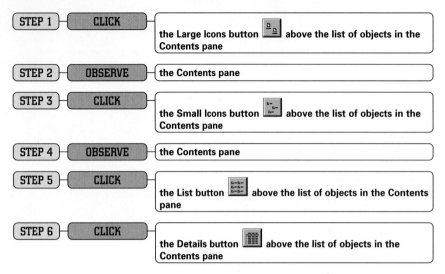

STEP 1 — CLICK — the Large Icons button [icon] above the list of objects in the Contents pane

STEP 2 — OBSERVE — the Contents pane

STEP 3 — CLICK — the Small Icons button [icon] above the list of objects in the Contents pane

STEP 4 — OBSERVE — the Contents pane

STEP 5 — CLICK — the List button [icon] above the list of objects in the Contents pane

STEP 6 — CLICK — the Details button [icon] above the list of objects in the Contents pane

To collapse the display of folders for the 3½ Floppy [A:] icon:

STEP 7 — CLICK — the minus sign to the left of the 3½ Floppy [A:] icon in the Tree pane

The folders located on the student disk are no longer displayed in the Tree pane. The Contents pane again displays the contents of the student disk.

A.c Creating a New Folder

You can create a new folder for an object in the Tree pane or the Contents pane. For example, you might want to add a folder to the student disk.
To add a folder to the student disk:

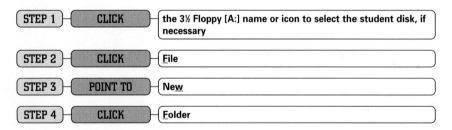

STEP 1 — CLICK — the 3½ Floppy [A:] name or icon to select the student disk, if necessary

STEP 2 — CLICK — File

STEP 3 — POINT TO — New

STEP 4 — CLICK — Folder

A new folder object is created in the Contents pane. The temporary name "New Folder" is selected and the insertion point is in the new folder's name box.
To name the folder:

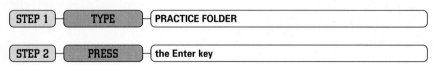

STEP 1 — TYPE — PRACTICE FOLDER

STEP 2 — PRESS — the Enter key

The new folder is named.

A.d Moving and Copying Folders and Files

You can select folders and files by clicking them. You can then copy or move them with the <u>C</u>opy and <u>P</u>aste commands on the <u>E</u>dit menu or shortcut menu, the Copy and Paste buttons on the Explorer toolbar, or with the mouse using the Drag-and-Drop method.

To copy a file to Practice Folder using the Drag-and-Drop method:

STEP 1	EXPAND	the display of folders on the student disk in the Tree pane
STEP 2	DISPLAY	the contents of the Word folder in the Contents pane
STEP 3	RIGHT-CLICK AND DRAG	the EXPLORER EXERCISE document name or icon across the separator bar into the Tree pane to the highlighted Practice Folder object
STEP 4	RELEASE	the mouse button
STEP 5	CLICK	<u>C</u>opy Here

The EXPLORER EXERCISE document is copied to Practice Folder. You can move a file(s) by following the same procedure and clicking <u>M</u>ove Here when the shortcut menu appears.

A.e Renaming Folders and Files

It is sometimes necessary to change the name of an existing file or folder. Suppose you need to rename the EXPLORER EXERCISE document file you copied to Practice Folder.

To rename the file in Practice Folder:

STEP 1	CLICK	the Practice Folder in the Tree pane to display the contents of the folder in the Contents pane
STEP 2	RIGHT-CLICK	the EXPLORER EXERCISE file in the Contents pane
STEP 3	CLICK	Rena<u>m</u>e
STEP 4	TYPE	RENAMED FILE
STEP 5	PRESS	the Enter key

The document file is renamed.

A.f Deleting Folders and Files

When necessary, you can delete a folder and its contents or a file by first selecting the folder or file. You can also delete multiple selected folders and files at one time.

To delete Practice Folder:

STEP 1	RIGHT-CLICK	Practice Folder in the Tree pane

STEP 2	CLICK	Delete

STEP 3	CLICK	Yes to remove the folder and its contents

The Practice Folder and its contents are deleted.

A.g Formatting a Disk

Usually disks are purchased already formatted. However, you may want to reuse a disk that contains files by removing the files. You can format a disk in Explorer or you can format a disk from the My Computer icon on the desktop.

To format a used disk, first *remove* the student disk and place a used disk with files you no longer want to keep in the appropriate disk drive. *Warning! When you format a disk, all the files on the disk are removed.*

To format a disk from the desktop:

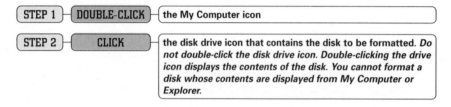

STEP 1	DOUBLE-CLICK	the My Computer icon

STEP 2	CLICK	the disk drive icon that contains the disk to be formatted. *Do not double-click the disk drive icon. Double-clicking the drive icon displays the contents of the disk. You cannot format a disk whose contents are displayed from My Computer or Explorer.*

To format a disk from Explorer:

STEP 1	CLICK	the down arrow on the Go to a different folder button

Start Menu ▼

STEP 2	CLICK	My Computer (scroll to view this option, if necessary)

STEP 3	CLICK	the disk drive icon in the Contents pane that contains the disk to be formatted. *Do not double-click the disk drive icon.*

Now you are ready to begin formatting the disk:

STEP 1	CLICK	File

STEP 2	CLICK	For**m**at

The Format 3½ Floppy [A:] dialog box appears. You specify the formatting options in this dialog box.

You must specify the disk capacity or how much data the disk can hold: 1.44 Mb (High Density) or 720 Kb (Double Density). It is important to format the disk with the correct capacity. A quick format is a faster process but does not check the disk for bad sectors. Use the Quick option only if you are certain the disk is good. The Full option erases files and checks the disk for bad sectors. You can add a label to the disk. For example, you might want to label a disk with your name or project to identify it from similar disks.

To continue formatting:

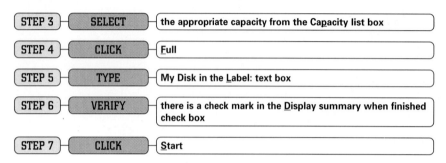

STEP 3	SELECT	the appropriate capacity from the Capacity list box
STEP 4	CLICK	Full
STEP 5	TYPE	My Disk in the Label: text box
STEP 6	VERIFY	there is a check mark in the Display summary when finished check box
STEP 7	CLICK	Start

The progress of the formatting procedure is illustrated by a moving blue bar at the bottom of the dialog box. When the process is complete, the Format Results dialog box appears showing the number of bytes of disk space available on the disk and any bad sectors.

To complete the formatting process:

STEP 8	CLICK	the Close button in the Format Results dialog box

At this point you could continue formatting disks by removing the disk and inserting the next disk to be formatted, changing the formatting options, if necessary, then clicking the Start button.

When you are finished formatting disks:

STEP 9	CLICK	the Close button in the Format dialog box

Close the Explorer application.

For more information on using all of the Explorer options to manage your folders and files, see online Help in Explorer.

Sample Language Skills Evaluation

Name: _____ Date: _____

A Spelling

Place a mark next to the words that are spelled incorrectly.

Examples: X Acident   ___ Genuine

1. ___ Alright
2. ___ Beauty
3. ___ Cofee
4. ___ Conture
5. ___ Description
6. ___ Enable
7. ___ Forteen
8. ___ Necesary
9. ___ Ordinary
10. ___ Opinion
11. ___ Pilar
12. ___ Privelege
13. ___ Recepe
14. ___ Salary
15. ___ Seperate
16. ___ Territory
17. ___ Toogether
18. ___ Truely
19. ___ Undo
20. ___ Verify

B Punctuation

Place a mark next to each sentence that is punctuated incorrectly.

Examples: ___ Correct punctuation is essential.
 X Effective writing, and speaking are important.

1. ___ Al's country house which is located on 105 acres is beautifully decorated.
2. ___ Hockey played with in-line skates is becoming more popular.
3. ___ However John did not feel that way.
4. ___ I learned all the rules and regulations; however, I never really learned to control the ball.
5. ___ In the parking lot by the red car we found a five dollar bill.

6. ___ Ollie is a warm gentle intelligent person.
7. ___ The author of the book , that I was editing, asked if she could see the manuscript.
8. ___ W.O. Mitchell's first book, *Who Has Seen the Wind*, was a best seller.
9. ___ We all enjoyed going to the zoo.
10. ___ Yes, you may go to the movies tonight.

C Grammar

Place a mark next to each sentence that is grammatically incorrect.

> **Examples:** **X** It ain't correct to use improper grammar.
> ___ I shall contact you at once.

1. ___ Regarding the concert tickets, the news are good.
2. ___ Neither the buyer or the seller is interested in that product.
3. ___ A group of managers are attending the convention.
4. ___ Since are last meeting significant problems have arose.
5. ___ It will take as many as three weeks to complete the report.
6. ___ We reported that the product performed superbly.
7. ___ Who did you send the report to?
8. ___ The financial and the personnel meetings was postponed.
9. ___ The load of bricks were dumped on the pavement.
10. ___ The glare on the computer screens has affected the video quality.

D Vocabulary

Place a mark in front of the word that is closest in meaning to the main word.

> ┌─ MAIN WORD ─┐
>
> **Examples:** **Big** ___ Small ___ Tiny ___ Red **X** Large

┌─ MAIN WORD ─┐

1. **Contract**	___ Agreement	___ Book	___ Touch	___ Notify
2. **Collate**	___ Staple	___ Clean	___ Arrange	___ Operate
3. **Transcribe**	___ Send	___ Copy	___ Circle	___ Exchange
4. **Endorse**	___ Stop	___ Prohibit	___ Rule	___ Sign
5. **Negotiate**	___ Gift	___ Confer	___ Touch	___ Notify
6. **Fasten**	___ Attach	___ Hasten	___ Diet	___ Eat
7. **Audit**	___ Hear	___ Present	___ Decide	___ Examine
8. **Duplicate**	___ Copy	___ Color	___ Presentation	___ Render
9. **Category**	___ Story	___ Group	___ Decision	___ Format
10. **Prudent**	___ Dull	___ Honest	___ Cautious	___ Careless
11. **Significant**	___ Frequent	___ Minor	___ Important	___ Written
12. **Critical**	___ Crucial	___ Fearful	___ Trivial	___ Painful
13. **Client**	___ Seller	___ Customer	___ Buyer	___ Broker
14. **Transmit**	___ Send	___ Pay	___ Change	___ Cross
15. **Revise**	___ Originate	___ Foresee	___ Edit	___ Plan

Sample Mathematical Skills Evaluation

Name: _____ **Date:** _____

A Equations

Place a mark in front of the number that answers the equation.

Example: 2+2=   __ 1   __ 2   __ 3   <u>X</u> 4

EQUATION	A	B	C	D
1. 9+3-2/2	__ 6	__ 5	__ 11	__ 15
2. (4-1+9)/2	__ 6	__ 4	__ 12	__ 19
3. 16-(8/2)+5	__ 8	__ 12	__ 15	__ 17
4. (22+5)/3-8	__ 1	__ 12	__ 4	__ 8
5. 9/(3+3-3)	__ 9	__ 6	__ 1	__ 3
6. 22+13-18/3x3	__ 12	__ 17	__ 8	__ 15
7. (8-16/4x2+3)	__ 3	__ 6	__ 8	__ 12
8. (5-3+6)/2x5	__ 12	__ 18	__ 20	__ 7
9. 26/(36+12-47)x2	__ 23	__ 13	__ 6	__ 19
10. (8x3/4+6)-2	__ 10	__ 6	__ 18	__ 12
11. 1+(9-5)/2x6+1	__ 8	__ 14	__ 20	__ 26
12. (7-4)/3x13+9-2	__ 14	__ 9	__ 20	__ 23
13. 24/8x(3+7-1)/9	__ 3	__ 12	__ 7	__ 15
14. (6x6+(8-2))/7x6	__ 36	__ 18	__ 26	__ 6
15. 2+(8/(2x1)-2)/2	__ 1	__ 3	__ 5	__ 7
16. (16+8)-(8/2x(2+2-1))	__ 6	__ 8	__ 18	__ 12
17. (15-3)/(((12x3+4)-10)/5)	__ 2	__ 4	__ 6	__ 8
18. 15/5x12+4-(30/6x3)	__ 14	__ 25	__ 36	__ 8
19. 8x3+((16-4)/4x5+2)	__ 34	__ 23	__ 56	__ 41
20. ((17+3)x3)-20/4x4-20	__ 20	__ 25	__ 45	__ 60

B Fractional and Decimal Equations

Place a mark in front of the number that equals the fraction given:

Example: $\frac{1}{2}$= ___ 0.1 ___ 0.25 ___ 0.33 X 0.5

EQUATION	A	B	C	D
1. $\frac{1}{4}$	___ 0.10	___ 0.25	___ 0.33	___ 0.50
2. $\frac{1}{2}$	___ 0.10	___ 0.25	___ 0.33	___ 0.50
3. $\frac{1}{3}$	___ 0.10	___ 0.25	___ 0.33	___ 0.50
4. $\frac{1}{10}$	___ 0.10	___ 0.25	___ 0.33	___ 0.50
5. $\frac{2}{4}$	___ 0.10	___ 0.25	___ 0.33	___ 0.50
6. $\frac{1}{100}$	___ 0.0001	___ 0.001	___ 0.01	___ 0.01
7. $\frac{33}{99}$	___ 0.10	___ 0.25	___ 0.33	___ 0.50
8. $\frac{1}{5}$	___ 0.10	___ 0.25	___ 0.33	___ 0.50
9. $\frac{1}{1000}$	___ 0.0001	___ 0.001	___ 0.01	___ 0.01
10. $\frac{15}{20}$	___ .25	___ 0.50	___ 0.75	___ 1.75
11. $\frac{9}{10}$	___ 90.00	___ 0.90	___ 9.00	___ 0.09
12. $\frac{12}{40}$	___ 1.20	___ 0.50	___ 0.30	___ 1.50
13. $1\frac{1}{3}$	___ 1.33	___ 13.00	___ 0.133	___ 1.50
14. $5\frac{1}{4}$	___ 5.22	___ 6.33	___ 5.14	___ 5.25
15. $16\frac{10}{40}$	___ 16.14	___ 17.14	___ 16.50	___ 16.25
16. $\frac{80}{20}$	___ 4.00	___ 0.16	___ 1.6	___ 0.04
17. $\frac{125}{1250}$	___ 0.125	___ 0.25	___ 0.10	___ 0.50
18. $45 + \frac{3}{4} + \frac{4}{12}$	___ 45.66	___ 45.50	___ 46.00	___ 46.35
19. $87 - \frac{1}{4}$	___ 85.66	___ 86.75	___ 88.00	___ 87.25
20. $99 - 66\frac{3}{4}$	___ 32.25	___ 155.75	___ 33.5	___ 35.75
21. $3\frac{1}{3} + 2$	___ $6\frac{1}{3}$	___ $5\frac{1}{3}$	___ $\frac{15}{3}$	___ 5
22. $5\frac{1}{2} - 3\frac{1}{4}$	___ $8\frac{1}{2}$	___ $2\frac{1}{8}$	___ $2\frac{1}{4}$	___ $2\frac{3}{5}$
23. $6\frac{3}{4} + 4\frac{1}{2}$	___ $14\frac{1}{4}$	___ $10\frac{3}{4}$	___ $2\frac{1}{2}$	___ $11\frac{1}{4}$
24. $15\frac{2}{3} + 37\frac{2}{5}$	___ $53\frac{1}{15}$	___ $52\frac{2}{3}$	___ $54\frac{1}{4}$	___ $51\frac{2}{15}$
25. $99\frac{1}{3} - 88\frac{1}{4}$	___ $9\frac{7}{8}$	___ $10\frac{5}{6}$	___ $10\frac{1}{4}$	___ $11\frac{1}{12}$

SOLUTIONS

SAMPLE LANGUAGE SKILLS EVALUATION SOLUTIONS:

A **Spelling**: 1. All right, 3. Coffee, 4. Contour, 7. Fourteen, 8. Necessary, 11. Pillar, 12. Privilege, 13. Recipe, 17. Together, 18. Truly.

B **Punctuation**: Sentences 1, 3, 5, 6, and 7 are punctuated incorrectly.

C **Grammar**: Sentences 1, 2, 3, 4, 6, 7, 8, and 9 are grammatically incorrect.

D **Vocabulary**: 1. Agreement, 2. Arrange, 3. Copy, 4. Sign, 5. Confer, 6. Attach, 7. Examine, 8. Copy, 9. Group, 10. Cautious, 11. Important, 12. Crucial, 13. Customer, 14. Send, 15. Edit.

SAMPLE MATHEMATICAL SKILLS EVALUATION SOLUTIONS:

A **Equations**: 1C, 2A, 3D, 4A, 5D, 6B, 7A, 8C, 9B, 10A, 11B, 12C, 13A, 14A, 15B, 16D, 17A, 18B, 19D, 20D.

B **Fractional and Decimal Equations**: 1B, 2D, 3C, 4A, 5D, 6C, 7C, 8B, 9B, 10C, 11B, 12C, 13A, 14D, 15D, 16A, 17C, 18C, 19B, 20A, 21B, 22C, 23D, 24A, 25D.

Proofreader's Marks

DEFINED		EXAMPLES

Paragraph	¶	¶ Begin a new paragraph at this
Insert a character	∧	point. Insrt a letter here.
Delete	ℓ	Delete these words. Disregard
Do not change	stet or	the previous correction. To
Transpose	tr	transpose is to around turn.
Move to the left	⌐	Move this copy to the left.
Move to the right	⌐	Move this copy to the right.
No paragraph	No ¶	No ¶ Do not begin a new paragraph
Delete and close up		here. Delete the hyphen from
		pre-empt and close up the space.
Set in caps	Caps or ≡	a sentence begins with a capital
Set in lower case	lc	letter. This Word should not
Insert a period	⊙	be capitalized. Insert a period⊙
Quotation marks	⌄⌄ ⌄⌄	Quotation marks and a comma
Comma	⋏	should be placed here he said.
Insert space	#	Space between thesewords. An
Apostrophe	⌄⌄	apostrophe is whats needed here.
Hyphen	=	Add a hyphen to Kilowatthour. Close
Close up	⌒	up the extra spa ce.
Use superior figure	⌄	Footnote this sentence. Set
Set in italic	ital. or ___	the words, sine qua non, in italics.
Move up	⌐‾‾‾⌐	This word is too low. That word is
Move down	⌊___⌋	too high.

Index